WOMEN IN REVOLUTIONARY PARIS, 1789–1795

WOMEN
IN REVOLUTIONARY PARIS
1789–1795

Selected Documents Translated
with Notes and Commentary by

Darline Gay Levy
Harriet Branson Applewhite
Mary Durham Johnson

UNIVERSITY OF ILLINOIS PRESS
URBANA AND CHICAGO

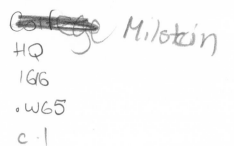
Illini Books edition, 1980

© 1979 BY THE BOARD OF TRUSTEES OF THE UNIVERSITY OF ILLINOIS
MANUFACTURED IN THE UNITED STATES OF AMERICA
P 8 7 6 5

This book is printed on acid-free paper.

Document No. 7, Chapter I, "Stanislas Maillard Describes the Women's March to Versailles, October 5, 1789," on pages 36–42: Reprinted with permission of Macmillan Publishing Co., Inc., from George F. E. Rudé, ed., *The Eighteenth Century,* pp. 198–205. Copyright © 1965 by The Free Press, a Division of The Macmillan Company.

Document No. 9, Chapter I, Police Deposition No. 343, Testimony from Marie-Rose Barré, on pages 49–50: From Philip Dawson, ed., *The French Revolution,* pp. 66–67. Copyright © 1967. Reprinted by permission of Prentice-Hall, Inc., Englewood Cliffs, New Jersey.

Document No. 7, Chapter II, "A Cook Testifies on Her Participation at the Champ de Mars," on pages 81–82: From George Rudé, *The Crowd in the French Revolution,* pp. 86–87. Copyright © 1959 Oxford University Press. Reprinted by permission of Oxford University Press.

LIBRARY OF CONGRESS CATALOGING IN PUBLICATION DATA

Women in Revolutionary Paris, 1789–1795.

Bibliography: p.
Includes indexes.
1. Women's right—France—History—Sources.
2. Women in politics—France—Paris—History—Sources.
3. France—History—Revolution, 1789–1799—Sources.
I. Levy, Darline Gay, 1939–   II. Applewhite, Harriet Branson.   III. Johnson, Mary Durham.
HQ1616.W65   301.41′2′0944   79–4102
ISBN 0-252-00855-3

To the memory of Beatrice Fry Hyslop

Contents

General Introduction   3

III. The Escalation of Women's Protest: January, 1792, through February, 1793   103

IV. Organized Feminine Political Power: Spring through October, 1793   143

Acknowledgments

THE EDITORS WISH TO THANK Professor Albert Soboul, the University of Paris, who read and commented on an earlier version of this manuscript; the Faculty Research and Travel Committee, Barnard College, for a grant to Darline Levy for research and collection of documents in Paris; Judith McBride, Virginia Lloyd, and Glenna Petersen for expert assistance in typing the manuscript.

A brief article summarizing subjects treated in this anthology was published in *Barnard Alumnae,* Spring, 1974, and reprinted in *The French Revolution: Conflicting Interpretations,* ed. Frank A. Kafker and James M. Laux, 2d ed. (New York, 1976).

WOMEN IN REVOLUTIONARY PARIS, 1789–1795

General Introduction

WOMEN FIND THEIR PLACE among the colorful images of revolutionary France, sometimes as real historical figures, more often as legends—Amazons, furies, heroines—or as invented characters—the Madame Defarges and the neoclassical goddesses of liberty. Such historical memories have distorted or suppressed the very real contributions that women made to the Revolution. In this anthology we focus on the political dimensions of that contribution, which involved women in changes of power and influence in Paris.

We have organized our documentation chronologically to demonstrate changes in women's political awareness and tactics during the six years of their active involvement in the Revolution. Chapter one documents Parisian women's aspirations and their initial reactions to the outbreak of the Revolution as well as their mass involvement in civil violence in October, 1789. The materials in chapter two illuminate the process of Parisian women's political education in revolutionary principles and their experience with revolutionary institutions between 1790 and 1792. Sources in chapter three treat Parisian women's activities during the critical revolutionary year 1792–93, while chapter four treats the brief period between the spring and fall of 1793 when one group of revolutionary women created an institution, the Society of Revolutionary Republican Women, to serve their overriding political interest in security and subsistence. Our documents in chapter five throw into relief the multiple dimensions of feminine citizenship during Year II of the Republic, with special attention to expressions of identification with Jacobin models and dissent from them. The sources in our final chapter document the phenomenon of Parisian women in revolt against the political and economic institutions of the Thermidorian oligarchy.

We believe this historical documentation illustrates revolutionary women's political roles, that is, their relationships with those in positions of governing authority and influence. Political and historical analysis indicates that most people are politically quiescent most of the time, that women tend to be less politically involved than men both over time and across cultural boundaries, and that it takes extraordinary circumstances to mobilize them.[1] In revolutionary Paris, women asserted themselves politically precisely in the context of such extraordinary circumstances: economic problems threatening their security dovetailed with power struggles and radical changes in authority; and the general Enlightenment quest for progress developed into the real opportunity for constitutional and legal reform.

Educated women made social, economic, and political demands that were radical even at a time of unlimited enthusiasm for reform.[2] They wanted a transformation of women's place in the family and in the economy, justifying their arguments on the grounds that women were the molders of future citizens and the repositories of society's values. They wanted legal equality of rights within marriage, the right to divorce, and extended rights of widows over property and of widowed mothers over their minor children. They wanted publicly guaranteed educational opportunities for girls, including vocational training for poor girls. They were concerned with the health of women and wanted public training, licensing, and support for midwives for all the provinces of France. They asked for guarantees for women's right to employment, the denial to men of specified professions like embroidery and dressmaking, and licensing procedures to limit entry into such professions. Olympe de Gouges took literally the title of the Declaration of the Rights of Man and Citizen, saying that it did not apply to women and drafting her own Declaration of the Rights of Woman, in which she demanded a representative institution for women. Less radical women became enthusiastic supporters. They planned festivals of freedom, organized clubs in which children were taught citizenship, offered prizes for recitations of the Declaration of Rights, organized workshops, and sewed for the troops. Some of these women understood the potential influence that could be gained from organization, and they attempted, largely unsuccessfully, to form correspondence societies and federations of women's groups.[3]

The demands of poor women—workers, market women, and the wives of *sans-culottes*—were less radical departures from past behavior,

---

[1]Jane S. Jaquette, *Women in Politics*, p. xiii.

[2]Jane Abray argues that such demands, if realized, would have transformed French culture more than did the abolition of monarchy. See Jane Abray, "Feminism in the French Revolution," *American Historical Review* 80 (February, 1975):43–62.

[3]For a survey of women's activities in revolutionary Paris, see Paule-Marie Duhet, *Les Femmes et la Révolution, 1789–1794*.

but paradoxically they were taken as a more serious threat by authorities because they dealt with the crucial political problem of supplying the Parisian populace with the means of its livelihood. Subsistence had long been considered an issue of particular concern to the women in Paris. They were the ones who stood in the bread lines and congregated in the streets and markets, and their behavior was volatile in times of shortages or increases in the price of bread, the dietary staple of the common people.[4] There is evidence to suggest that women were sometimes more willing than men to combine legal tactics, such as petitioning, with the resort to violence which at least implicitly questioned the legitimacy of the prevailing government.[5] The women risked all sorts of measures: shouting and demonstrating in the spectator galleries of the national legislature and Section assemblies, circulating seditious petitions, making insulting remarks to local and national magistrates, and protesting in food riots and popular insurrections. The most effective measures were incidents of *taxation populaire,* where crowds frequently dominated by women seized merchandise from shopkeepers and grocers, distributed the goods to all customers equally at *le prix juste,* the "just price" (determined by the participants) and then returned the proceeds to the merchants.

In 1793 some of the *femmes sans-culottes* participated in the Society of Revolutionary Republican Women, the first political interest group for common women known in western history.[6] The organization was founded by an actress and a chocolate maker; it counted common women among its members and represented the opinions and interests of the working poor, cooperating with or confronting male-dominated institutions—Section assemblies, popular societies, and the National Convention. Tolerated by authorities for barely half a year, the Society was an important indicator of the extent and limits of organized women's political influence.

Parisian women's participation in politics can be explained only within the context of the whole Revolution—its antecedents, its leaders, its issues, its institutional changes, and its dramatic events. When

[4]See George Rudé, *Paris and London in the Eighteenth Century: Studies in Popular Protest.*

[5]On the morning of July 16, 1791, the day before the massacre on the Champ de Mars, two women made the proposal to the Cordeliers to knock down statues of kings which still decorated the squares and bridges of Paris. The president rejected their proposal "out of prudence." Albert Mathiez, *Le Club des Cordeliers pendant la crise de Varennes et le massacre du Champ de Mars,* p. 124, cited from *Babillard,* July 17, 1791.

[6]See Margaret George, "The 'World Historical Defeat' of the Républicaines-Révolutionnaires," *Science and Society* 40, no. 4 (Winter, 1976–77):410–37. See also Marie Cerati, *Le Club des citoyennes républicaines révolutionnaires.*

the Revolution came, processes that nationalized the French political struggle had been under way for at least a century.[7] Issues that had once been local or regional had become national. Royal ministers, intendants, parlementary magistrates, provincial officers, tax farmers, taxpayers, aware citizens—all were caught up in the expansion of the issues that concerned them. The accelerating pace of change was interweaving economic transformations, demographic changes, intellectual developments, political and administrative reforms, and so on. Thus, the nationalization of politics was not limited to issues of royal centralization and its consequences, but included also the implications of the Enlightenment, social and cultural changes.

Social issues raised by Enlightenment writers contributed to this nationalizing process. Legal reform was one issue of particular relevance to women. France before the Revolution had no national legal system, and so the legal status of women differed from province to province.[8] It was generally true that forms of legal equality originating in the Middle Ages had been abolished or were no longer applied in the eighteenth century. For example, noblewomen had lost seigneurial rights to plead cases or adjudicate disputes within their territories, and Parisian working women had lost most of their exclusively female guilds that protected their economic rights. Concern for civil rights and just punishment had ameliorated some conditions for women; for example, the sentence for female adultery had been reduced in some places from public whipping and imprisonment to a two-year prison term. By and large, women were legally totally subservient to their husbands or fathers in virtually all areas of marriage contracts, inheritance laws, property and tax laws, and child custody arrangements. Marriages were indissoluble. Only proof of her husband's death freed a wife, even if she was deserted, although she could get legal separation if she was abused and her life endangered by her husband. When the publicists began calling attention to these matters in tracts, pamphlets, and petitions, they were speaking to conditions that prevailed throughout France. Their propaganda had a nationwide circulation. The boldest among them asked for nothing less than full legal equality for the women of France, whether single, married, or widowed.

[7]Charles Tilly, Louise Tilly, and Richard Tilly, *The Rebellious Century, 1830–1930,* esp. pp. 26–29.

[8]The best summary is Léon Abensour, *La Femme et le féminisme avant la Révolution française.* See also: Jean Portemer, "Le Statut de la femme en France depuis la Réformation des coutumes jusqu'à la rédaction du Code civil," *Recueils de la Société Jean Bodin pour l'histoire comparative des institutions* 12:447–97.

Another social issue was a national system of education. The seventeenth-century treatises of Fénelon and Madame de Maintenon's school at St. Cyr had generated considerable interest in programs for educating women. A royal ordinance of 1724 mandated compulsory universal primary school education; paid schoolteachers were to be sent to all parishes, but the government was not energetic in enforcing this law.[9] Nonetheless, on the local level, and in Paris in particular, philanthropists, curés, nuns, and local officials were sometimes successful in their attempts to set up neighborhood primary schools. Education became a major concern of women publicists during the Revolution; they frequently made the moral argument that poor girls without any training had no recourse but prostitution if they lost their family support. Many of the cahiers of 1789 included demands that the government provide education for girls.

For a century before the Revolution the French state had grown in scope and power, and the royal bureaucracy had been increasingly centralized. While some Enlightenment publicists urged the extension of administrative organizations and processes into areas such as education and legal reform where women would be positively affected, others joined an Enlightenment protest against certain consequences of centralization and nationalized the issue of protection for the individual against government expansion of its spheres of influence. Women writers in the Third Estate joined the Enlightenment protest against certain consequences of this centralization, labeled royal absolutism. Typically, they opposed not the tendency of rationalizing absolutists to attack collective privileges, but rather the threat those absolutists' operations posed to the individual's right to free and full self-expression.

A small minority of educated women among the *hautes bourgeoises* imitated women of the liberal aristocracy by organizing salons. There ideas circulated about the creation of a new free society; there the philosophes and their feminine supporters and hostesses occasionally debated the necessity of providing women with educational opportunities and legal rights. One philosophe, Condorcet, brought together explicitly feminist themes in his prerevolutionary writing, and in a political journal in 1790 he explicitly advocated political and legal equality for women, restricting the suffrage, however, to women of property.[10]

[9]Abensour, *La Femme et le féminisme*, p. 52.

[10]A. Condorcet O'Connor and M. F. Arago, *Oeuvres de Condorcet*. 12 vols. (Paris, 1847). The following essays discuss the question of women's rights: "Lettres d'un Bourgeois de New Haven

Other writers selectively incorporated feminist themes, while a hand-
ful of articulate women publicists, like Olympe de Gouges, Madame de
Coicy, and many obscure authors, male and female, who opted for
anonymity, popularized and broadcast feminist ideas as their contribution to the flood of pamphlets and brochures written before and during
the opening months of the Revolution. They borrowed ideas from the
Enlightenment establishment (but also drew heavily upon a French
feminist tradition which can be traced to the literature of the late
Middle Ages and Renaissance), giving forceful expression tó women's
demands for education, economic and political rights, and even benefits
of comprehensive welfare programs. Some of these demands implied
expansion of government services; others frankly presupposed deliberate
policies of laissez-faire.

Royal administration also affected the subsistence problems that were
so important in the lives of the common women of Paris. Traditionally,
women protestors would put pressure on municipal authorities at the
Hôtel de Ville, not on monarchical authorities. Beginning with the
reign of Louis XIV, the focus of the bread issue shifted from the local to
the national level.[11] Migration and population growth swelled the dis-
proportionate size of Paris and made it necessary for ministers and
officials to search for grain supplies outside localities that had been
traditional suppliers. As attempts were made to rationalize the distribution of grain on a national basis, protesters began aiming at national as
well as local authorities. This gradual process intensified in the 1760s
amidst policy debates and policy reversals reflecting conflicts over principle and struggles for power between proponents of free trade and
supporters of mercantilism. During frequent disturbances, women of
the people learned how to make their economic grievances known to
state officials; they learned the names of ministers responsible for economic policies which affected their ability to find employment and food.
Although royal troops quashed prerevolutionary popular disturbances
like the Flour War of 1775, they could not eradicate popular hatred of
royal ministers and policies that disrupted the traditional modes of food
distribution and pricing.

The growth of royal government affected basic issues other than food
supply. Working women of the Third Estate upheld their traditional
privileges of membership in guilds and participation in religious and

---

à un Citoyen de Virginie" (1787), vol. 9, pp. 1–123; "Essai sur la Constitution et les Fonctions
des Assemblées provinciales" (1788), vol. 8, pp. 115–659; and "Essai sur l'admission des
femmes au droit de la cité" (1790), vol. 10, pp. 119–30.

[11] See Tilly, Tilly, and Tilly, *Rebellious Century*, pp. 33, 50–51.

secular ceremonies. But they found these privileges jeopardized by royal ministers and officers, often professionally trained men whose chief concerns were developing policies for efficient methods of tax collection and promoting the interests of the state over all parochial or corporate interests. The grievances of working women often fell on deaf ears. As they lacked armed force, organization, and leadership, their efforts to call attention to their economic plight were frustrated.

All these trends—intellectual, social, political, and economic—had increased the number of people, both men and women, who were aware of the implication of politics for their personal lives. The same trends broadened the horizons of the politically aware, bringing them into contact not only with local and regional authorities, but with national officials as well. But it was the circumstances of the Revolution itself which allowed Parisian women to stake out the field of their political participation, progressively enlarge its scope, and intensify its impact. It is those revolutionary circumstances that we now examine systematically.

The nationalization of the political struggle that we have traced in the *ancien régime* was accelerated, intensified, and centered in Paris during the Revolution. A key part of these processes was the alteration or creation of political institutions that could serve both as stimuli to political activity and as channels for political participants. Female participants—and they came from every class and social category in Paris—learned to use these institutions. When the Estates General was announced, women authors were among the publicists, making sure that issues such as education, divorce, and public health facilities were targets of reform or new legislation. When the Estates General had become the National Assembly, committed to writing a constitution, women were among the crowds from Paris who secured its removal from Versailles and reestablishment in Paris. Important inspiration continued to come from the activities of constitution drafting and lawmaking, especially between 1789 and 1791 and between 1791 and 1793.

The revolutionary press, with its rapid and constant production of journals and pamphlets, has long been acknowledged for its contribution to revolutionary politics. Educated women contributed to and read the journals. It is estimated that more than two-thirds of the men and more than one-third of the women in Paris were minimally literate.[12]

[12]The only systematic attempt to calculate literacy rates in revolutionary France was based on signatures on marriage contracts. It does not include figures for Paris. For 1786–90 the female literacy rate for the Department of Seine-et-Oise was 30–39 percent. Since urban literacy was

But since journals were read aloud and debated in public places where common women congregated, the women undoubtedly picked up some of the language and content of revolutionary debate. Oral political communication in Paris is an important part of the explanation for the political activities of women. Paris was the most populous urban center of the late eighteenth century, and women encountered each other daily in the streets, the cafés, the markets, the stalls, the gaming halls of the Palais Royale, and later on in the workshops, breadlines, Section assemblies, popular societies, and galleries of clubs and national legislatures. Women were hardly confined to home and church. This kind of street-level contact meant that rumors spread rapidly, observers could be easily harangued to take part in a demonstration or go to the scene of a disturbance, and popular societies could do their organizing.

Paris became the revolutionary capital, the headquarters of the national legislatures and the central Jacobin Society. Government was no longer centered among the nobility at Versailles, but in Paris in the national legislatures, the Commune, and the Section assemblies, all of which had galleries open to the public. With such institutions literally in their midst, government could become an immediate daily experience to the women of Paris. It was easier to learn about politics, make demands, express enthusiasm, or lodge protests.

The functions of these institutions in provisioning Paris in war and revolution became particularly central. Historians of popular movements in the Revolution note that these *journées* involving recurrent subsistence crises were the ones where women predominated in the crowds. Economically secure women frequently supported the economic and subsistence demands of poor women.

The hardships of the revolutionary years came after several generations of comparative biological security and, equally crucially, after several immediately prerevolutionary decades of relative psychological and physical insecurity. The eighteenth century had seen an end to the devastating famines and deadly plagues of early modern France; women, excluding those in the underemployed or unemployed floating population of Parisian destitutes, had come to expect the reasonably steady supply of bread and other necessities, selling at a reasonable price, which would assure their well-being. But it is also true that bread riots and the Flour War in the decade of the seventies had fortified latent fears of

---

usually greater, it may be estimated that 35–49 percent of Parisian women during the Revolution were at least able to sign their marriage contracts. The data are from: Michel Fleury and Pierre Valmary, "Les Progrès de l'instruction élémentaire de Louis XIV à Napoléon III d'après l'enquête de Louis Maggiolo (1877–1879)," *Population* 12 (1957):71–92.

dearth while reinforcing rioters and their sympathizers in the ᵉ that once again violence could prove to be a potent, effective weaᵖ the war against fear and hunger. When the early months of the Revo. tion coincided with a bread and flour shortage and a sudden price increase, poor women became desperately afraid that they could not hold their families together and might slip into abject poverty.[13]

Such circumstances pitted the poor against authorities they felt were responsible for assuring their livelihood, particularly in a time of bad harvests, inflation, and foreign and civil war.

Women in Paris engaged themselves in Revolutionary politics for many reasons in addition to their economic needs. Particularly striking in these documents is evidence of a sophisticated grasp of the implications of revolutionary events, even among the illiterate poor. We find women who could not sign marking a petition on royal executive authority, a cook testifying that she reads revolutionary journals, a wigmaker's wife asserting her citizen rights. Such revolutionary mobilization was made possible fundamentally by the opening of elective assemblies, clubs, and popular societies which women could attend and in some cases join. Beginning as proselytizing institutions to teach the sovereign people their rights, these organizations became places where women could participate directly in drafting petitions, sending delegations, and lodging protests.

Other revolutionary institutionalization which facilitated feminine political activities included the creation of the National Guard, whose radical members were sympathetic to and ready to support popular economic demands; the *levée en masse* (national conscription), which required the mobilization of the entire society and alerted women to the connection between political-military questions and the question of subsistence for civilians; the continuous flux in political factions which dominated the Paris Commune and the national assemblies; and popular insurrections, the *journées,* which played a crucial part in revolutionary radicalization between 1789 and 1795.

Not only did the patterns of revolutionary institutionalization we have been discussing facilitate women's expanding participation, but this participation also affected new or changed institutions. The democratization of Section assemblies and popular societies made it easier for

---

[13]For discussion of material conditions of existence for women in prerevolutionary France, and for material on women's participation in protest movements during periods of subsistence crisis, see: Olwen H. Hufton, "Women and the Family Economy in Eighteenth Century France," *French Historical Studies* (Spring, 1975), pp. 1–22; Steven L. Kaplan, *Bread, Politics, and Political Economy in the Reign of Louis XV,* 2 vols. (The Hague, 1976), vol. 1, pp. 90–92.

ngside men of their same occupational and
edly the presence of wives and neighbors also
equally new to political activity. The most
: female participation transformed a male in-
n's march to Versailles, which ended with the
ssembly back to Paris. Along with the National
an men, women were assertive and boisterous
d cheering the first group of deputies as they
brought the government literally into the midst of
the people.

The Thermidorians, who came to power in July, 1794, dismantled or
transformed these institutions, which had proven so beneficial for the
women of Paris. Under the Thermidorians, democratized institutions
gave way to oligarchical ones, popular insurrections were weakly supported by radical members of the National Guard and the Convention,
and popular clubs and general assemblies were dominated by men of
property; a white terror was unleashed to punish the perpetrators of the
Red Terror. After Thermidor, women ceased political activity, returning only during the brief tragic *journées* of Germinal and Prairial, when
they participated in the final popular uprisings of the Revolution and
initiated marches to local and national representatives to demand bread
and a restoration of the rights of the people.

We would suggest in conclusion that the economic, constitutional,
and political crises of the Revolution generated institutions in which
political roles for women could be developed and multiplied and the
impact of their participation intensified. We feel that this focus on the
relationship between women and political authorities leads to the most
historically sound explanation of women's behavior. Their multiple
goals and definitions of issues provide us with evidence of their transformation into citizens and participants in democratic politics.

I

Feminine Revolutionary Expectations and Activism: 1789

IN MAY, 1789, Louis XVI convoked a meeting of the Estates General—the first in 175 years.[1] Within six weeks the Third Estate and many lower clergy united against the first two Estates; spokesmen for the Third Estate proclaimed themselves the National Assembly, representing a nation of Frenchmen, and in Paris, electors for the Third Estate remained in session as the core of a new municipal government.

On July 14, artisans and working people in the capital participated in the conquest of the Bastille, a symbol of oppressions under the Old Regime. Simultaneously, peasants in the countryside engaged in a series of violent *jacqueries;* they demanded their freedom from feudal obligations and assaulted nobles unwilling to relinquish feudal rights. So threatening were the peasant uprisings that on the night of August 4–5, secular and religious representatives of the first two Estates surrendered their feudal privileges; municipalities, provinces, and towns followed suit. Later that month the Estates General issued the Declaration of the Rights of Man and Citizen and began preparing the first written constitution for the French monarchy.

As women in Paris became aware of the revolutionary significance of these dramatic events, they began expressing aspirations for a regenerated society. Through petitions, organized marches, and acts of violence they exerted pressure on national legislative and executive authorities, attempting to make both responsive to women's sometimes conflicting needs for protection, security, guaranteed subsistence, fiscal

---

[1]The first of the revolutionary assemblies, the Estates General, sat from May 6 to June 17, 1789. On June 17 the Third Estate and most of the lower clergy declared themselves the National Assembly; on June 27 the King ordered the nobles and upper clergy to join. The National Assembly sat until September, 1791. It was replaced by a newly elected body, the Legislative Assembly, which was in session until September, 1792. The legislature under the First Republic was the National Convention, which sat from August, 1792, until 1795.

stability, steady employment, occupational training, and civil rights. Representatives of a Parisian guild for working women frankly demanded the restoration of guild privileges jeopardized by free-market legislation. In another document included here, women of the Third Estate do not ask for the vote or the right to elect female deputies to the Estates General; rather, they demand protection for professional rights in women's trades and guaranteed public primary education for girls. However, in other political literature educated female elites from among the liberal aristocracy and the upper bourgeoisie prepared pamphlets and wrote letters professing faith in the Estates General and demanding civil rights, including liberal legislation on marriage, divorce, and inheritance.

During the summer of 1789 the majority of Parisian women—aside from the aristocratic women who joined their husbands and fathers in exile—greeted the Revolution with enthusiasm. Prominent *bourgeoises* deposited their jewels and money with the National Assembly to help solve a national financial crisis, and a small number of Amazons volunteered to serve with the National Guard.

Our information about the revolutionary aspirations of common women outside the guilds comes primarily from eyewitness accounts of summertime activities in Paris. Women were among the crowds at the Bastille on July 14, but there is no reason to suspect that they planned the operation along with men in the National Guard.[2] A few days later, women took bouquets to the newly elected mayor of Paris, Bailly, and the commander-in-chief of the National Guard, Lafayette.

By late summer, economic problems began to stimulate more active protest. Bad harvests and speculation endangered the supply of grain for Paris and raised bread prices to new highs. In addition, unemployment surged among artisans, merchants, and domestics who catered to aristocrats as the numbers of emigrating nobles increased. Women were particularly affected by the decline in the luxury trades and services.

Issues of bread and unemployment were the traditional concerns of women of the people, but by August they were beginning to act on these concerns in new and untraditional ways. We include in this chapter a document to illustrate the almost daily processions of market women, laundresses, and working men to give thanks to the patron saint of Paris for sparing the city in the July crisis. But these processions—several each day and provided with impressive escorts of Na-

---

[2]George Rudé, *Paris and London in the Eighteenth Century: Studies in Popular Protest*, pp. 132, 133.

tional Guardsmen—usually included a trip to the Hôtel de Ville to present Lafayette with a bouquet or a loaf of bread. These symbolic demonstrations indicate an untraditional alliance of the women with the National Guard and the women's untraditional awareness that their economic interests would be represented by the new bourgeois government in Paris.[3]

Tensions in Paris reached their zenith in early October. The King had called for additional mercenaries to protect him, and the Queen welcomed royalist troops at a feast where the national tricolor was insulted. Patriotic Parisian guards and the women of the people were incensed by such unpatriotic behavior.

On the morning of October 5, Parisian women from the central market districts and the faubourgs sounded the tocsin for a popular insurrection. They converged on the Hôtel de Ville and exhorted Lafayette to lead them in a march to Versailles to demand bread from the King and the National Assembly. Lafayette hesitated to support such protest, but radical Guardsmen joined the women and offered armed support for the procession. The demands of middle-class radicals for political reforms were combined with the demands of poor women for economic reforms. From the standpoint of participants in the October march, the popular uprising was successful. After several violent incidents at Versailles, the King agreed to assure a regular supply of bread to Paris and to consent to revolutionary legislation prepared by the National Assembly. The King also agreed to return to live in Paris under popular surveillance.

Eyewitness accounts of women's behavior during the October Days provide us with evidence that women were beginning to transform themselves into *citoyennes*. The women probably did not grasp the intricacies of the debate over the constitutional provisions for the royal veto—the president of the National Assembly, Mounier, recounted that they chastised him for his support of "Monsieur le Veto"—but they did show that they understood the roles of the deputies,[4] and in demanding the Assembly's relocation in Paris, they revealed their awareness of the Assembly as the vital center of the regime's political life.

On the evening of the march to Versailles, the women occupied the Assembly's meeting hall; one observer noted that they "voted" along with the deputies on motions and amendments relevant to a decree

---

[3]George Rudé, *The Crowd in the French Revolution*, pp. 66, 67. For the evidence, see document 1 below, this chapter.

[4]Jean-Joseph Mounier, *Faits relatifs à la dernière insurrection* (n.p., n.d. [1789]).

concerning the circulation and distribution of grains and "exercised . . . the function of the legislative power and the executive power."[5] Their treatment of the King indicates another development: the erosion of their image of his inviolable sovereignty. On his return trip to Paris they surrounded his carriage with pikes bearing the heads of his murdered guards and chanted that they were bringing back the baker, the baker's wife, and the baker's apprentice—hardly traditional modes of demonstrating respect and loyalty to a fatherly monarch.

The pattern of the October insurrection is of central importance for understanding the Parisian women's involvement in the Revolution from 1789 to 1795. The alliance between the radical wing of the National Guard and the women of the people had provided women with the armed force and leadership necessary for conducting their crusade for economic security. Such alliances would recur in 1792, 1793, and 1794 when political and economic crises converged. It was not until 1795 that this alliance broke down. Once middle-class radicals withdrew support for popular protest, the women found themselves incapable of influencing the course of events.

The October Days generated two political myths. Contemporary conservative and moderate writers maintained that the October women were "furies" and "harlots" who had been dragged out of the gutter and bribed by the Duc d'Orléans in his effort to supplant Louis XVI as the constitutional monarch. Such individuals also argued that the October Days were an indication of the violence and anarchy which would be unleashed if the will of the people prevailed.[6]

Observers who held radical views argued in the opposite manner: the October women were heroines; they aspired to liberty, and when they saw the Revolution in jeopardy, they rose up to save the nation from royalist hordes who surrounded the King; these female patriots had intended to make a peaceful march to Versailles (although some of them carried pikes), but royalists had insinuated themselves into the crowds and incited women to acts of violence.[7]

Although the right and the left differed in their opinions of the October women, neither side disputed the fact that women predominated in the October march and displayed extraordinary tenacity in demanding bread and patriotic loyalty from the King. Of all the popular

[5]*Révolutions de Versailles, Dédiées aux dames Françoises, no. 1* (n.p., n.d. ["du samedi 3 octobre au (deletion in text) du même mois"]), p. 18.

[6]A spokesman for the right was Jean-Joseph Mounier.

[7]See document 7 below, this chapter.

insurrections during the Revolution, the October Days stand out as the women's insurrection. The women were making their traditional demand for stable supplies of bread at prices they could afford. What was dramatically new was their target—the King and the deputies instead of the government of the city of Paris.

Less violent middle-class women would continue to insist that the National Assembly make good its commitment to rights and liberties by institutionalizing both in laws benefiting women.

Both middle-class women and working-class women had appropriated newly nationalized issues and had restated them to represent their interests, and they were entering into dialogue and confrontation with new national authorities, executive and legislative, to satisfy their needs and demands.

1. Petition of Women of the Third Estate to the King

Source: *Pétition des femmes du Tiers-Etat au Roi, 1er janvier 1789*
(n.p., n.d.), in Bibliothèque historique de la Ville de Paris,
12,807, vol. 1, no. 17.

These petitioners, women of modest means, appeal directly to
the King because they do not conceive of the Estates General as
an institution truly representative of the nation. They urge the
King to intervene personally to satisfy their demands for a solid
practical and moral education and for exclusive rights to practice
feminine trades. Their stated objectives are to become honorably
self-supporting and to prepare themselves for their roles as
educators of the young.

———————————

Sire,

At a time when the various orders of the state are busy with their
interests, when everyone is trying to assert his titles and his rights, when
some people are worrying about recalling centuries of servitude and
anarchy, when others are making every effort to shake off the last links
which still bind them to the imperious remains of the feudal system,
women—continual objects of the admiration and scorn of men—
women, wouldn't it be possible for them also to make their voice heard
amidst this general agitation?

Excluded from the national assemblies by laws too well consolidated
for them to hope to break, they do not ask, Sire, for your permission to
send their deputies to the Estates General; they know too well how great
a role interest would play in an election and how easy it would be for the
representatives [*les élus*] to impede the freedom of the votes.

We prefer, Sire, to place our cause at your feet; not wishing to obtain
anything except from your heart, we address our complaints and confide
our miseries to it.

The women of the Third Estate are almost all born without fortune; their education is very neglected or very defective: it consists in their being sent to schools at the house of a teacher who himself does not know the first word of the language he is teaching. They continue going there until they are able to read the service of the Mass in French and Vespers in Latin. Having fulfilled the first duties of religion, they are taught to work; having reached the age of fifteen or sixteen, they can make five or six *sous* a day. If nature has refused them beauty, they get married without dowry to unfortunate artisans, lead aimless, difficult lives stuck away in the provinces, and give birth to children they are incapable of raising. If, on the contrary, they are born pretty, without culture, without principles, without any idea of morals, they become the prey of the first seducer, commit a first sin, come to Paris to bury their shame, end by losing it altogether, and die victims of licentious ways.

Today, when the difficulty of subsisting forces thousands of them to put themselves up for auction, when men find it easier to buy them for a spell than to win them over forever, those whom a happy penchant inclines to virtue, who are consumed by the desire to learn, who feel themselves led by a natural taste, who have overcome the deficiencies of their education and know a little of everything without having learned anything, those, to conclude, whom a haughty soul, a noble heart, a pride of sentiment cause to be called *prudish,* are forced to throw themselves into cloisters where only a modest dowry is required, or forced to hire themselves out when they do not have enough courage, enough heroism, to share the generous devotion of the daughters of Vincent de Paul.

Also, several, solely because they are born girls, are disdained by their parents, who refuse to set them up, preferring to concentrate their fortune on the head of a son whom they designate to carry on their name in the capital; for it is good that Your Majesty understands that we also have names to keep up. Or, if old age finds them spinsters, they spend it in tears and see themselves the object of the scorn of their nearest relatives.

To prevent so many ills, Sire, we ask that men not be allowed, under any pretext, to exercise trades that are the prerogative of women—such as seamstress, embroiderer, *marchande de mode,* etc., etc.; if we are left at least with the needle and the spindle, we promise never to handle the compass or the square.

We ask, Sire, that your benevolence provide us with the means of putting to use the talents with which nature will have furnished us, notwithstanding the impediments which are forever being placed on our education.

May you assign us positions, which we alone will be able to fill, which we will occupy only after having passed a strict examination, after trustworthy inquiries concerning the purity of our morals.

We ask to be enlightened, to have work, not in order to usurp men's authority, but in order to be better esteemed by them, so that we might have the means of living out of the way of misfortune and so that poverty does not force the weakest among us, who are blinded by luxury and swept along by example, to join the crowd of unfortunate beings who overpopulate the streets and whose debauched audacity is a disgrace to our sex and to the men who keep them company.

We would want this class of women to wear a mark of identification. Today, when they go so far as to adopt the modesty of our dress, when they mingle everywhere in all kinds of clothing, we often find ourselves taken for them; some men are mistaken and make us blush because of their scorn. It would be necessary that under pain of having to work in the public workshops for the benefit of the poor (it is known that work is the greatest punishment that can be inflicted on them), they never be able to remove this mark. . . . . [*sic*] However, it occurs to us that the empire of fashion would be destroyed and one would run the risk of seeing many too many women dressed in the same color.

We implore you, Sire, to set up free schools where we could learn our language on the basis of principles [and] religion and ethics. May one and the other be offered to us in all their grandeur, entirely stripped of the petty applications which attenuate their majesty; may our hearts be formed there; may we be taught above all to practice the virtues of our sex: gentleness, modesty, patience, charity; as for the arts that please, women learn them without teachers. Sciences? . . . they serve only to inspire us with a stupid pride, lead us to pedantry, go against the desires of nature, make of us mixed beings who are rarely faithful wives and still more rarely good mothers of families.

We ask to come out of the state of ignorance, to be able to give our children a sound and reasonable education so as to make of them subjects worthy of serving you. We will teach them to cherish the beautiful name of Frenchmen; we will transmit to them the love we have for Your Majesty, for we are willing to leave valor and genius to men, but we will challenge them over the dangerous and precious gift of sensitivity; we defy them to love you better than we; they run to Versailles, most of them for their interests, and when we, Sire, see you there, with difficulty and with pounding hearts, and are able to gaze for an instant upon your August Person, tears flow from our eyes. The idea of Majesty, of Sovereign, vanishes, and we see in you only a tender Father, for whom we would sacrifice our lives a thousand times.

2. THE SPECIFIC GRIEVANCES OF THE MERCHANT FLOWER SELLERS OF THE CITY AND FAUBOURGS OF PARIS

Source: *Doléances particulières des marchandes bouquetières fleuristes chapelières en fleurs de la Ville et faubourgs de Paris* [1789], in Charles-Louis Chassin, *Les Elections et les cahiers de Paris en 1789,* 4 vols. (Paris, 1888–89), vol. II, pp. 534–37.

In this cahier, written to express grievances of women who made their living in Paris as flower sellers, the petitioners revere the King, and at the same time they expect the Estates General, and particularly the Third Estate's representatives, to function as their national spokesmen, but they also argue that rights consecrated under law and by tradition are valid, whatever the disposition of King and Estates might be. These women sent their cahier to the electors of the Third Estate at the Archevêché, to city officials, to Necker, and, finally, to the Estates General.

———————◆———————

The liberty accorded to all citizens to expose before the nation's representatives the abuses which assail them from all sides is without doubt a sure sign of impending reform.

In this confidence, the *marchandes bouquetières* formerly comprising the *communauté des maîtresses bouquetières et marchandes chapelières en fleurs* of the City and Faubourgs of Paris venture to address themselves to you, our Lords (the Estates General). It is not for ordinary abuses they ask correction. It is their trade, their whole existence, which they lost by the doubtless involuntary error of one of His Majesty's former ministers, which they reclaim at this time.

Even before forming a *communauté* and constituting themselves as a *corps de jurande,* the *marchandes bouquetières* already had statutes which they enforced among themselves under the authority and jurisdiction of the *prévôt* of Paris or of his lieutenant-general of police.

This kind of *jurande,* as imperfect as it was, undoubtedly prevented abuses. However, it was soon realized that these precautions would not be adequate for maintaining order unless the responsibility for internal discipline was placed in the hands of the *bouquetières*. Consequently, they were established as a *communauté*.

In 1735, thanks to the kindheartedness of Louis XV, the *maîtresses bouquetières* obtained verification of their *communauté* and new regulations which were ordered executed by *lettres-patentes* of November 26, 1736, [and] registered in Parlement on December 18, 1737.

The *maîtresses bouquetières* who had undergone a three-year apprenticeship and who had paid substantial fees for the *maîtrise* were peacefully plying their trade when they found themselves suddenly deprived of it by the suppression of their *communauté*.

The ministers' oppressive silence, the menaces with which they were armed—doubtless without their knowledge—and the repellent coldness of their clerks stifled their [the *bouquetières'*] cries at that time, but today, when a better order is in the making, they hope for everything from the Prince's justice and from that of the Estates.

In the eyes of anyone else except the enlightened representatives of the nation, the petitioners' reclamation perhaps would not seem worth the sacrifice of some of the precious time being allocated to the examination of the major interests which will occupy them. But they [the *bouquetières*] need not fear being rebuffed. They know, these worthy representatives of the French people, that they have a greater responsibility towards the most indigent class in particular. The more unfortunate a man is, the more sacred are his rights, especially where his trade constitutes all the wealth he has. Its protection cannot fail to be of concern to the nation's deputies and to hold their attention.

Besides, the petitioners' reclamation is bound up with an important issue which is submitted to the Estates for a decision: that of knowing whether it would be useful or not to allow every individual an indeterminate liberty to engage in all kinds of commerce.

Let the petitioners be allowed to venture some reflections here which may perhaps pave the way for a decision on this capital issue.

In the regulation of commerce and trade, two things should be taken into consideration. The entire *corps* should be organized so that each individual who commits himself to a trade can earn a living for himself and his children. However, access to trades, and above all to those which are designated in particular for the class with meager means, should not be made so difficult that the industry of the poor is discouraged and emulation stifled.

This combination, on which the general happiness and the prosperity of commerce rest, necessarily would be destroyed by indeterminate liberty.

Too great a facility allowed under the edicts of 1776 and 1777 has made all the professions only too acutely aware of the inconveniences of this liberty. A large number of merchants does not produce—far from it—the salutary effect which it would appear must have been expected from competition. Because the number of consumers does not increase in proportion to the number of artisans, the latter necessarily hurt one another; they can obtain the buyer's preference only by lowering the price of their goods. Distress and the need to sell at a low price force them to turn out shoddy [goods] or to feign ruin, which brings mortal blows to commerce.

The more restricted a trade is, [and] the fewer resources it holds out, the more important it is to reduce the number of competitors. Unfortunately, since the suppression of their *communauté,* that is what the petitioners have found out. Their trade, although limited, offered them, before this suppression, a means for making a living and raising their children. Today, when everybody can sell flowers and arrange bouquets, their modest gains are divided up to the point that they can no longer make enough to live on. The lure of this gain, restricted though it may be, and even more, a strong propensity for laziness, nonetheless determined a crowd of young people of the feminine sex to enter the petitioners' trade; and because their trade cannot feed them, they look to libertinage and the most shameful debauchery for the means they are lacking. The petitioners' cause is also that of morals.

The flower trade in itself does not suffer any the less from this anarchy. There is no more policing of the market. All the unprincipled girls whom no law, no decency can restrain, throw themselves on the goods which the flower growers bring, pillage them or crush them, [and] arbitrarily set the price. And only too often it happens that because of this, the flower growers lose the precious fruit of their hard work. It's because of this [situation] that brawls arise during which these hawkers are backed up by soldiers and by disreputable characters. It is because of this that you get this abuse which set in when liberty was accorded in the trade of the *marchandes bouquetières:* girls who are not merchants have thought up the idea of fastening orange blossoms with pins or artificial flowers which they attach to the aforementioned branches [or] they attach several carnations together and put them on cards and sell them as a single one.

All these abuses, which can only be ended with the reestablishment of the *communauté,* are contrary to order and discouraging for the growers, who devote themselves to the cultivation of flowers. The inconveniences produced by these disorders have been felt in all times, and it is because of them that in 1731 the new statutes for the *communauté des bouquetières maîtresses* were confirmed.

Therefore, the petitioners dare expect from the equity of the Estates the reestablishment of their corporation. Besides, this is a justice that is due them since they paid the King considerable sums for enjoying the advantages of their trade, advantages they are deprived of by too much competition and the disorders it brings with it.

The petitioners ask that a police force be provided to stop large numbers of people who, claiming free trade, hang around the market every night (and especially the nights before holidays for patron saints), waiting for the flower growers and intending to abuse their good faith. They lay waste to the markets, either arbitrarily or by leave of the authorities, before the usual hour for selling the above-mentioned flowers. These same people have strayed from honesty to the point of going off into the countryside, where they lay waste to the flower beds and orange groves belonging to seigneurs and private homes.

The former *journalières bouquetières* are reduced to the most extreme poverty by the different kinds of people who have taken to selling flowers. Since liberty was declared in this branch of trade, the petitioners have been pained to see mothers of families without work, [women] whom they used to support with wages of thirty *sols* a day, plus food; four *livres,* ten *sols* for two and one-half days' work during the minor holidays; and nine *livres,* also for two and one-half days, during the principal holidays—which allowed them to raise their little families.

Liberty, which all orders of the State reclaim, cannot constitute an obstacle to the petitioners' request. Liberty is an enemy of license, and citizens are free so long as they obey only the laws which they impose upon themselves.

The petitioners entrust their just reclamation to the deputies of the Third Estate above all. They [the deputies of the Third Estate] more than the others [that is, more than the deputies of the First and Second Estates] are their [the petitioners'] representatives, their friends, their brothers, and it is up to them to plead the cause of indigent people.

Based on these considerations, let an irrevocable order be promulgated, with interdictions, from His Majesty to the effect that under no pretext whatsoever shall a *marchande bouquetière* or other person be permitted to buy or sell flowers before 6 A.M. between [the religious holidays of] Pâques and Saint-Martin, and also before 6 A.M. between Saint-Martin and Pâques.

The petitioners will not cease addressing vows to the heavens for the protection and prosperity of the nation's representatives.

Signed: the above-mentioned *marchandes,* represented by Madame Marlé, syndic of the corporation

3. The Fishwives of Paris Pay Homage to the Third Estate

Source: *Compliment des dames poissardes à leurs frères du Tiers Etat* [1789], in Charles-Louis Chassin, *Les Elections et les cahiers de Paris en 1789,* 4 vols. (Paris, 1888–89), vol. III, pp. 252–53.

The *poissardes* (fishwives) traditionally enjoyed special status among the *menu peuple.* They were given prominent places in ceremonial processions, and whenever there was a royal birth, the *poissardes* had the privilege of going to Versailles to verify the existence and sex of the royal infant. Their couplets addressed to the Third Estate in the summer of 1789 reflect their confidence that the King would join the Third Estate to protect the interests of his people. According to the bookseller Hardy, the *poissardes* received a gratification from the Estates of three hundred *livres.* Hardy also tells us that the author of this *Compliment* was the poet Maréchal (as noted in Chassin, *Les Elections,* vol. III, p. 252).

━━━━━◆━━━━━

As all hearts are united today to direct their prayers to heaven for the prosperity of our monarch and his *august family* as well as for the *successful* reestablishment of the realm's finances and the guarantee of a lasting tranquility for the Fatherland, grant us, Messieurs, that animated with the most respectful zeal for your persons, we may be allowed to glorify ourselves in your eyes for the choice that has just been made in our favor, when you were named, by public acclaim, to sustain the interest of the people, to which you belong, the French people, and to [work] with as much zeal for its [the people's] king. Wisdom, equity, disinterestedness, profound knowledge, and a thousand other virtues that exist among you, Messieurs, were the sole reasons you were chosen, and assure the happiness which awaits us. Our prayers for the preservation of your precious days will cease only with the [end] of our own.

Deign to allow the raptures of our joy to burst forth in the couplets which follow:

(To the tune: *Vous qui de l'amoureuse ivresse*)

If the clergy, if the nobility, / My good friends / Treat us with such rudeness / and disdain / Let them all fancy themselves capable of ruining the State / While waiting, we will drink / to the Third Estate.

In the face of Supreme Justice / Not more than for us / will their artifice serve them / and their ire / Would it have escaped their memory / that their luster derives, as does their glory / from the Third Estate?

We all owe to its Power / respect, esteem / But to what do we owe our birth? / It's to chance. / The first who made himself Master / was a soldier. / He was King; from whom did he hold the Kingship? / From the Third Estate.

You, who consider us scum / So politely / just as we pay you the *taille* most nobly. / Long live the Savior of France! Necker vivat! From where does this hero spring? / From the Third Estate.

From Louis, our Great Monarch, / Oh! The Great Heart! / He wills, he executes, he marks out for us our happiness. / Let us defend, love with zeal, / serve the State. / Forever faithful to Louis may it be. / The Third Estate!

4. A Woman Recounts Her Role in the Conquest of the Bastille

Source: Marguerite Pinaigre, "Pétition adressée à l'Assemblée nationale," in A.N., F^{ic} III, Seine 71.

The second of the great popular insurrections of 1789 was the conquest of the Bastille. Male participants were hailed as heroes who had saved the Revolution. Many were listed on registers as Vainqueurs de la Bastille, and wounded or crippled *vainqueurs* and widows and children of *vainqueurs* who died during the assault were awarded pensions. Few accounts single out the participation of women, although the name of one woman, Marie Charpentier, does appear on lists of *vainqueurs*. Marguerite Pinaigre's petition reveals that the common women did join their men in the uprising and identified themselves among the defenders of the rights of the people. In deferential but forthright language, Femme Pinaigre asks that the National Assembly recognize services which she, along with her husband, rendered the nation.[1]

[1] The translators would like to thank Jennifer Westfall for valuable assistance in transcribing and interpreting this document.

Legislators:

The person named here, Margueritte Piningre [*sic*], wife of Sieur Bernard Vener, one of the Vainqueurs de la Bastille, has the honor of appearing today before your august assembly to reclaim the execution of the decree issued by the Constituent Assembly in his [her husband's] favor in 1789. This intrepid citizen, who has the misfortune of being crippled for the rest of his days without ever being able to work again in his life because of wounds received on all parts of his body, yes, Legislators, not only has this dear citizen fought in the conquest of the Bastille with the greatest courage, but furthermore, his *citoyenne* wife, who is present here, worked equally hard with all her might, both of them having resolved to triumph or to die. It is she who ran to several wineshops to fill her apron with bottles, both broken and unbroken, which she gave to the authorities to be used as shot in the cannon used to break the chain on the drawbridge of the Bastille. Therefore, by virtue of these legitimate claims the petitioner believes herself justified in coming before the National Assembly today to advise it concerning the non-execution of laws relative to conquerors who were severely maimed, as was the petitioner's husband. This law awards a pension to those who are really crippled and without the means for earning their living. Such is the situation of the latter, who is offering to provide evidence in the form of authentic statements. Nevertheless, he still has not been awarded this pension which he so richly deserves, he as well as his wife, as a consequence of the dangers they faced. The only gratification which this citizen has received is a small sum of four hundred *livres,* which since 1789 has barely sufficed to care for him and to help him get over the severe wounds he suffered.

Under these circumstances, and in the light of such a compelling account, the petitioner dares hope, Messieurs, for your justice and your usual generosity. May you be willing to take under urgent consideration the object of a request which is becoming as pressing as it is urgent,— assuming that surely you would not allow one of the most zealous and intrepid Vainqueurs de la Bastille to languish any longer bent under the weight of the indigence to which he is presently reduced, along with his wife and his children, who expect his every minute to be his last— because from this period [July 14, 1789] on he has always been ill and continues to suffer cruelly every day. The petitioner expects the favor of the representatives of the French nation, to whom she will never cease to offer her most heart-felt gratitude.

[signed] Marguerite Pinaigre

5. WOMEN ARTISANS SALUTE THE NEW LEGISLATURE AND
   PLEDGE THEIR SUPPORT

Source: [Madame Rigal], *Discours prononcé par Mme. Rigal, Dans une assemblée de femmes artistes et orfèvres, tenue le 20 septembre, pour délibérer sur une Contribution volontaire* (n.p., n.d. [1789]), in A.N., F^{ic} III, Seine 71.

In this document Madame Rigal exhorts a meeting of *femmes artistes* and silversmiths to donate money to the National Assembly to help prevent national bankruptcy. Note her argument that bankruptcy would endanger not only the professional interests of women in her audience but also a new national interest.

———————

Mesdames and Mesdemoiselles,
    Your choice of me honors me infinitely, because it is a proof of confidence and an occasion for zeal. However, I ought to be frightened at the prospect of speaking, but I reassure myself with the thought that here I need neither eloquence nor reserve. We share the same sentiments; they will shed light on one another. They will come alive together. Of all the bonds which unite sensitive hearts, none is more powerful than participation in a just and generous action.
    Liberty,—and we see this,—elevates, [and] exalts all hearts. If it has produced a few bitter fruits, it promises us happier and more salutary ones. The elite among the French citizenry works for the restoration of the State. As they cannot all be legislators, our compatriots at least can all make themselves useful. The brilliance of knowledge is a distinguishing mark of some; others distinguish themselves by the brilliance of sacrifices. Our sex is excluded from arduous labors, but it is allowed to engage in two very worthwhile occupations—the exercise of the delicate virtues, and heroic sacrifices.
    The time has come to [activate] them on behalf of France.

Either through mistakes in administration or through [fault of] circumstances, this entire vast empire is threatened with destruction—notwithstanding the acknowledged probity of our monarch; notwithstanding the unexampled genius of his minister. The State's public wealth is in danger, and personal fortunes would succumb with it if they [those holding private wealth] were to hesitate to come—to fly—to its aid. All classes of society are dependent upon one another to such an extent, and they are so closely bound to government, that no branch of government can fall without crushing the greater part of society. The arts and commerce would be the first exposed to perish. See even now how much they are suffering and languishing since the public treasury has been in trouble and monetary circulation has been declining. The capitol of the arts threatens to become its tomb.

We are *artistes;* we are *citoyennes;* we are either mothers or sisters or wives of *artistes* and citizens. Our children or our brothers or our husbands showed their courage in securing the deliverance of the Fatherland. The Fatherland is our common family. Our sex is eminently endowed with the spirit of family life. Who is more sensitive than we to public calamities? Who is more disposed to pity, to humanity, to useful generosity? Who among us can resist the voice of the poor, however it makes itself heard?

A poor one, one of our own, who interests us all, offers himself to our vision with the most touching and majestic traits: this is the Fatherland. If we could dispose of our goods, all our goods would be consecrated to [the Fatherland]. One [possession] is left for our use, which vanity employs for an ephemeral triumph—these are our ornaments, so dear to beauty, so varied by fashion, so vaunted and sought after by national taste and foreign imitation.

Here is the offering we must make with enthusiasm, French women. We do not need citations from the example of either the Romans or the Spartans. The heart of Frenchmen and the honor of Frenchmen have no rival, no equal in the universe. These are not found as virtues studied in history, but [rather they are] our natural sentiments which are both independent of education and superior to obstacles. They manifest themselves in our theatres and in our hamlets. Two virtuous farmers from Champenil set the example for their sex. Several women *artistes* from Versailles set an example for our own [sex]. Their noble gesture was transmitted to us and through us will be communicated to all the women of France.

Ah! If this general movement contributes to the restoration of a failing empire! If, through the simple recounting of our feeble efforts, all good citizens, all rich proprietors, all opulent capitalists were to become united as we are for the salvation of the Fatherland! If only so many treasures kept under lock and key . . . would open for the benefit of the public treasury! If only personal interest heeded the advice of the general interest! If only the trembling miser understood that with the ruin of the state he will be crushed on piles of gold and will die for his crimes!

Yes, if a horrible bankruptcy occurs, the crime will no longer be that of the administration; it has exhausted its ingenuity to avoid this disaster. It will be the crime of perverted citizens who hide their wealth, who refuse their contributions, and who allow power to fall and revenues to dry up. No crime is more fatal or more dishonorable. If it takes place, the empire will dissolve and the monarchy will be lost. All branches of commerce will dry up. All our works of art will be suspended. One hundred million arms will demand work in vain, and subsistence. They will be reduced to brigandage and to criminality. An insensitive wealth will find itself punished, divested by a despairing indigence. Cities will become deserts. Lands will go uncultivated. Foreign banks will flee from our counters. All French merchants will be banished from ports [that will be] opened to other peoples. Our mediators will not dare approach the courts of allies. In the end our name will be stricken from all transactions and defamed in the mouths of all. This epoch will be the shameful epoch of the monarchy.

No, it must become the brilliant epoch, the auspicious Egeria. A king, the friend of his people, a people the friend of its king, will contract a new alliance; all social ranks will come together, not to mingle, but to provide mutual reinforcement. The National Assembly will prepare for us an existence which will be, so to speak, immortal. In order to serve us, the wisest and most upright administrators will resist the excess of work, the injustice of cabals, the ingratitude of frivolous hearts, the greatest torture for a generous heart. Working together, our legislators and our ministers will overcome fatality and will subjugate intrigue. But their beneficence would come too late, would be useless, if the finances of the state were left any longer in paralysis and absolute impotence. While the National Assembly is busy with regenerating them [the finances of the state] on a grand scale, we dare hope to help on a small scale. We bring the widow's mite to the altar of the Fatherland. Companions of the arts, subjects of the state, let us ennoble our frivolous adornments, let us sanctify worldly displays by sacrificing them to the public need; before taking them back and renewing them, let us wait until the nation is no longer in mourning or in [a state of] want. May luxury become a virtue, and may the Arts, which give luster to an empire, contribute to its renaissance and sustenance.

6. ACTS OF THANKSGIVING AND DEMONSTRATIONS OF STRENGTH

Source: Siméon-Prosper Hardy, "Mes Loisirs," vol. VIII, fols. 431, 443, 479, in B.N., Mss. fr., vol. 6687.

This document provides evidence that by mid-summer of 1789, women of the people were participating *en masse* in public ceremonies of thanksgiving in alliance with the newly constituted National Guard. Hardy tells us that these demonstrations alarmed some observers; it is possible to view them as dress rehearsals for the march to Versailles.[1]

[1]Our attention was called to the significance of these midsummer marches by George Rudé, *The Crowd in the French Revolution,* p. 67.

Wednesday, August 12.

On this day, in the morning, fishwives from the Market of Saint-Jean en Grève and from several other markets are seen passing along rue St. Jacques in very large numbers and in very good order. [They] were going, as were all those seen on preceding days, to offer Ste. Geneviève a superb bouquet and a crown of orange blossoms along with a bread to bless. They were marching two by two to drumbeat and to several other instruments, preceded, accompanied, and followed by the bourgeois militia.

Friday, August 21.

Toward the hour of noon, a kind of procession of girls and women is seen once again passing along the rue St. Jacques, [a procession] which one would say came from the Quartier Saint-Eustache, accompanied by soldiers from the bourgeois militia and by musical instruments; these girls and these women returned from Ste. Geneviève to drumbeat with two consecrated breads, five large brioches, bouquets, and two branches of vines decorated with bunches of grapes which they were going to offer to the Holy Virgin in the metropolitan church, having to go afterwards to the Hôtel de Ville. Several people were heard criticizing and censuring these multiplied and daily gatherings of *citoyennes,* who appeared, however, to have no objective other than that of performing solemn thanksgiving to the Supreme Being for the visible protection he just accorded to Parisians.

Thursday, September 17.

Today, beginning at five in the morning, crowds went to the bakers, as [had happened] the day before, to ask for bread there. Once again it was necessary to station riflemen there [at the bakers] until the entire distribution [of bread] was completed. It was distressing to note that people were trying to work up anxiety in order to get feelings running very high, while reasonable people believed that with the precautions being taken daily as well as with the hopes one should have concerning the bounty of the new harvest, no one would experience the misfortune of lacking bread if each person limited himself to his usual consumption without committing the imprudence of hoarding out of false fear a larger quantity than this consumption called for.

Toward the hour of noon, rioting women went in large numbers to the Hôtel de Ville to complain about the bakers. They were sent for an audience at four in the afternoon and for some kind of answer from the mayor of the city and the representatives of the commune. These women said publicly "that men didn't understand anything about the matter and that they wanted to play a role in affairs."

7. STANISLAS MAILLARD DESCRIBES THE WOMEN'S MARCH TO VERSAILLES, OCTOBER 5, 1789

Source: Stanislas Maillard's testimony to the Châtelet
Commission, in *Procédure criminelle instruite au Châtelet de Paris*, 2
vols. (Paris, 1790), vol. I, pp. 117–32, reprinted from George
Rudé, ed., *The Eighteenth Century* (New York, 1965), pp.
198–205.

Stanislas Maillard, a National Guardsman and Vainqueur de la
Bastille, testified before the commission established by the
Tribunal du Châtelet in 1790 to investigate the events of October
5, 1789. Maillard gives a full account of the political objectives
of women participants and their tactics (including their use of
violence). Note that he rejects Lafayette's authority, targeting the
National Assembly as the agency responsible for distributing
subsistence.

———————

Stanislas-Marie Maillard, twenty-six years of age, captain in the Bastille
Volunteers, residing in the rue Béthizi at Paris, in the parish of St.
Germain l'Auxerrois, testified

That at seven o'clock in the morning of October 5 last he went to the
City Hall to lodge a complaint on behalf of the volunteers. The city
council was not in session, but the rooms were filled with women who
were trying to break in all the doors of the rooms in the City Hall. This
determined him to go down to the headquarters of the National Guard
in order to receive the instructions of M. de Gouvion as how best to
remedy and prevent the destruction that might be wrought by these
women. M. de Gouvion requested him immediately to stay with him
and to help him to calm the people. At that moment news was brought
to M. de Gouvion of a riot that had broken out in the Faubourg St.
Antoine, and, fearing that the company of volunteers stationed at the
Bastille, at the entrance to the Faubourg, had not been supplied with

ammunition, M. de Gouvion gave him an order for the delivery of three hundred cartridges for the volunteers. He (the present witness) then made off to the district of St. Louis-la-Culture, where he had the order countersigned; went on to the place where the volunteers were stationed, found, on inspection and after enquiry, that they had enough ammunition for their defence, and consequently made no use of the order. The workers at the Bastille now advanced on the volunteers standing under arms in the courtyard, but Mr. Hulin, their commanding officer, and he himself addressed the workers with courtesy and assured them that their arms would only be used against the enemies of freedom, and not against themselves as they appeared to fear, and to convince them of this they ordered the volunteers to lower their arms. When calm had been restored and the workers had left the place de la Bastille, he left Mr. Hulin and in accordance with M. de Gouvion's request to give him assistance (M. de Gouvion being alone), returned alone to the City Hall. On arrival he found it at first impossible to enter the building, which was occupied by a large crowd of women who refused to let any men come in among them and kept repeating that the city council was composed of aristocrats. He himself was taken for a member of the council, as he was dressed in black, and entry being refused him, he was obliged to go and change his clothes. But as he went down the steps of the building, he was stopped by five or six women, who made him go up again, shouting to their comrades that he was a Bastille Volunteer and that there was nothing to fear from him. After this, having mingled with the women, he found some forcing the downstairs doors and others snatching papers in the offices, saying that that was all the city council had done since the revolution began and that they would burn them. Supported by a certain Richard Dupin, he urged them to keep calm, but these women kept saying that the men were not strong enough to be revenged on their enemies and that they (the women) would do better. While he was in the courtyard, he looked around and saw a large number of men go up, armed with pikes, lances, pitchforks, and other weapons, having compelled the women to let them in. They then flung themselves on the doors that the women had begun to beat, broke them down with great hammers that they had with them and with crowbars that they found in the City Hall, and took all the arms they could find and gave some to the women. He then received word that a number of women had arrived with torches to burn the papers in the building, so he dashed out [and] flung himself upon them (there were but two) as they approached the City Hall, each bearing a lighted torch; he snatched the torches from their hands, which nearly cost him his life, as they were intent on carrying out their design. He prayed them to send a deputation to the council to demand justice and to describe their plight, as they were all in need of bread, but they replied that the whole council was composed of bad citizens who deserved to be hanged from lamp posts, M. Bailly and M. de Lafayette first of all. . . .

. . . Mr. Maillard . . . , continuing his evidence, said that to avert the danger and misfortune that threatened both Mm. de Lafayette and Bailly and the City Hall, he thought it best to go once more to staff headquarters, where he only found present M. Derminy, M. de Gouvion's aide. Whereupon he (the witness) told M. Derminy that these women would not listen to reason and that, having destroyed the City Hall, they intended to proceed to the National Assembly in order to learn all that had been done and decreed up to the present date. He told these ladies that the National Assembly owed them no reckoning and that if they went there, they would cause a disturbance and would prevent the deputies from paying serious attention to the important business arising from the present situation. As the women persisted in their plans, he thought it wise to repair once more to M. Derminy and acquaint him with their resolution, adding that if the latter thought fit, he would accompany them to Versailles in order to prevent and to apprise them of the danger to which they were exposing themselves by embarking on so rash a venture. To this M. Derminy replied that he could not give him an order of this nature, which would be against the citizens' interests, but that he (the witness) might do as he pleased, provided that what he did did not endanger the public peace. In reply, he assured M. Derminy that the proposed action would have no such results and that it was, in fact, the only means of relieving the City Hall and the capital; moreover, by these means the districts could be alerted, and, while the women marched four leagues, the army would have time to avert the evils that these ladies were proposing to commit.

The witness now seized a drum at the entrance to the City Hall, where the women were already assembled in very large numbers; detachments went off into different districts to recruit other women, who were instructed to meet them at the place Louis XV. . . . But as the people were assembled in great numbers, and this square was no longer suited as a place of meeting, they decided to proceed to the place d'Armes, in the middle of the Champs Elysées, whence he saw detachments of women coming up from every direction, armed with broomsticks, lances, pitchforks, swords, pistols, and muskets. As they had no ammunition, they wanted to compel him to go with a detachment of

them to the arsenal to fetch powder, but he made use of the order given
him by M. de Gouvion and displayed it to them, claiming that the order
had been made out for them but there was no powder in the arsenal
(though he knew that the contrary was true). . . . And now by means of
prayers and protestations he succeeded in persuading the women to lay
down their arms, with the exception of a few who refused, but whom
wiser heads among them compelled to yield. . . .

Meanwhile, he had acquired the confidence of these women to the
extent that they all said unanimously that they would have only him to
lead them. A score of them left the ranks to compel all the other men to
march behind them, and so they took the road to Versailles with eight or
ten drums at their head. They now numbered about six or seven thousand and passed through Chaillot along the river. There all houses were
closed up, for fear, no doubt, of pillage, but in spite of this, women
went knocking at all the doors, and when people refused to open, they
wanted to beat them in, and removed all sign-boards. Observing this,
and wishing to prevent the ruin of the inhabitants, he gave the order to
halt and told them that they would discredit themselves by behaving in
such a manner and that if they continued to do so he would no longer
march at their head, that their actions would be looked on unfavorably,
whereas if they proceeded peaceably and honestly, all the citizens of the
capital would be grateful to them. They yielded at length to his remonstrances and opinions and discreetly continued on their way to Sèvres.
On the way, however, they stopped several couriers and carriages of the
court coming from the direction of Versailles for fear (as they said) that
the Pont de Sèvres be closed to stop them passing—but without harming these persons in any way. Arriving at the Pont de Sèvres, he gave the
order to halt, and, to prevent mischief, he asked if there were any armed
men there; but instead of the inhabitants of Sèvres to whom he addressed this question giving any satisfactory reply, they merely stated
that Sèvres was in a state of the greatest consternation, that all houses
were closed, and that it would be impossible to find any refreshment for
these ladies. . . .

[Several of the men having been left behind at Sèvres,] he and the
women continued on their journey to Versailles. Past Viroflay they met a
number of individuals on horseback who appeared to be bourgeois and
wore black cockades in their hats. The women stopped them and made
as if to commit violence against them, saying that they must die as
punishment for having insulted, and for insulting, the national cockade;
one they struck and pulled off his horse, tearing off his black cockade,
which one of the women handed to him (the witness). He ordered the

other women to halt . . . and came to the aid of the man whom they were ill-using; he obtained his release on condition that he should surrender his horse, that he should march behind them, and that at the first place they came to he should be made to carry on his back a placard proclaiming that he had insulted the national cockade. . . . [The same treatment having been meted out to two other passers-by, and two of the women having mounted their horses,] he drew the women up (as far as it was in his power to do so) in three ranks and made them form a circle and told them that the two cannons that they had with them must be removed from the head of their procession; that although they had no ammunition, they might be suspected of evil intentions; that they would do better to give an air of gaiety than to occasion a riot in Versailles; and that as the city had not been warned of their proceedings, its inhabitants might mistake their purpose, and they might become the victims of their own zeal. They consented to do as he wished; consequently, the cannons were placed behind them, and he invited the women to chant "Long live Henri IV!" as they entered Versailles and to cry "Long live the king!"—a cry which they did not cease to repeat in the midst of the citizens awaiting them, who greeted them with cries of "Long live our Parisiennes!" So they arrived at the door of the National Assembly, where he told them that it would be imprudent for more than five or six of them to appear. They refused, all wanting to go in, whereupon a guards' officer, on duty at the National Assembly, joined him and urged that not more than twelve of the women should enter. . . .

After much discussion among the women, fifteen were chosen to appear with him at the bar of the National Assembly; of these fifteen he only knew the woman Lavarenne, who has just been awarded a medal by the Paris city council. Entering the assembly, he urged the women to be silent and to leave to him the task of communicating to the assembly their demands, as they had explained them to him on the way; to this they consented. He then asked the president's leave to speak. M. Mounier, who was then president, granted him leave, and he told them that two or three persons, whom they had met on the way driving in a carriage from the court, had informed him that they had learned that an abbé, a member of the assembly, had given a miller two hundred *livres* to stop him from grinding corn, with the promise to give him the same every week. The National Assembly insisted that he should name this individual, but he could not satisfy their wishes, as he could remember neither the names of those whom these persons denounced nor the names of the accusers themselves; all that he could remember was that the latter lived in the rue de Plâtre Ste. Avoye. As the assembly persisted in demanding the name of the accused, M. de Robespierre, deputy of Arras, rose to speak and said that the stranger admitted to their august assembly was absolutely right, that he believed there had been talk of it that very morning, and that the Abbé Gregoire could throw further light on the matter; hence, he (the witness) was relieved of the obligation of doing so. He (the witness) now once more addressed the assembly and said that to restore calm, allay public disquiet, and avert disaster, he begged the gentlemen of the assembly to appoint a deputation to go to the Life-Guards in order to enjoin them to adopt the national cockade and make amends for the injury they were said to have done to it. Several members raised their voices and said it was false that the Life-Guards had ever insulted the national cockade, that all who wished to be citizens could be so freely, and that no one could be forced to be so. Speaking again and displaying three black cockades (the same that were spoken of earlier), he said that, on the contrary, there should be no person who did not take pride in being so and that if there were within this august assembly any members that felt dishonored by this title, they should be excluded immediately. Many applauded these words, and the hall rang with cries of "Yes, all should be so and we are all citizens." In the midst of this applause he was handed a national cockade, sent in by the Life-Guards, which he showed to all the women as a proof of their submission, and all the women cried, "Long live the king and the Life-Guards!" He once more asked leave to speak and said that it was essential also, in order to avert misfortune and to allay the suspicions that had been spread in the capital concerning the arrival of the Flanders Regiment at Versailles, to withdraw this regiment, because the citizens feared it might start a revolution. [The assembly now agreed to appoint a deputation to wait upon the king and put forward the women's demands. Meanwhile, angry words were exchanged with the clerical members of the assembly, and it was rumored that the Life-Guards had fired on the women outside.]

As he spoke, a dozen women entered the National Assembly and said that the Life-Guards had just fired on them, that one had been arrested, and that they were waiting for him (the witness) to come down before deciding on the manner of the death he had merited. At that moment the sound of musket fire could be heard; this caused alarm in the assembly, and he was urged by several deputies to hasten down in order to put a stop to these mischiefs. He went down surrounded by the women and observed a Life-Guard, who was being held by the bridle of his horse; the man wished to dismount, but the women prevented him, though without doing him any injury other than to hurl abuse at him. When the Life-Guard saw him advance to speak to him, he drew a sword and cut through his reins; the point of the sword struck a woman on the shoulder, and he fled. He (the witness) made to run after him, but he could not catch him, and the Life-Guard, as he fled, discharged his pistol at him but failed to hit him. He (the witness) then returned to the National Assembly, having enjoined the women not to approach closer to the royal palace. At eight o'clock in the evening the president returned with his deputation from their audience with the king. He repeated the king's words before the assembly; the women listened respectfully, as their intent was to restore calm among his people. Then the president read aloud five papers relative to the demands addressed by the Parisian National Guard to the National Assembly and to the king concerning the food supply. His Majesty had commanded that two officers should accompany him (the witness) back to Paris, but the women objected to this, and all said that they alone should escort him. The five papers were entered in the registers of the assembly, and copies were handed to him by Viscount Mirabeau; immediately afterwards he returned to Paris with a part of the women in a carriage of the court. In the avenue de Versailles, as they rode, they encountered the Parisian National Guard.

Arriving in Paris, he gave orders to be taken directly to the City Hall, which he entered escorted by some 150 women, who went ahead of him into the hall where sat the representatives of the commune, the mayor presiding. He (the witness) gave an account of all that had taken place and, having first read them aloud, handed to the mayor the five papers entrusted to his care (as has been related above). . . . At six o'clock in the morning of Tuesday, October 6, the mayor besought the women to withdraw to their homes, which they did; but eight or ten of them escorted him (the witness) to his dwelling, which was then the Hôtel de Grenelle St. Honoré in the street of the same name. At eight o'clock in the morning of this same day, ten to twelve women came to fetch him and compelled him to march with them to meet the National Guard and present the Marquis de Lafayette with a laurel branch on his return from Versailles. But a messenger whom they encountered told them that he was ordered to have the Tuileries palace prepared to receive His Majesty, who was coming to Paris that evening. The women urged him (the witness) to go with them to meet His Majesty. So he went with them, and they met the king at Viroflay. They mingled with the women who escorted the king's carriage and returned to Paris to the City Hall, and here he left all these women. And that is all he knew of the matter.

8. FOURNIER L'AMERICAIN DEPICTS THE OCTOBER DAYS

Source: F.-A. Aulard, ed., *Mémoires secrets de Fournier l'Américain* (Paris, 1890), pp. 27–35.

Fournier l'Américain wrote a secret memoir on his revolutionary career four years after the October Days, at the height of the Terror, when it was fashionable to associate oneself with the *journées*. Unlike Maillard and other deponents in the 1790 Châtelet investigation, Fournier emphasizes his willingness to defy constituted authorities. While his memoir highlights principally his own contributions, it is also valuable for showing the interaction between women and radical National Guards—a liaison that was critical in making the *journée* a success.

———————◆———————

. . . When I saw my brothers crying with hunger on the fifth of October, I could no longer hold in my feelings. The detestable aristocratic and royalist horde had plotted to submit the nation to slavery by starvation and saw no other way to force this nation to renounce its plans for conquering its liberty. That day, at 7 A.M., I heard cries of general alarm and the tocsin, which was being sounded. I ran to the Hôtel-de-Ville. I found the people there, who, when they saw me, cried out: "Fournier, lead us to Versailles, where we want to go and ask for bread." I answered that I would go if I could assemble a sufficient number of armed troops. The battalion of the Vainqueurs de la Bastille was the first to start moving, and having come to an understanding with the women, it went off to Versailles, where, in the middle of the place d'Armes, it seized despotism's bodyguards and troops, who were posted there.

I felt I shouldn't waste a minute. I ran through Paris rallying the greatest number possible of good citizens.

When I arrived at Sainte-Eustache, I found in command d'Ogny, my successor, under whom the citizens were refusing to march. D'Ogny was base enough to turn to me and urge me to assemble them. The public safety was at stake; I allowed myself no other consideration. I had only to say to my former comrades, "Brothers, do you recognize me?" Immediately all companies took up arms. Will you believe that on the spot d'Ogny had the impudence to station himself beside me, *at the head* of these same companies, which [then] went to the Hôtel-de-Ville? There a fight broke out over whether d'Ogny or I should remain in command. A fair number of citizens and troops went over to my side. Then it was remarked that we were missing a standard for our rally. I went to get the flag with the celebrated motto *Destruction des tyrans.*

When I returned to the Hôtel-de-Ville, I found all the people and the French Guard, who called out to me, "To Versailles, Fournier, lead us!" I sounded the call to arms, and everyone willingly rallied.

Then, d'Ogny came out of the Hôtel-de-Ville. "Who gave you the command to sound the call to arms?" he asked the drummers. "I did," I answered, stepping forward. "Who gave you the order to do that?" he retorted. I told him in the strongest tone: "The tocsin and the sovereign people." Then he uttered some threatening remarks against me which I cut off by going after him with my naked sword. He fled into the Hôtel-de-Ville, where I pursued him.

But reflection caused me to let this coward go so I could busy myself with the sycophant Lafayette, whom I found in one of the suites of the Hôtel-de-Ville at work drafting important motions which were neither mine nor the people's. I addressed him and said: "General, the people are asking for you below, on the Place-de-Grève. You must go out at once; the time has come. The people want to make the trip to Versailles to look for bread. I exhort you not to delay." Lafayette obeyed. I went out immediately. He came over to my column, where, addressing me [carrying] a little brochure in his hand, he said: "Fournier, what's this? You, on whom I have counted most heavily for detachments for a forty- or fifty-league hike to search for grain—are you going to let me down today?"

This obvious trap set to divert us from the major objectives on our minds had no hold on me. "Yes, General," I retorted, "I am going to let you down today. We must go to Versailles, and it is time to get started." Having replied, I took up my role as commander. "Attention! Left face! To Versailles! . . ." Right then, two women went over to Lafayette and said, pointing with their fingers at the notorious street lamp, "À Versailles, ou à la lanterne!" After these remarks he left, [and] we left.

But these scoundrels of ours had agreed among themselves to use every means to cause the enterprise to fail. D'Ogny had become

Lafayette's lieutenant. He marched at his side. We had only gotten up to the Pont-Neuf when they forced us to make our first stop. The general and d'Ogny came over to me and said: "We must not leave without ammunition. You could go get some at the District Sainte-Eustache." I was very suspicious that this bait covered still another hook. That is why I was on my guard. I consented to go with my first column to look for ammunition, but I told my second [column] to wait for me at the end of the Champs-Elysées, along with the general, and not to lose sight of him.

What a surprise I had when I arrived at Sainte-Eustache to find d'Ogny there and to hear him call out to the troops inside the church and [to those] in battle formation: "Put down your arms! Everyone home! I order you in the name of the general." Indignant, I cried out, "Citizens! Stop where you are!" Immediately, I ripped off my epaulettes, I stamped on them, and I cried out with all my might: "That coward who has just dared order citizens to go home deserves to be stamped on, like this." I reattached my epaulettes and said to my troops: "Citizens, whoever loves me will follow me"; and to the women: "Your children are dying of hunger; if your husbands are perverted and cowardly enough not to want to go look for bread for them, then the only thing left for you to do is to slit their throats."

The effect of this speech was most deadly for d'Ogny. It had scarcely been delivered before the women fell upon him and dealt him so many fist blows and kicks in the stomach that they forced him to march along. He died shortly afterwards, following complications from this treatment, which he had merited only too well.

I went back to the Champs-Elysées to rejoin my detachment, which I had left on the Pont-Neuf, and then it looked as if we were off to Versailles at last.

When we were opposite the manufactory of Sèvres, a carriage came by identifying itself as Lafayette's trains. It was led by eight post-horses. Eight to ten men in the uniform of national cavalry were on the *impériale,* on the seat, and behind. All along our lines, they cried out: "Attention. Coming through. These are the trains of the general." At this word, "of the general," I stopped the carriage and said, "This could be the devil's carriage. I'm stopping it to find out what's inside." Immediately a swarm of *mouchards* and *coupe-jarrets* encircled me and let the carriage get through. I ask whether they might not have been mixed up in planning a joint getaway by the king and the general, because at this very hour and minute the ever-active and patriotic National Guard of Versailles and the Vainqueurs de la Bastille, who, as I mentioned earlier,

were the first to leave, and out in front, stopped the royal trains at
Versailles, just below the Orangerie, and had them returned to a safe
place.

The perfidious intentions of this wretched Lafayette cannot be in
doubt when it is recalled that he had the armed citizens make five or six
stops between Paris and Versailles, in the middle of a downpour of rain
and the most awful weather, which made it impossible to get there until
sometime between midnight and 1 A.M. That way, d'Estaing was given
time to prepare all the criminal maneuvers of the court and the
traitor-general. This d'Estaing gave up his post with the National Guard
of Versailles with the express intention of making himself more useful at
the château. But when I was informed of his treason, I took over the
corps de garde of the former French Guard and its artillery range, where I
established special security. . . .

[Fournier l'Américain goes on to explain that he had tried unsuccessfully
to prevent the general massacre on the sixth of October. Later that
morning:]

    . . . I addressed five or six of these women who, with the name and
outward appearance of *poissardes,* conceal moral qualities, and above all,
judgment, which always makes it possible for them to value sound
advice. I stooped to their level of intelligence and borrowed Père
Duchesne's style, and while putting fist to nose, I told them: "Damn my
ass, [*Sac . . . b . . . esses*] don't you see that Lafayette and the king are
fucking you up [*vous c . . .*] when they tell you they are going to meet
in private to get bread for you? Don't you see that it's a ruse to put you
off and to give you your chains back, and famine? The whole damned lot
should be taken away to Paris. . . ."

No sooner had I spoken these words and followed them up with the
gesture of hanging my hat on the tip of my sword, and crying, "To
Paris! To Paris with the king!" than fifty thousand voices repeated this
same cry, "To Paris!" And then, we left. . . .

We set off again.

I was delegated to go ahead in order to give the municipality of Paris
the news that the master of Versailles was arriving in Paris, and that the
people, who wanted it that way, were escorting him back.

Source: *Réimpression de l'Ancien Moniteur, seule histoire authentique et inaltérée de la Révolution française, depuis la réunion des Etats-Généraux jusqu'au Consulat,* 32 vols. (Paris, 1847), vol. II (May, 1789–November, 1799), pp. 542–44, testimonies LXXXIII, LXXXV; Barré testimony from *Procédure criminelle instruite au Châtelet de Paris* (Paris, 1790), Deposition 343, as reprinted in Philip Dawson, ed., *The French Revolution,* pp. 66, 67.

Twenty-five women were called to testify before the Châtelet Commission investigating the October Days. Three of them, Madelaine Glain, Jeanne-Dorothée Delaissement, and Marie-Rose Barré, provide different perspectives on feminine participation. Glain acted as a spokeswoman before the National Assembly and then was one of three women to carry the Assembly's decrees back to the Mayor and the Commune of Paris. Delaissement was a much less observant and comparatively inactive follower. Barré, another leader, was deputized to the King and was later called upon to testify on behalf of Saint-Priest, who was accused of insulting the deputies.

———

Deposition Number LXXXIII

Madelaine Glain, forty-two years old, a *faiseuse de ménage,* wife of François Gaillard, an office clerk in the District de l'Oratoire with whom she lives on rue Froidmanteau, no. 40, testifies that, having been forced, as many women were, to follow the crowd that went to Versailles last Monday, October 5, and having arrived at Sèvres near the porcelain manufactory, [and] a gentleman with a black decoration having asked them where they were going, they answered that they were going to ask for bread at Versailles. This gentleman urged them to behave themselves, but a woman whom the declarant knew to be a prostitute and who since then has been living with Lagrement, a soft drink peddler on rue Bailleul, having said that she was going to Versailles to bring back the queen's head, was sharply reproached by the others. Having arrived at the streets leading to Versailles, this same woman stopped a mounted Royal Guardsman, to whom she delivered many insults, threatening him with a bad, rusty sword which she held open in her hand. This Royal Guardsman said that she was a wretch, and in order to [make her] release the bridle of his horse, which she was holding, he struck her a blow which inflicted an arm wound. Having come at last to the Château with the intention of informing His Majesty concerning the motives of their proceedings, she, the declarant, found herself locked in, that is to say, her skirts caught on two spikes of the gate, from which a Swiss Guard released her. After that she went with the other women to the hall of the National Assembly, where they entered, many strong. Some of these women having asked for the four-pound loaf at eight *sols,* and for meat at the same price, she, the declarant, called for silence, and then she said that they were asking that they not be lacking bread, but not [that it be fixed] at the price these women were wanting to have it. She did not go with the deputation to the Château but returned with Sieur Maillard and two other women to the Hôtel-de-Ville in Paris to bring back the decrees they were given at the National Assembly. Monsieur the mayor and the representatives of the commune were satisfied and received them with joy. Then she, the declarant, was led by the National Guard to the District de l'Oratoire to convey this good news. She cannot give us any news concerning what happened at Versailles on the sixth, but she learned, without being able to say from whom, that someone named Nicolas, a model in the academy, who lived at the home of Poujet, rue Champfleuri, on that day, Tuesday, had cut off the heads of two Royal Guards who had been massacred by the people, and since then the above-mentioned Nicolas has not reappeared in the *quartier.*

Deposition Number LXXXV

Jeanne Dorothée Delaissement, age twenty-eight, a mistress seamstress, widow of Philippe Brenair, living in Paris, rue Mauconseil, at the house of the wheelwright, opposite rue Française, stated that on last Monday, October 5, in the morning, she, the declarant, was forced to go, as many other women were, with the crowd that wanted to go to Versailles. The women who dragged her in first led her to the Hôtel-de-Ville and then to Versailles. She saw nothing worth mentioning along the way. She knows that an individual whom she did not know at that time, but whom she came to know afterwards, named Maillard went to a great deal of trouble to keep order among the women, who were armed with pikes, sticks, pieces of iron, and other things, and that he succeeded in getting them to disarm *en route*. When they arrived at Versailles, a soldier dressed in a blue costume, who she learned was in the Regiment of Flanders, told her, in answer to her questions about people they should be suspicious of, that the Flanders Regiment would do them no harm, but that they must beware of the Royal Guards, who, during a meal, had trampled the *national cockade*. She, the declarant, did not go the Château or to the meeting hall of the National Assembly, etc.

Deposition 343
June 18, 1790

Marie-Rose Barré, age twenty, unmarried, a lace-worker, residing at 61, rue Meslay, upon oath . . .

Deposes that on October 5, last, at about eight o'clock in the morning, going to take back some work, she was stopped at the Pont Notre Dame by about a hundred women, who told her that it was necessary for her to go with them to Versailles to ask for bread there. Not being able to resist this great number of women, she decided to go with them. At the hamlet at the Point-du-Jour, two young men, unknown to her, who were on foot and going their way, told them that they were running a great risk, that there were cannon mounted at the bridge at Saint Cloud. This did not prevent them from continuing on their way. At Sèvres they had some refreshments; then they continued on their way toward Versailles. The two young men of whom she spoke met them near Viroflay and told them that they had escaped at Saint Cloud but that at Versailles they would be fired on. But they continued on their way. At Versailles they found the King's Guards lined up in three ranks before the palace. A gentleman dressed in the uniform of the King's Guards, who, she was told, was the duc de Guiche, came to ask them what they wanted of the king, recommending peaceful behavior on their part. They answered that they were coming to ask him for bread. This gentleman was absent for a few minutes and then returned to take four of them to introduce them to the king. The deponent was one of the four. Before taking them to the king, he led them to the comte d'Affry, who requested that they be introduced to His Majesty right away, which was done.

They spoke first to M. de Saint-Priest, and then to His Majesty, whom they asked for bread. His Majesty answered them that he was suffering at least as much as they were, to see them lacking it, and that so far as he was able he had taken care to prevent them from experiencing a dearth. Upon the king's response they begged him to be so good as to arrange escorts for the flour transports intended for the provisioning of Paris, because according to what they had been told at the bridge in Sèvres by the two young men of whom she spoke earlier, only two wagons out of seventy intended for Paris actually arrived there. The king promised them to have the flour escorted and said that if it depended on him, they would have bread then and there. They took leave of His Majesty and were led, by a gentleman in a blue uniform with red piping, into the apartments and courts of the palace to the ranks of the Flanders Regiment, to which they called out, "Vive Le Roi!" It was then about nine o'clock. After this they retired into a house on rue Satory and went to bed in a stable. She does not know the names and addresses of the three women introduced to the king with her. Tired from the trip, having a swollen foot, she did not go Tuesday to the palace or the Place d'Armes, knows nothing, as a witness, of what happened there, and came back to Paris between four and five o'clock in the afternoon of that day in a carriage.

She adds that a fortnight later a gentleman whom she heard called M. de Saint-Paul came to her place and asked her to go to a court commissioner to make a formal declaration of what M. de Saint-Priest told her on Monday, October 5, at Versailles, when she presented herself to speak to the king. As the deponent did not know a court commissioner, Saint-Paul suggested Maître Chenu. The deponent remarks that she was then living on rue du Four at the corner of rue des Ciseaux. . . . The commissioner . . . took her declaration . . . in which she sets forth that having heard it said, by the two young men mentioned above, that of seventy wagons of flour intended for Paris only two had arrived, she informed M. de Saint-Priest of this, and he answered that as the grain shortage was equally bad everywhere, it was not surprising that the inhabitants of places where flour passed through stopped it for their supply. Besides, the threshing season had not yet arrived, which caused the provisions to be smaller than they should be. . . . She told the commissioner that the minister did not say to her what was being attributed to him by the public: "When you had only one king, you had bread; now that you have twelve hundred of them, go and ask them for it," that in fact she did not hear the minister say this. Which is all that the deponent said she knows . . . and she has signed. . . .

10. A Liberal Journalist Attempts to Integrate the Insurrectionary Deeds of the Women of the People into the Mythology of the Revolutionary Establishment

Source: Anon. "Par un homme de lettres connu, qui va publier un ouvrage intitulé *La France vue dans l'avenir*" [author's note to title], *Les Héroïnes de Paris, ou L'Entière liberté de la France, par des Femmes. Police qu'elles doivent exercer de leur propre autorité. Expulsion des Charlatans, &c., &c., le 5 Octobre 1789* [n.p., n.d.], in B.N., Lb³⁹ 2411.

With this patriotic polemic the author of *Les Héroïnes de Paris* contributed to the invention of a myth which the triumphant notables were ready to use to confer respectability on the October events. The pamphleteer lauded women for their energy, their courage, their character, and their unwillingness, in general, to resort to violence, and he appealed to them to continue functioning in their role as a vigilante police force.

———◆———

Too much confidence was doing us in. Even our enemies warned us about it without realizing they were. Their scandalous triumphs, their noisy orgies, which already enlightened us about their detestable plans for July 13, have just betrayed them once again. The wicked, however crafty they may be, however accomplished in crime, always betray themselves. Heaven and their own hearts undo their most cunning and secret operations.

We can flatter ourselves that yes! our liberty is strengthened. It needed that much. It could have endured but a minute longer; it was being ruined on all sides. . . . . [*sic*] And it's the women who restored it to us! In what immortal glory they have just enveloped themselves. And with what order[1] and courage they went almost ten thousand

[1]On the banners which flew before them, they had hung a scale on which, in truth, they were going to weigh our destinies. They took the liberty of heeding the justice which this scale

strong, to get an accounting from the worthy supporters of despotism
for the latest crime they had just committed and which, in effect, was
the last for some of them. The horrible crime, this crime of *lèze-nation*,
was to have prepared in cold blood for a celebration where it had been
decided that at the conclusion the *national cockade* would be proscribed,
and in its place everyone would put on black cockades, and in truth,
pockets were filled with black cockades to be put on solemnly in the
midst of the gay festivities of the banquet. This new Saint-Bartholomew
was plotted as gallantly as that of last 13 July and that of 24 August,
1572. . . .

The cockade, which saved us, and which the king wanted to wear,
was thrown down with spite and kicked underfoot by guests. This
outrage was addressed less to the cockade than to the nation. They
would willingly have mixed in with the wine from Champagne a few
drops of our blood, which is called [the blood] of the *riffraff*, and which
they were hoping would soon be flowing more abundantly. These
gentlemen were making there what they so congenially refer to as a
prelibation.[2]

They tell us, by way of justifying themselves, that the districts of
Paris gave parties before they did; but [those parties] were a little
different. Besides, it must be acknowledged that in general the best
citizens, or above all, the most prudent ones, did not propose them.
They did better at the District des Petits-Augustins; they used the
money from their celebration for a patriotic offering.

After the most bountiful harvest we were without bread; appropriate
measures were taken to see to it that we would be without any. They
were going to block off Paris, reduce it to the utmost extremity. Factual
proofs exist. Our brothers in the provinces would have come to our aid;
but they would not have been able to come fast enough. They would

---

designates, and they observed it religiously. What damage have they done? What have they
taken without payment? And whom have they punished, if not their aggressors or other guilty
parties long since condemned by the public? Would the aristocrats, in the place of the women of
the people, have been as delicate? In the following note, observe how they used to behave on
another issue, [one] which affects women's morals; they still think pretty much along these same
lines.

[2]This word comes from the Latin and means to begin to drink. The French nobility used to
use it to designate a barbaric right which it appropriated to itself, and which was also in use in
several other realms. When two young people from the country got married, the seigneur of the
village enjoyed the right of sleeping with the new wife on the marriage night. As a result of this
horrible custom, the first child born of each marriage was almost always the fruit of an adultery.
Is it surprising that with this vexation, and so many others, the people became malicious and
contracted all the vices for which they were reproached?

have found us either all dead or with only a minute left to live. Providence alone saved us, and by using the feeblest means, in order that we derive all the glory from it. She [Providence] inspired the women with the resolution to liberate the Fatherland; she made them succeed. They got it out of the king that he would come to live among us; nothing more was needed. We must say in their praise what the Jewish women said about David when he vanquished the giant Goliath and cut off his head: "Saul killed a thousand of our enemies. David killed ten thousand."

The aristocrats tell a sour joke. They tell us that Providence chose from a very beautiful class of society and heroines that she wanted to use to save us. She chose them from La Halle, from the Marché de l'Abbaye, and tomorrow they will go to the cabaret to celebrate their victory.

This reproach is serious. It must be answered. Let us see, first of all, how any useful and legitimate revolution can be made by a great people in a case where repeated abuses have created too great a disproportion among the individuals who compose it.

Some well-stocked heads, some good citizens, write, speak, [and] show the necessity of shaking off a degrading and intolerable yoke. The people listen to them; they are surprised not to have thought all that out the way [the publicists] do. They become angry with themselves for having submitted to slavery for too long; they get riled up; they arm themselves; they cannot be held back. Soon the revolution is made. But is it possible that it could be made by those same people who prepared [the way for] it? Their numbers are so small, and ordinarily so weak!

The women, who have just carried off the [revolution] we are celebrating, are, you say, haranguers, and what heroic feelings for honor could they have? I answer that underneath disadvantageous exteriors (and these exteriors themselves are the deadly work of the rich people, as I will show in another work) the women of the people hide a fine character which finds expression when needed. It gets denigrated gradually because a careless and crude education, which rich people would be angry to see them pass up,[3] leads them back to vices which misery makes almost inevitable for them. But find them a gentler and more honest existence like the one they will soon have, at last, and you will see virtues flower and be sustained among them. You will also see the advantages that they will have over our ladies who pride themselves on

---

[3]There are still people to be found who are unjust enough to allege that the people must not know how to read or write; that they must not be enlightened; that they must live in ignorance, for fear that they might learn the value of liberty and no longer be willing to let themselves be enchained.

sentiment, and even over those who give some proofs [of such senti-
ment], because they have nerve, energy—what the *deplorable health of
the society of beautiful people* no longer tolerates in the women who have the
misfortune to live that way.

I repeat: those who have just saved us deserve our full gratitude, and
as the beginning of a repayment, we must give them some advice from
which they will undoubtedly profit. They must not embark upon any
more expeditions which could degrade them. They must sustain the
glory they have acquired; they must show themselves worthy of the
beautiful role they have just played out before all of France. They should
take upon themselves a respectable self-discipline, and one which would
do them infinite honor. This would include never drinking in excess (a
horrible thing in women because they must always be the very incarna-
tion of softness and modesty), but also not allowing drunkenness in
men. They are capable of exercising this empire over them. That would
ward off and prevent quarrels. Also, they should not entertain themselves watching charlatans recently brought back to Paris by the aristocrats to distract us, to cause us to turn away from our duties, to make
us neglect the means for repelling the evils that are being prepared for
us. The charlatans must be chased away or forced to work; they are
dangerous men. Women would also have to prevent lack of respect for
the clergy and for titled people. They have it in for the clergy, above all,
and certainly it has its faults, but it must be recalled that in that class
there are some very respectable men, and it is always setting a bad
example to despise those who attend the altars. Besides, they cannot,
and do not wish to harm us; they made all the sacrifices asked of them.
The English, who have been free far longer than we, have a very generous custom in their too frequent fights [complete] with head blows and
fist fighting: as soon as one of the two champions falls, the other holds
out his hand to raise him up, and they embrace. Let us imitate them as
far as formerly privileged persons are concerned—that is to say, the
nobles and the priests.

Finally, the women would also have to stop the guards at the tollgates
from letting green or rotten fruits through for transport to the markets.
The people, and above all the children, get poisoned eating these fruits;
they contract lingering illnesses which consume them and are due to this
cause and [are also caused by] spoiled grain, which we have been eating
for several months now, but which at last will be used, no doubt about
that, to make starch.

11. A Defender of Laboring Poor Women Supports Welfare Legislation

Source: *Motion de la pauvre Javotte, députée des pauvres femmes, Lesquelles composent le second ordre du Royaume depuis l'abolition de ceux du clergé et de la noblesse* (Paris, 1790), in B.N., Lb^{39}, 3489.

This pamphlet was the work of a publicist who clearly empathized with the plight of nobility, clergy, and unprivileged women. In the aftermath of revolutionary triumphs bringing benefits principally to the elites, the author challenges the new revolutionary government to take on the obligation of providing for the security and welfare of poor women, functions which the privileged orders were no longer in a position to discharge.

Foreword

It is very surprising that the thousand and one journals which inform the public daily, all saying the same thing, never said anything at all about the motion of poor Javotte or about her admission among the nation's representatives. We hasten to correct this insulting oversight, which could have ignited a civil war between poor women and incapable writers, a war all the more formidable because we know from the campaign of '89 how much less philosophically the penmen go at one another than the swordsmen do.

Preliminary Speech of Poor Javotte

Messieurs,

You do me the honor of receiving me in your midst. I see that there are twelve hundred of you to represent half the nation, and I stand alone to answer for the confidence of the other [half]. Nonetheless, Gentlemen, I assure you that I am not in the least intimidated.

My instructions are very simple, and I do not intend to exceed them.

I hold my powers from my constituents, and I will not take any from philosophy. Just allow me to precede my motion by a brief history, as you have had your decrees preceded by the Declaration of the Rights of Man.

In this way, Messieurs, it will be easy for me to make you understand that the Revolution has done nothing for poor women; that the inequality of advantages perpetuates masculine aristocracy at their expense; and that, forced to see in you the privileged sex, they look upon themselves as the second order of the realm ever since [the orders] of the clergy and nobility have been abolished. Let us get to my history.

I was born in a province the name of which I no longer know.[1] My parents, who were extremely poor, had many children, and we, who were many mouths to feed, were a shabby-looking lot. In the vicinity of our miserable cottage there lived several of these impertinent privileged people who, despite philosophy, enjoyed rights which their ancestors acquired while elevating the French monarchy. One of them makes my father concierge at his château; the wife of another takes my mother in with her; still another (these nobles had a rage for protecting!) transforms my three ragged, starved, and rascally brothers—one into a well-dressed clerk; the second into a very well nourished gamekeeper; and the youngest into a very well mannered seminarian. I still had a poor hunchbacked sister and an old tonsured uncle. The former despaired of finding a husband, and the latter despaired of finding a benefice. A good marquise who could not do the impossible placed my sister in a convent, my uncle at the head of her parish, and me at the head of my uncle's household.

One fine day (one might have said that this was by magic!) we found ourselves very far removed from the ills which had haunted our entire existence—content, happy, already consoled for the past, and what is sweet after hopeless days, assured for the future. However, how pitiful we were! These great people, who did some good for us, were not our equals.

But look, here is how we learned about the Rights of Man.

The château of my father's benefactor is philosophically pillaged. . . . [*sic*] no more agent; my mother's protectress is patriotically forced to flee. . . . [*sic*] no more retreat; they religiously set fire to the seminary where my youngest brother serves God . . . , he flees without his cassock. In republican fashion they batter down the tollgate where my older brother serves the King. . . . [*sic*] he escapes in his night-

---

[1]That has been happening to many people for some time now.

shirt. . . . . [*sic*] It would have been asking for too much if the third, who aristocratically killed off the rabbits, could have done as the other two did, but the poor devil had some democratic lead in his legs!

Temples, altars, refuges of modesty, ministers of religion, nothing is respected. My pathetic sister saved a remnant of her virtue only because of her pitiful figure, and my saintly uncle saves a piece of life only because of a grenadier's coat-tails; each one runs as he can, crying: VIVE LA NATION.

One beautiful night (because there were many lanterns in the street) we are all reunited on the quay which leads to the Place de Grève— father, mother, brothers, uncle—homeless, without bread or assistance or hope! It was a superb moment! because we were the equals of all the great people who will no longer do any good.[2]

However, as we were hungry, our heads bowed humbly before who- ever was willing to throw down a few *liards* to relieve our misery, and we remarked to one another: it's not enough to be the equals of the great ones, we must find bread.

But how do you find it? Philosophy took it from everybody. "Let's go ask the government," says my uncle, "for a spade and twenty *sols,* because it is still necessary to keep alive, even after you have been robbed, grilled, roasted, and thrashed, and even though you know the Rights of Man."

My father, my uncle, and my brother went to ask for work; they got it after much trouble. My mother, my sister, and I asked for some also; we were told that there wasn't any for women. "Are there then no poor women in this city?" I ask. "There aren't any other kind," said a thou- sand voices around me, in all the streets, at all the doors, along the avenues, in the districts, at the shows, before the National Assembly. "You won't get anywhere without forcing your way through our wretched groups, without feeling yourself pressed by our feeble hands; without feeling to the depth of your soul our cries, our tears, our supplications, our reproaches. Oh! It's very sad, it's very sad for a magnificent city, where there are so many pleasures, so many charities, and so many people who make the laws!"

These were my new companions speaking. I studied them. So many subjects worthy of pity surrounded me! "Yes, it is very sad," I repeated, "It is very sad! And even the facility of obtaining alms is very depress- ing,[3] when it encourages only laziness. The stare of a woman I noticed

[2]With what could they do it?

[3]It is only too necessary in France! The humanity of Frenchmen apparently wants to buy back the wrongs of their government.

on my right and whose expression had about it something at once severe and touching, stopped me. "You have just heard," she told me, "that the state is doing nothing for us; tell me what can compensate for its oversight? Is it to an alms-giving charity that the care of so many thousands of citizens must be confided? Can one become useful to society only if forced? Your father and your brothers work; without this aid, they would perish. You have the same needs as they, but the government doesn't have the same concern for you. What resources are left when, all at once, support is taken away, and means, and even hope, without which there is no courage?"

"My mother," I answered, "does dressmaking [*fait la toilette*] and everything that relates to fashion; my sister knows how to do lacemaking and dressmaking. I can do cutting and embroidery." "You can do everything," said a poor old woman at my left, "everything you have to do to end up at the Hôpital. The embroiderers are bankrupt, the *marchandes de mode* close their shops, the dressmakers lay off three-fourths of their workers, and soon the ladies of quality won't have *femmes de chambres*. A poor dressmaker [*couturière*], even in good times, didn't earn enough to buy shoes, and those who had handsome Peters had stupid lovers, but all these Peters, my dear child. . . ."

I interrupted her, "I want to be honest and to work." "You will die of hunger." "I hope not; my uncle gave me a good education. I had a fine enough hand, and I learned everything you have to know to be employed in a trading firm [*maison de commerçant*]." "Only men are employed in trading companies [*maisons de commerçant*]." "I copy music very accurately." "Only men copy music." "I worked even harder at drawing, even at painting." "Only men know drawing and painting."[4] "I play the harp, the guitar, I play the harpsichord passably well, I will give lessons to young ladies." "Only men give lessons to young ladies." "Okay," I retorted, becoming impatient, "if men do everything that women would do better in their place. . . . Still, I see *bureaux d'écrivains* and I will write as these men do." "Do you have money to pay a mistress?" "They are going to abolish them." "They are going to abolish them. They are going to. They are going to!" repeated the old woman. "Okay. Yes! We will be very well off as far as everything that's going to come is concerned, but while waiting, everything that has come to be is killing us."

"Men," continued my neighbor on the right, "are favored by the government from the beginning of their lives; we are abandoned by it

---

[4]That is quite natural, because the *écoles de dessein* are only for men.

until the end of ours. There are several free schools for them; there are almost none for us. Think of giving them talent: they want to teach us nothing but the catechism. We were hoping that the nation's representatives, who came together to correct abuses, would concern themselves for a moment with our fate, but until now, they have been able to think only about the Jews and the actors."

While they were talking this way, a terrible thought overpowered me. Do they want to force women whom fate deprives of everything to see in the corruption of their morals the only means open to them? I hastened to dismiss this cruel idea. Enlightened charity, I thought, will have come to our aid by then; it will have formed consoling establishments for those among us who fear neither fatigue nor night work, who shudder only at the idea of opprobrium. A kind of phantom whose slow and weak voice reached me with difficulty answered: "I know about these consoling establishments. SEVEN *Sols,* that's what I found there to ward off death. . . [*sic*] SEVEN *Sols* are the wages for a day's work on which I was never able to support myself. . . . [*sic*] To work for eighteen hours without rest, without stopping. . . . . [*sic*] To devour in haste the inadequate nourishment which SEVEN *Sols* can procure! . . . [*sic*] And beneath a half-open roof, on damp wet straw, to see a new day coming, new exertions. . . . [*sic*] and no new strength! Ah, tell me whether one should shrink from the grave only to find such charity!"

I stop here. . . . . . [*sic*] No, I will not try, Gentlemen, to say what I was feeling. At the gaze of these eyes washed out in tears, this forehead lined by long years of pain, my heart could scarcely stand its throbbing; it seemed to me that it was trying to expand to be able to embrace all the evils whose image was reproducing itself before my eyes. Ah! You have never seen her, you, who want to assure the happiness of your Fatherland, you, whose infinite labors we bless. But, while the cry goes up from all directions, "We are going to perish!" this Fatherland will thrust only one cry into your hearts: Save my children. Please deign to consider these many victims: some of them right before your eyes, with their tears and their despair; others holding their useless courage in the heart of most avid indigence; all pointing to the neglect of legislators in all ages.

What! We have seen patriotism distribute her caution and rewards to find offenders and the guilty, and will we not see a patriot honor himself with the more beautiful care of saving *citoyennes* for the State?

Oh! If nature makes us the weaker [sex], then she indicates to humanity where aid must be increased; [she indicates] to the laws where resources must be found. She says to all hearts: "Protect the sex in which I have placed the sweetest virtues, because while its means are more limited, its responsibilities are more extensive; because morals depend on it; because, finally, it's in this sex that the title of mother resides— mother, Oh Fatherland! the dearest, the first in your sight; and you lose more when we cease being upright than when we cease to exist."

There, Gentlemen, is what I had to tell you, and here are the vows of your unfortunate *citoyennes*. I wanted to put it in the form of a motion which wouldn't waste anyone's time. Excuse a little singularity in a woman.

Motion of Poor Javotte

Let the National Assembly deign to consider the fate of unfortunate women.

II

Women and Constitutional Monarchy: 1790–91

THE TWO YEARS following the October Days were a period of relative social calm in the revolutionary capital. The supply and price of bread were stabilized, and incidents of popular protest were less frequent and less widespread than they had been in 1789. Politically, these years were a period of active reform as the men in the National Assembly drafted the Constitution of 1791. Women's politics exhibited similar variety. Middle-class women continued to press for specific legislation to ameliorate the condition of women. Some of them attempted to organize women into clubs that would foster their interests. Some radical middle-class women congregated at the Cordeliers Society, which vowed to serve as the watchdog for the interests of the sovereign people and propagate democratic and, by 1791, even republican ideals. The women who took an active part in Cordelier meetings and demonstrations were well educated; several of them were respected journalists, printers, and merchants.

Women continued to pressure the National Assembly, but the deputies did not write the legislation they considered so urgent: the right to divorce, equal primary educational opportunities for girls, and regulations on women's health. Many of the liberal reforms that were in fact introduced—legislation affecting the fiscal regime, state-church relations, administrative organization, and justice—were or would soon become politically controversial in the eyes of women. The suffrage provisions of the Constitution of 1791, for example, were passed with no serious consideration of female suffrage. Men were divided into two categories. Active citizens, entitled to participate in local and national elections and to join the National Guard, were those who paid taxes equivalent to at least three days' wages. Passive citizens were men who did not meet that tax qualification; they were excluded from political bodies and the National Guard.

These suffrage requirements were among the laws soon to become a source of conflicts among the Assembly, Paris city government, and common people of Paris. The great majority of Parisian *sans-culottes* were classified as passive citizens. Bourgeois economic policies incorporated into the Constitution also discriminated against the *sans-culottes*. Workers were forbidden to strike or form associations to protect their own interests. The Assembly established national workshops for men and women under bourgeois supervision and restricted public aid to all able-bodied men and women who had failed to find jobs with private employers. The workshops were needed because the emigration of nobles and clergy curtailed employment in the luxury trades and services that catered to nobles. Women were heavily represented in these trades.

For Parisian women, the significant political development of the period 1790–91 was the creation of new opportunities for their involvement in clubs and popular societies. One of the earliest clubs in which women actively participated was the Cercle social, founded in January, 1790. By fall it was explicitly favoring women's issues, and some prominent women came to speak before it. Also noteworthy was the earliest of the truly popular societies, the Société fraternelle des patriotes de l'un et l'autre sexe, Défenseurs de la Constitution. Women were admitted to full membership in this society and also served as officers.[1]

Originally, the fraternal societies functioned as educational institutions rather than as political pressure groups. Most speakers favored the constitutional monarchy and thought of the clubs as places to discuss and teach citizens their rights and obligations in the regenerated state. Middle-class women were often entrusted with such tasks as organizing civic ceremonies and delivering patriotic speeches. The women of the people also flocked to the patriotic societies, which became the center of local social life as the churches closed and the priests departed.

Three women members of the Société fraternelle, Etta Palm d'Aelders, Théroigne de Méricourt, and Pauline Léon, were active in revolutionary politics during the period 1790–91. D'Aelders, a Dutch woman, had been in Paris since 1774; she addressed the Cercle social on women's rights twice in the late fall of 1790.[2] In February, 1791, she introduced an ambitious plan to form women's patriotic societies in each Section of Paris and in each of the eighty-three Departments—all to be

[1]Marc de Villiers, Baron du Terrage, *Histoire des clubs de femmes et des légions d'Amazones (1793–1848–1871)* (Paris, 1910), chap. 2; Isabelle Bourdin, *Les Sociétés populaires à Paris pendant la Révolution* (Paris, 1937).

[2]Marc de Villiers, *Histoire des clubs,* chap. 2; Marie Cerati, *Le Club des Citoyennes Républicaines révolutionnaires* (Paris, 1966).

coordinated by a *"cercle central et fédératif."* One society was founded on March 23, with d'Aelders as its secretary, but it failed to expand for lack of support when the Paris Sections did not send representatives. Her announced goal was to set up schools and workshops to teach a skill to poor girls. Although she never got her schools, she did use her subscription money to buy apprenticeships for three girls. Her club survived until she became a suspect in the fall of 1792; she emigrated to Holland in January, 1793.

Théroigne de Méricourt, also a member of the Société fraternelle, had been a participant in the Women's March in October, 1789. In the first three months of 1790 she was in a short-lived society called Amis de la loi, which was dedicated to teaching the people their rights.[3] She tried, unsuccessfully, to found a women's society and later became an ardent advocate of an armed female battalion.

Pauline Léon was already the most radical of the three; in 1793 she became one of the leaders of the *femmes sans-culottes.* In the spring of 1791 she was a member of a fraternal society in her Section and of the Société fraternelle, and she was an associate of the Cordeliers. In March she addressed to the National Assembly a demand that women have the right to bear arms.

Early in 1791 members of the fraternal societies, men and women, became involved in more radical political activities as expressions of a developing triple distrust: of aristocrats, of the National Assembly, and of the King. Their denunciations of aristocrats became more heated. They armed themselves, seized contraband articles from merchants, and disrupted sessions of the Club monarchique, an organization of nobles and conservatives which won the particular enmity of the fraternal societies because it distributed food at below-market prices to the indigent to win their support.[4] Women also joined the protests against certain new laws, especially the prohibition against collective petitions and the Le Chapelier law abolishing guilds and prohibiting any professional or workers' organizations.[5] When Louis XVI, who had refused earlier to approve legislation nationalizing the church, acerbated the constitutional crisis by fleeing the capital with the royal family in late June, the ultrapatriotic Cordelier Society opened a campaign to replace the monarchy with a republic; Cordeliers canvassed national workshops and fraternal societies to solicit popular support for their movement.

---

[3]Marc de Villiers, *Histoire des clubs,* chap. 4.

[4]Bourdin, *Les Sociétés populaires,* pp. 53, 54.

[5]Albert Mathiez, *Le Club des Cordeliers pendant la Crise de Varennes et le Massacre du Champ de Mars* (Paris, 1910), p. 28.

The Cordelier campaign ended in tragedy. A short time after the King's flight to Varennes, a peaceful rally was held at the Champ de Mars; thousands of men and women attended in order to sign a petition demanding Louis XVI's replacement and a popular referendum on executive authority. The issue of executive authority occupied the full attention of the political clubs and popular societies as they debated, drafted petitions, and exchanged deputations. Women affiliated with these organizations were involved in the mounting challenge to royal legitimacy. They were deputized by fraternal societies, they participated in debate in the Cordeliers and other clubs, and they were among the petition signers on the Champ de Mars.

Lafayette, on the pretext that the gathering was seditious, brought the National Guard to the Champ de Mars to disperse the crowd. When it failed to disband quickly enough, the guard opened fire; approximately fifty demonstrators were killed. Within weeks, leading Cordeliers were arrested or forced to flee into exile. Women were also among those arrested for participation in the demonstration on the Champ de Mars. The list included Etta Palm d'Aelders; the wife of the butcher Legendre, who was active in Section politics; the wife of a well-to-do wine merchant; and the owner of Hébert's print works.[6]

The massacre on the Champ de Mars represented a dramatic and violent rupture within the Third Estate. The representatives of Paris and of the nation had authorized the National Guard to fire on the people of Paris. The wealthy middle classes were polarized against the shopkeepers, artisans, and workers of Paris. The *menu peuple* acted out an intense involvement in the legal and constitutional question of executive legitimacy at a time when bread prices and general economic conditions were stabilized.

In September the constitution was completed and ratified, however reluctantly, by the King. Opposition to the constitutional monarchy was temporarily muted by general enthusiasm for the new government. Typical was the speech by Louise Robert, wife of the president of the Société fraternelle, coupling enthusiasm for the Revolution with glorification of women's domestic duties.

A note of discord is found in a unique feminist document, the Declaration of the Rights of Woman. Its author, Olympe de Gouges, argued that such a document was made necessary because the Constitution of 1791 and its preamble, the Declaration of the Rights of Man and Citizen, were silent on the issue of women's rights. De Gouges was the

[6]*Ibid.*, pp. 198, 199, 203, 211, 266, 267.

daughter of a butcher from Montauban. After an early and unsuccessful marriage she came to Paris without her husband; in 1778 she began to produce plays. Poorly educated, she wrote in a barely legible hand and spelled phonetically. In 1788 she turned her energies to politics and wrote several tax reform proposals. In the early years of the Revolution, she, too, tried unsuccessfully to organize a female society. In 1793 she would be guillotined as a reactionary royalist, but in 1791 her feminist manifesto stands out as a strident denial of faith in the Constitution of 1791. It would take a deepening military crisis, mounting distrust of the King, and recurring subsistence crises to generalize opposition to the constitutional monarchy.

1. SPEECH BY THE CITOYENNES OF THE RUE DU REGARD TO
   THE CORDELIERS CLUB, FEBRUARY 22, 1791

Source: Club des Cordeliers, Société des amis des droits de
l'homme et du citoyen, *Extrait des délibérations du 22 février 1791*
(Paris, 1791), in Bibliothèque historique de la Ville de Paris,
10,065, no. 67.

This speech is an exhortation to the men of the Cordeliers to be
firmer in their opposition to aristocrats and others who might
undermine the accomplishments of the Revolution. These women
accept their own roles as wives and mothers, but do not hesitate
to accuse male revolutionaries of becoming slipshod; they
threaten that they will become militant if the men do not rouse
themselves. They have defined the Cordeliers Club as an
organization to defend national security and to oversee national
leaders.

———————◆———————

Citoyennes of the rue du Regard, faubourg Saint-Germain, to their courageous brothers of the Cordeliers Club, greetings and perseverance!
    In the bosom of our households, engaged in having our children
memorize the sacred principles of the constitution, which our husbands
and brothers have sworn to be vigilant in supporting and realizing, we
learn with sadness and fear of the destruction which threatens the
Fatherland and of the attacks by the enemies of the public weal, who
delude themselves with expectation of making a counterrevolution in
giant steps. Where, we said then, where are the men of July 14? Where
are the heros who made themselves sentinels atop the debris of the
Bastille, always watchful over liberty? Where is that family of twenty-
five million brothers who promised one another to fly to the aid of our
common home in time of calamity? Are they no more, these children of
liberty? Have they disappeared with the dungeons of the Bastille which
fell under their blows? We also, we are worthy of fighting, of dying for
the Fatherland. Listen, brothers of the Cordeliers Club, we have left our

shelters where the duties of maternity secluded us; we have momentarily interrupted our domestic labors; we are reunited; we have spoken of the misfortunes which from all sides assail the still fragile edifice of liberty. Here is what your sisters say, the *citoyennes* of the rue du Regard.

Brothers, rely no longer on the faith of perfidious men or imbeciles who traitorously invite you to the security of death, to the confidence of slaves.

Brothers, watch, watch with more exactitude and severity than ever over the governing of the state. We will follow you day and night; how wretched for you if the ship breaks apart before you call the public strength to its aid! You will have lost our respect.

Brothers, escape the vain and frivolous display of eloquent words; speak only to act; never act with hope of gaining fame. Your reward shall be within yourselves, if you do your duty.

Brothers, remain forever in arms; do not in this crisis succumb to the memory of past deeds; in order to plunge you back into slavery, your enemies will seize the moment of abandon when you are singing hymns to liberty.

Brothers, until now we have been honored and proud to be called your companions.

We have consoled ourselves for our inability to contribute to the public good by exerting our most intense efforts to raise the spirit of our children to the heights of free men. But if you deceive our hope, if the machinations of our enemies blind you to the point of rendering you insensible at the height of the storm, then indignation, sorrow, despair will impel and drag us into public places. There, we shall fight to defend liberty; until you have conquered it you will not be men. Then we shall save the Fatherland, or, dying with it, we will uproot the torturous memory of seeing you unworthy of us.

Brothers, our alarms are imaginary; they will never be realized; we want to believe in you as in ourselves. Your vigilance is ever the same; we already owe [you] much for it. We shall praise you for it if free souls know how to praise or need to be praised. Greetings and perseverance to our brave brothers of the Cordeliers Club. We commend the Fatherland to you; we cease speaking of it with you only in order to converse with our children about it.

At the bottom of this address are the following signatures: Femmes Rouiller, Grenier, Lolay, former baroness de Villepail, Trusson, widow Lefebvre, Saint-Jean, Bonpaix, Damour, Douce, daughter Valentin, Bourgeaux, Pascal, Bertier, Merk, Berttok, Mullei, LeFranc, Guinand.

I am, with the warmest cordiality, your brother Kolly [or Holly], of the Cordeliers Club, February 23, 1791.

2. Etta Palm d'Aelders Proposes a Network of Women's Clubs to Administer Welfare Programs in Paris and Throughout France

Source: Etta Palm d'Aelders, *Lettre d'une amie de la vérité, Etta Palm, née d'Aelders, Hollandoise, sur les démarches des ennemis extérieurs et intérieurs de la France; suivie d'une adresse à toutes les citoyennes patriotes, et d'une motion à leur proposer pour l'Assemblée nationale, lue à l'Assemblée féderative des amis de la vérité, le 23 mars 1791* (n.p., n.d.), in Bibliothèque historique de la Ville de Paris, 12,807, vol. 1, no. 15, pp. 16–31.

In this pamphlet d'Aelders speaks to two questions: first, the question of France's foreign and domestic friends and foes, and second, the question of how patriotic women already involved in a men's political society might organize an exclusively women's circle to maximize their usefulness as administrators of welfare. D'Aelders' thoughts on the second subject are reprinted here.

———————

. . . My fellow citizens, my brothers, if my feeble voice could reach your heart, if my zeal for the happiness of Frenchmen could inspire you to some extent, then listen to me. Rally around the tree of the constitution; it is the tree of life. Watch over the sacred fasces of the union; it is the bulwark of your liberty. Go, abjure on the altar of the Fatherland all hatred and partial enmity, all personal jealousies. Relegate to contempt, to anathema, whoever dares malign his brother; may love of the Fatherland, of liberty, of fraternity, be in your hearts as on your lips; let us all seek out ways of supporting one another, of succoring the unfortunate, of regenerating morals, of cherishing virtue, and of contributing, each of us, individually and in general, to making the French people the happiest people in the world. May your union and your happiness be blessed by all the nations.

In the eighty-three Departments, armed citizens united to defend the constitution. Do you not believe, Gentlemen, that these wives and mothers of families could join together, following their example, to make it [the constitution] loved? The Société des amis de la vérité is the first to have admitted us to patriotic sessions. Creil, Alais, Bordeaux, and several others followed your example. Would it not be useful to form, in each Section of the capital, a patriotic society of *citoyennes*, female friends of the truth, whose general and federative circle would be supervised by you, Gentlemen, and would invite the fraternal societies of the eighty-three Departments to correspond with them. Each circle of *citoyennes* would meet in each Section as frequently as they believed useful for the public good and following their own particular rules; each circle would have its own directorate, which would meet once a week as a general staff under the supervision of the directorate of the friends of the truth. Thus, it would be in a position to supervise efficiently the enemies harbored in the midst of the capital and to differentiate the genuinely poor person in need of his brothers' aid from brigands called out by enemies. And the directorate of the central circle, corresponding with patriotic societies in the Departments, would propagate enlightenment and would make it possible to break up more easily the plots hatched by malevolent persons.

It is up to you, Gentlemen, friends of the truth, to develop the full utility of such an establishment. I would want to propose to my *concitoyennes* a means of demonstrating that they are worthy of the justice just rendered them by the august representatives of the nation; that they yield nothing to you in zeal for supporting your strengthening of their work.

These circles of women could be charged with overseeing the establishment of wet nurses. Ah! How urgent that a maternal view be taken of this administration, where a culpable negligence makes nature tremble. Yes, young women from the country, arriving in this huge capital without friends, without acquaintances, abandoned to themselves, without work and wandering around, prey to all kinds of seduction, often return home with their souls debased, their blood polluted. And innocent victims confided to these creatures are immolated or condemned to a painful existence and countless infirmities. A thousand other motives not any the less worthy of interest argue the necessity of a strict supervision of this administration to give healthy and robust men to a future generation.

Ah! Isn't this the field of honor where we must gather our laurels? These societies of *citoyennes* could be charged, in addition, with supervising public education. Wouldn't it be natural that charity schools, given over for the most part to ignorant people brought up with all kinds of prejudices, be under the immediate supervision of enlightened and virtuous *citoyennes?* Zealous women patriots would take care to teach children the rights of men, respect and obedience for the law, the duty of citizens, the decrees of the National Assembly, and, finally, the revered names of France's regenerators instead of legends of the saints and the almanac of miracles.

These women's clubs could be charged in addition with investigating the conduct and the need of unfortunate people requesting aid from the Section—which would be easy, using the central circle where *citoyennes* from all the Sections would gather, because giving isn't everything, but giving well is. For example, a poor woman about to become a mother, deprived of all the assistance her condition calls for—doesn't she have sacred rights to our aid?

Woe to those among us who could look pitilessly upon their like, overwhelmed with misery, on a pallet of pain, bringing into the world an innocent victim whose cries, weakened by need, are calls for the preservation of life.

Woe to whoever, at the sight of this, does not share her clothing to cover her [the impoverished mother], and her necessities of life to aid her.

Thus, by establishing a society of women in each Section, by means of a light contribution of a crown a month, a fund, for example, could be formed for indigent women (once expenses were deducted), and they could designate from their group a directress and commissioners charged with keeping a register of those who asked for their assistance.

These commissioners would be charged with going into humble dwellings to inform themselves concerning morals, conduct, or misfortunes of the indigent and with bringing consolation along with aid to their unfortunate brothers. In this way the distance between the rich and the poor would be narrowed infinitely. In this way charity would be excited in the one, courage and patience in the other. The morals of both would be purified and egoism destroyed, and the wealthy man, object of jealousy and envy, would become an object of love and veneration to his brother in indigence.

This, Gentlemen, is a plan worthy of your attention. It is up to you. to the friends of the truth, to develop its full usefulness. I dare assure you that the courageous *citoyennes* who supported you with such passion in raising the altar of the Fatherland, on which you swore no longer to be anything other than a people of brothers, will applaud my project. Already they burn to show all Europe that if, when they were degraded under despotism, pleasing frivolity was their lot, then when they are restored to the dignity of their being, they will be the model for all civic virtues.

Citoyennes patriotes, to whom the august representatives of the nation have just given imprescriptible rights of nature of which a cowardly avidity, an unjust tyranny, deprived you, you no longer will be sacrificed to the avidity of a brother or immolated to your parents' pride. No longer will you be buried from the beginning of your existence in these odious caverns where you were forced to suffocate the heart's sweetest sentiments. No longer will it be a crime for you to be sensitive to the voice of nature.

Glory, immortal glory to the legislators of France, for having restored to the weakest but largest portion of humanity their rights—by decreeing equality of distribution [of properties]. But would it not be your duty to lay evidence of your gratitude at the feet of the august Senate which has just given you a civil existence?

Therefore I make the formal motion that from among the women who are friends of truth, a deputation be named to go to the bar of the National Assembly to bear respectful and grateful witness before the representatives of France to what they just did for them and to promise these worthy fathers of the people that they will inspire their children with the same respect, the same love, for the constitution and the most ardent zeal in propagating moral and civil virtues.

This discourse, having received a unanimous vote, and its printing having been requested of the federative assembly, Madame d'Aelders proposes to those *citoyennes* who were present that they meet the following Saturday at the printing establishment of the Cercle social. I committed several of my friends to join us there, and this is how I experienced the joy of forming the Société patriotique de bienfaisance, called *Amies de la Vérité,* to the success of which I have pledged all my attention and my entire life.

3. Petition to the National Assembly on Women's Rights to Bear Arms

Source: Pauline Léon, *Adresse individuelle à l'Assemblée nationale, par des citoyennes de la Capitale, le 6 mars 1791* (Paris, n.d.), in B.N., Le[33] 3x. 22.

Pauline Léon was a member of the Cordeliers Club in 1791; in 1793 she served as president of the radical women's club, the Society of Revolutionary Republican Women (see chapter 4). This document was drafted at a time when, under law, only members of the National Guard could bear arms. Léon demands legislative authorization for a women's militia so that women could defend their homes against aristocrats. She insists that women are as essential as men in the armed defense of the Revolution. This document shows that women are redefining their rights as their perceptions of national needs change.

———————

Legislators:

Patriotic women come before you to claim the right which any individual has to defend his life and liberty.

Everyone predicts that a violent shock is coming; our fathers, husbands, and brothers may be the victims of the fury of our enemies. Could we be denied the joy of avenging them or of dying at their sides? We are *citoyennes,* and we cannot be indifferent to the fate of the fatherland.

Your predecessors deposited the Constitution as much in our hands as in yours. Oh, how to save it, if we have no arms to defend it from the attacks of its enemies?

Yes, Gentlemen, we need arms, and we come to ask your permission to procure them. May our weakness be no obstacle; courage and intrepidity will supplant it, and the love of the fatherland and hatred of tyrants will allow us to brave all dangers with ease. Do not believe, however, that our plan is to abandon the care of our families and home, always dear to our hearts, to run to meet the enemy.

No, Gentlemen. We wish only to defend ourselves the same as you; you cannot refuse us, and society cannot deny the right nature gives us, unless you pretend the Declaration of Rights does not apply to women, and that they should let their throats be cut like lambs, without the right to defend themselves. For can you believe the tyrants would spare us? No, no—they remember October 5 and 6, 1789. . . [in text]. But, you say, men are armed for your defense. Of course, but we reply, why deprive us of the right to join that defense, and of the pleasure of saving their days by using ours? Do they know the number and strength of our hidden enemies? Have they but one fight to fight? Is our life dearer than theirs? Are our children not orphaned by the loss of their fathers as much as their mothers? Why then not terrorize aristocracy and tyranny with all the resources of civic effort [*civisme*] and the purest zeal, zeal which cold men can well call fanaticism and exaggeration, but which is only the natural result of a heart burning with love for the public weal?

Without doubt, Gentlemen, the most joyous success will crown the justice of our cause. Well then, we shall have the pleasure of having contributed to the victory. But if, by the wiles of our enemies or the treachery of some on our side, the evil ones win victory, then is it not cruel to condemn us to await in our homes a shameful death and all the horrors which will precede it? Or—an even worse misfortune—to survive the loss of what we hold most dear, our families and our liberty?

No, Gentlemen, do not imagine it. If, for reasons we cannot guess, you refuse our just demands, these women you have raised to the ranks of *citoyennes* by granting that title to their husbands, these women who have sampled the promises of liberty, who have conceived the hope of placing free men in the world, and who have sworn to live free or die—such women, I say, will never consent to concede the day to slaves; they will die first. They will uphold their oath, and a dagger aimed at their breasts will deliver them from the misfortunes of slavery! They will die, regretting not life, but the uselessness of their death; regretting moreover, not having been able to drench their hands in the impure blood of the enemies of the fatherland and to avenge some of their own!

But, Gentlemen, let us cast our eyes away from these cruel extremes. Whatever the rages and plots of aristocrats, they will not succeed in vanquishing a whole people of united brothers armed to defend their rights. We also demand only the honor of sharing their exhaustion and glorious labors and of making tyrants see that women also have blood to shed for the service of the fatherland in danger.

Gentlemen, here is what we hope to obtain from your justice and equity:

1. Permission to procure pikes, pistols, and sabres (even muskets for those who are strong enough to use them), within police regulations.
2. Permission to assemble on festival days and Sundays on the Champ de la Fédération, or in other suitable places, to practice maneuvers with these arms.
3. Permission to name the former French Guards to command us, always in conformity with the rules which the mayor's wisdom prescribes for good order and public calm.

Signed,

Léon, *fille,* etc.

Something more than three hundred signatures follow.

4. A CALL FOR AN END TO SEXUAL DISCRIMINATION

Source: Etta Palm d'Aelders, *Adresse des citoyennes françoises à l'Assemblée nationale* (n.d. [Summer, 1791]), in Bibliothèque historique de la Ville de Paris, 12,807, vol. 1, no. 15, pp. 37–40.

In this document Etta Palm d'Aelders exhorts the National Assembly to legislate complete equality of rights for women, but her specific concerns are with equality between spouses in laws affecting marriage and equal opportunity for education. She articulates the most radical feminist thought of the high enlightenment, grounding constitutional propositions in laws and rights of nature.

Gentlemen,

The chains of Frenchmen have fallen with a crash; the sound of their fall caused despots to grow pale and shook their thrones; an astonished Europe fixed an attentive eye on the star that illuminates France and on the august senate which represents a people who join the love of being just to the will to be free.

Yes, Gentlemen, you have broken the iron sceptre in order to replace it with the olive branch; you have sworn to protect the weak. It is a question of your duty, your honor, your interest, to destroy down to their roots these gothic laws which abandon the weakest but [also] the most worthy half of humanity to a humiliating existence, to an eternal slavery.

You have restored to man the dignity of his being in recognizing his rights; you will no longer allow woman to groan beneath an arbitrary authority; that would be to overturn the fundamental principles on which rests the stately edifice you are raising by your untiring labors for the happiness of Frenchmen. It is too late to equivocate. Philosophy has drawn truth from the darkness; the time has come; justice, sister of liberty, calls all individuals to the equality of rights, without discrimination of sex; the laws of a free people must be equal for all beings, like the air and the sun. For too long, alas, the imprescriptible rights of nature have been misprized; for too long, bizarre laws, the worthy product of centuries of ignorance, have afflicted humanity; finally, for too long, the most odious tyranny was consecrated by absurd laws.

But Gentlemen, article XIII of the code of civil order [*code de police*], which was presented to you by the Constitutional Committee, surpassed the most unjust thing done in barbarous centuries; this is a refinement of despotism [designed] to render the constitution odious to the female sex and, by degrading our lives while flattering your conceit, to lull you to sleep in the arms of a slave and thus to dull your energy the better to rivet your chains.[1]

Majestic legislators, would you weight down with chains the hands that have helped you with so much ardor to raise the altar of the Fatherland? Will you make slaves those who have contributed with zeal to making you free? Will you stamp a brand on the forehead of a Clelia, a Veturia, a Cornelia? No. No. Conjugal authority should be only the consequence of the social pact. It is wisdom in legislation, it is in the general interest to establish a balance between despotism and license, but the powers of husband and wife must be equal and separate. The laws cannot establish any difference between these two authorities; they must give equal protection and maintain a perpetual balance between the two married people. Wouldn't it be unjust to assign to the husband all the ease of vice, while the wife, whose fragile existence is subject to countless ills, would have the full difficulty of virtue for her share?

Fathers of the country, do not sully your immortal work by such a clashing stain; doubtless a moral code is necessary for you, but morals are the work of time and education. They are not commanded; abuse of

[1]The article in question appears in *Projet de Loi sur la police municipale et la police correctionnelle presenté par le Comité de Constitution; imprimé par ordre de l'Assemblée nationale* (Paris, 1791), p. 22: "The charge of adultery can be pursued only by the husband and only through the correctional police. But this action will always be brought in the first instance before the district court and the appeal will be made before the seven district courts designated by law. A woman convicted of this offense will be punished, depending on the circumstances, by one year, eighteen months, or two years of imprisonment and by forfeiture of matrimonial arrangements established in her favor. The dowry will not be confiscated; the husband will have control of it no matter what clauses are contained in the marriage ceremony, on the condition, however, that he provide an allowance for board, at the judge's discretion. The husband at any time can put an end to the sentence by stating his willingness to take his wife into his home. The woman's accomplice will be condemned to a fine of one-eighth of his fortune and to a prison term of three months." [Translators' note.]

liberty is a natural consequence of the oppressive regime of the indissolubility of marriage and of the dull and enervated education of the cloisters, haunts of ignorance and fanaticism which you destroyed in your wisdom. You will complete your work by giving girls a moral education equal to that of their brothers; for education is for the soul what watering is for plants; it makes it fertile, causes it to bloom, fortifies it, and carries the germ productive of virtue and talents to a perfect maturity.

Representatives of the nation, in the name of your honor, in the name of saintly liberty, vote down the unjust and unpolitic code; it would be the apple of discord in families, the tomb of liberty. Constraint withers the soul; the slave thinks only of breaking his chains, of having his revenge for servitude. Doubtless the Committee, in order to present you with this odious article, consulted the theologians and not the philosophers. Well! Consult only your heart; it will instruct you better than the maxims of the jurisconsults of preceding centuries—these men, turned grey in despotism, who take the avidity of their soul for an effect of virtue. Nature formed us to be your equals, your companions, and your friends; we are the supports of your infancy, the felicity of maturity, and the consolation of your old age, sacred titles to your gratitude.

5. Women Sign a Petition to the National Assembly on the Fate of the King

Source: Albert Mathiez, *Le Club des Cordeliers pendant la crise de Varennes et le massacre du Champ de Mars,* pp. 112–15, reprinting the text of the petition to the National Assembly of July 14, 1791, with signatures, from A.N., C. 75, no. 737.

Members of the Cordeliers Club and the popular societies went together to the Champ de la Fédération on July 14, 1791. There, they drew up and signed a petition to the National Assembly concerning the political future of the King. That afternoon, they brought it to the Assembly. Among the signers were forty-one women, grouped separately from the men. It may be assumed that these women understood the issues treated in the petition, and that therefore they were prepared to stand up and be counted for opinions on royal legitimacy and on the issue of democratic control of the national legislature.

———————————

Petition to the National Assembly
Said to be [the petition] of the hundred.

Gentlemen,

Frenchmen chose representatives to give them a constitution, not to restore a leader who betrays and breaks his most sacred oaths, a leader who has expressed the most perfidious intentions and those most destructive of this great work to which they have all contributed. Rightly alarmed by the dangerous inclinations of your committees, we come to place in your midst our just fears and to ask of you, in the name of the Fatherland, in the name of this sacred liberty which it has conquered, to work speedily to dissipate them [these fears].

When the Romans, this first free people, saw that the Fatherland was in danger and that it was a question of decreeing on the interests of everyone, they assembled as a people. The senators came and took from their assemblies the essence of the deliberations they were dictating, and the Senate never pronounced alone concerning such important interests.

The citizens present here come therefore with this [character] which they hold from the Romans, with this character of liberty which they will preserve until they die, to ask of the Nation's representatives that they not legislate anything definitive concerning the fate of Louis XVI until the desires of the commoners [*les communes*] of France have been expressed and until the voice of the mass of the people has been heard.

Therefore, make this sacred commitment to await the expression of this public voice before pronouncing on a question which affects the whole nation and which the powers you have received from it [the nation] do not embrace.

Fear lest you yourselves crown the perfidious atrocities of our enemies by delivering your country over to all the horrors of a civil war.

Finally, consider that you cannot and must not prejudge anything concerning questions of this nature, and that any decree which is not circumscribed within the boundaries prescribed for you would be declared null and at the same time would take on the character of the most terrible outrage against the rights of the sovereign, the people, the people.

Paris, Thursday, 14 July, 1791, at one o'clock in the afternoon. [The signatures follow. Among them were the following "signatures of women, sisters, and Roman women":]

Veuve de la Garde, Guit, Bigant, Haranger, Lapeyre, A. Perré, Tiollet, Melin, Lardy, Brillon, Lavoisier, Grantille, Guillot, *Veuve* Maillard, *Femme* Bresson, Cottard, *La Veuve* Brault, Mancontuc, *Mademoiselle* Barbet, Delattre, *Veuve* Delivet, F. Reboulet, Majeau, *La veuve* Donneux, *Femme* Pierret, Goffrois, Goutte, Mony, F. Boutheron, Breton, Coubet, *Veuve* Lucidor, Bachellet, Benoist, Corbin, *Femme* Lair, Thibaust, Décret, F. Lejeune, F. Janssns [*sic*], F. Chantroi.

6. A Shopwoman and Champ de Mars Petitioner Asks for Protection from the Jacobins Against Revolutionary Officials

Source: Account in *Mercure universel* of a meeting of the Jacobin Society on July 15, 1791, as reprinted in Marcel Reinhard, *La Chute de la Royauté,* p. 482.

This young shopwoman was a member of a fraternal society. On July 14 she had been deputized by her society to present a petition, probably a version of the preceding document, to the National Assembly on the subject of a popular referendum on royal legitimacy. However, while there, she was threatened by the mayor and a National Guardsman. The following day, as a member of another deputation "of thousands" bearing a petition to the Jacobin Club asking that members sign the Champ de Mars petition individually, this young woman was prepared to exploit her contact in an effort to obtain justice.

———————

Session of July 15, 1791

. . . A young woman from the deputation:

M. le président, I ask you for a favor for myself and my sister. Today we were deputized to the National Assembly by our fraternal society in order to present our petition. At the door of the National Assembly my sister and I were stopped by an officer of the National Guard, whom I did not know, and who had a blue ribbon and a red ribbon, with crosses in his buttonhole. When we told the Mayor and this officer that we brought a petition, they rebuffed us and prevented us from entering, threatening us and saying that tonight they would kidnap us, and that my shop, which is in the street . . . [in text] would be closed and razed. *M. le président,* I ask you, I pray you to accord me the protection of the Society.

(Commissioners were named to investigate these facts.)

7. A Cook Testifies on Her Participation at the Champ de Mars

Source: Cross-examination by the police commissioner of the Section Fontaine de Grenelle of Constance Evrard, twenty-three-year-old cook, 64 rue de Grenelle, in Archives, Préfecture de Police, Paris, Aa 148, fol. 30, xx, as paraphrased by George Rudé, *The Crowd in the French Revolution*, pp. 86–87.

This document is a police interrogation of a cook, Constance Evrard, who was arrested on July 17 and charged with insulting the wife of a National Guardsman who was at the Champ de Mars when the massacre took place. The cook's testimony gives evidence of the sophisticated and informed awareness of *femmes sans-culottes*. Evrard, having attended meetings of the Cordeliers Club and the National Assembly, knew that the aim of the petition was to reorganize executive power, and, in addition, she was a regular reader of radical political journals.

Q. Had she been to the Champ de Mars?
A. Yes, she had been there with Madame Léon and her daughter.
Q. Why had she been there?
A. To sign a petition *"comme tous les bons patriotes."*
Q. What was the petition about?
A. She understood its aim was *"à faire organiser autrement le pouvoir exécutif."*
Q. Did she often to to public meetings?
A. She had sometimes been to the Palais Royal and the Tuileries.
Q. Did she belong to any club?
A. She had sometimes been to the Cordeliers Club, though not actually a member.
Q. Had she been with any particular group in the Champ de Mars?
A. She had been on the "autel de la patrie" and signed the petition.

Q. Had she thrown stones or seen any stones thrown?

A. No.

Q. Who had invited her to sign the petition?

A. No one, but she had heard various people say that there was a petition to sign in the Champ de Mars.

Q. Was it true that her name had appeared in the papers?

A. Yes, her name had appeared in *Les Révolutions de Paris*, because she had expressed grief at the death of Loustalot.

Q. What papers did she read?

A. She read Marat, Audouin, Camille Desmoulins, and very often, *L'Orateur du peuple*.

8. A Boy's Testimony Concerning an Illiterate
   Woman Signing the Petition at the Champ de Mars,
   July 17, 1791

Source: One testimony from a copy of the proceedings of the
inquiry into the Champ de Mars incidents, in A.N., F⁷ 4622.
The copy was made by one of the accused, the lawyer Buirrette
de Verrières, and is reprinted in Albert Mathiez, *Le Club des
Cordeliers pendant La crise de Varennes et le massacre du Champ de
Mars,* p. 247.

This testimony from an eleven-year-old boy is one of several
documents attesting to the presence of illiterate women among
the petition signers at the Champ de Mars, and indicating
women's active political involvement in the events following the
King's attempt to flee into Belgium.

———————————⬩———————————

Thursday, 28 July, 1791, eleven o'clock in the morning.

In the presence of Joseph-Daniel Quiret and Jean-Louis Berthe, both
notable adjuncts from the Section des Quatre-Nations.

Jean-Pierre Belletoise, aged eleven years, native of Chaillot, son of
Jean Belletoise, locksmith, with whom he lives in Chaillot . . . [in
text].

States that on Sunday, 17 July, the current month, he went walking
around five o'clock to the Champ de la Fédération; that he saw many
people up on the altar of the fatherland; that he heard the words *King*
and *National Assembly* spoken, but he didn't understand what was said
about them; [that] he heard that the public was being persuaded to
come to sign; that he saw several people go up to sign; among them,
with her children, [was] an old woman, who, not knowing how to
write, had one of her children sign for her; that, in the evening, he heard
it said that the red flag would arrive, that he looked around to flee; that
he noticed that on the altar of the fatherland they were saying that good

citizens had to remain there; that he also heard it said that M. de Lafayette had come at three o'clock, and having been questioned on the motive that brought him there, he [Lafayette] had answered that [he had come] in the name of the law; people had answered that his brains would be blown out for the nation; that he [Belletoise] made his escape along the water's edge.

9. ADDRESS BY THE WOMEN OF LA HALLE TO THE
   NATIONAL ASSEMBLY, AUGUST 27, 1791, AS THEY MAKE
   A DONATION OF MONEY

Source: *Adresse des dames de La Halle à l'Assemblée nationale, séance du 27 août 1791, au soir* (n.p., n.d.), in B.N., Le²⁹ 1729.

This is an address by the marketwomen to the National Assembly in the last month of its existence as they offer valuable items as a gesture of support for the work of the Revolution. Note the explicit denial of political involvement, despite the dramatic impact upon Paris of the King's flight in June and the shooting on the Champ de Mars in July.

Gentlemen:

Since your courage broke the shameful irons of slavery that weighed upon the French people for so many centuries, and since your wisdom has given this great people a truly admirable Constitution, which will generate our glory and happiness, and since all nations envy it, the citizens of all classes feel themselves warmed by the sacred fire of patriotism.

The idea of liberty enlarged souls, enflamed spirits, electrified hearts. To acquire it no sacrifice is too dear; in safeguarding it, life itself counts for nothing.

The market dwellers, for whom all politics and all refinements are foreign, know no other virtue than to be useful and informed on behalf of their Fatherland.

Our husbands and sons have enlisted beneath the flag; we ourselves come to place our offering on the altar of liberty in the august temple of the nation and its laws. We are eager to contribute, insofar as we can, to the support of the generous Frenchmen who fly to the frontiers to defend them against traitors and tyrants who wish to give us back our chains.

Formerly we were a guild, a confederation dedicated to the Virgin, patroness of France. In dedicating a cult to her, we had ornaments and silver plate in a treasure chest deposited in the Church of the Sepulchre.

Today we have no other guild than the French, no other confederation than patriots, no other cult than liberty. Hence, we consecrate to the defense of the Fatherland the funds of a rent contract, the silver, silver plate, and ornaments we have in a coffer. Since the Virgin is the protectress of France, she will receive as fitting homage our self-sacrifice for her. Our offering is no greater than twelve hundred to fifteen hundred *livres,* but, Gentlemen, it is the offering of the poor, the widow's mite, and this coin is precious when offered from the heart.

Virtuous legislators, saviors of the Fatherland, deign to accept the just tribute of our respect, of our recognition, and of our love.

To Monsieur, the President of the National Assembly

Monsieur:

The women codfish sellers in La Halle, from the brotherhood of Saint-Louis, have the honor of informing the National Assembly that on November 2, 1789, they brought to the treasury the funds of their brotherhood, amounting to the sum of three thousand *livres.* They brought the receipt to M. Bailly so that this sum could be offered as an outright gift to the nation. We have carefully followed various journals [appearing] at this time and we noted that this sum was not inserted in your minutes. They dare hope, M. le Président, that you will be willing to allow them to profit from the moment when their sisters make their gift, to humbly request that you insert the two amounts which their hearts and devotion to the Fatherland inspired them to donate.

The President's Reply

Mesdames,

It is not one of the lesser benefits of the Constitution to have destroyed the spirit of individual corporations, so as to make of all Frenchmen only a family of brothers closely united by the indissoluble and sacred bond of love of Fatherland.

In consecrating today to the public cause what previously had been only a symbol of union between a few individuals, you give a new proof of patriotism which had distinguished you to such great advantage since the beginning of the Revolution.

As a token of our satisfaction, the National Assembly invites you to attend the session.

10. The Declaration of the Rights of Woman

Source: Olympe de Gouges, *Les Droits de la Femme* (Paris, n.d. [1791], in B.N., E* 5568.

De Gouges was a butcher's daughter from Montauban who wrote several plays and a number of pamphlets on the coming Estates General. In this work de Gouges states that the Declaration of the Rights of Man and Citizen is not being applied to women. She implies the vote for women, demands a national assembly of women, stresses that men must yield rights to women, and emphasizes women's education. She addresses *Les Droits de la Femme* to the Queen, trusting perhaps that the Queen could be converted to the cause of political rights for women and become principal spokeswoman for a feminist program. De Gouges' allegiances are complexly divided between royalty and the national legislature.

To the Queen: Madame,

Little suited to the language one holds to with kings, I will not use the adulation of courtiers to pay you homage with this singular production. My purpose, Madame, is to speak frankly to you; I have not awaited the epoch of liberty to thus explain myself; I bestirred myself as energetically in a time when the blindness of despots punished such noble audacity.

When the whole empire accused you and held you responsible for its calamities, I alone in a time of trouble and storm, I alone had the strength to take up your defense. I could never convince myself that a princess, raised in the midst of grandeur, had all the vices of baseness.

Yes, Madame, when I saw the sword raised against you, I threw my observations between that sword and you, but today when I see who is observed near the crowd of useless hirelings, and {when I see} that she is restrained by fear of the laws, I will tell you, Madame, what I did not say then.

If the foreigner bears arms into France, you are no longer in my eyes this falsely accused Queen, this attractive Queen, but an implacable enemy of the French. Oh, Madame, bear in mind that you are mother and wife; employ all your credit for the return of the Princes. This credit, if wisely applied, strengthens the father's crown, saves it for the son, and reconciles you to the love of the French. This worthy negotiation is the true duty of a queen. Intrigue, cabals, bloody projects will precipitate your fall, if it is possible to suspect that you are capable of such plots.

Madame, may a nobler function characterize you, excite your ambition, and fix your attentions. Only one whom chance has elevated to an eminent position can assume the task of lending weight to the progress of the Rights of Woman and of hastening its success. If you were less well informed, Madame, I might fear that your individual interests would outweigh those of your sex. You love glory; think, Madame, the greatest crimes immortalize one as much as the greatest virtues, but what a different fame in the annals of history! The one is ceaselessly taken as an example, and the other is eternally the execration of the human race.

It will never be a crime for you to work for the restoration of customs, to give your sex all the firmness of which it is capable. This is not the work of one day, unfortunately for the new regime. This revolution will happen only when all women are aware of their deplorable fate, and of the rights they have lost in society. Madame, support such a beautiful cause; defend this unfortunate sex, and soon you will have half the realm on your side, and at least one-third of the other half.

Those, Madame, are the feats by which you should show and use your credit. Believe me, Madame, our life is a pretty small thing, especially for a Queen, when it is not embellished by people's affection and by the eternal delights of good deeds.

If it is true that the French arm all the powers against their own Fatherland, why? For frivolous prerogatives, for chimeras. Believe, Madame, if I judge by what I feel—the monarchical party will be destroyed by itself, it will abandon all tyrants, and all hearts will rally around the fatherland to defend it.

There are my principles, Madame. In speaking to you of my fatherland, I lose sight of the purpose of this dedication. Thus, any good citizen sacrifices his glory and his interests when he has none other than those of his country.

I am with the most profound respect, Madame,

Your most humble and most obedient servant,

de Gouges

The Rights of Woman

Man, are you capable of being just? It is a woman who poses the question; you will not deprive her of that right at least. Tell me, what gives you sovereign empire to oppress my sex? Your strength? Your talents? Observe the Creator in his wisdom; survey in all her grandeur that nature with whom you seem to want to be in harmony., and give me, if you dare, an example of this tyrannical empire. Go back to animals, consult the elements, study plants, finally glance at all the modifications of organic matter, and surrender to the evidence when I offer you the means; search, probe, and distinguish, if you can, the sexes in the administration of nature. Everywhere you will find them mingled; everywhere they cooperate in harmonious togetherness in this immortal masterpiece.

Man alone has raised his exceptional circumstances to a principle. Bizarre, blind, bloated with science and degenerated—in a century of enlightenment and wisdom—into the crassest ignorance, he wants to command as a despot a sex which is in full possession of its intellectual faculties; he pretends to enjoy the Revolution and to claim his rights to equality in order to say nothing more about it.

Declaration of the Rights of Woman and the Female Citizen

For the National Assembly to decree in its last sessions, or in those of the next legislature:

Preamble

Mothers, daughters, sisters [and] representatives of the nation demand to be constituted into a national assembly. Believing that ignorance, omission, or scorn for the rights of woman are the only causes of public misfortunes and of the corruption of governments, [the women] have resolved to set forth in a solemn declaration the natural, inalienable, and sacred rights of woman in order that this declaration, constantly exposed before all the members of the society, will ceaselessly remind them of their rights and duties; in order that the authoritative acts of women and the authoritative acts of men may be at any moment compared with and respectful of the purpose of all political institutions; and in order that citizens' demands, henceforth based on simple and incontestable principles, will always support the constitution, good morals, and the happiness of all.

Consequently, the sex that is as superior in beauty as it is in courage during the sufferings of maternity recognizes and declares in the pres-

ence and under the auspices of the Supreme Being, the following Rights
of Woman and of Female Citizens.

Article I
Woman is born free and lives equal to man in her rights. Social
distinctions can be based only on the common utility.

Article II
The purpose of any political association is the conservation of the
natural and imprescriptible rights of woman and man; these rights are
liberty, property, security, and especially resistance to oppression.

Article III
The principle of all sovereignty rests essentially with the nation,
which is nothing but the union of woman and man; no body and no
individual can exercise any authority which does not come expressly
from it [the nation].

Article IV
Liberty and justice consist of restoring all that belongs to others; thus,
the only limits on the exercise of the natural rights of woman are
perpetual male tyranny; these limits are to be reformed by the laws of
nature and reason.

Article V
Laws of nature and reason proscribe all acts harmful to society;
everything which is not prohibited by these wise and divine laws cannot
be prevented, and no one can be constrained to do what they do not
command.

Article VI
The law must be the expression of the general will; all female and
male citizens must contribute either personally or through their representatives to its formation; it must be the same for all: male and female
citizens, being equal in the eyes of the law, must be equally admitted to
all honors, positions, and public employment according to their capacity
and without other distinctions besides those of their virtues and talents.

Article VII
No woman is an exception; she is accused, arrested, and detained in
cases determined by law. Women, like men, obey this rigorous law.

Article VIII

The law must establish only those penalties that are strictly and obviously necessary, and no one can be punished except by virtue of a law established and promulgated prior to the crime and legally applicable to women.

Article IX

Once any woman is declared guilty, complete rigor is [to be] exercised by the law.

Article X

No one is to be disquieted for his very basic opinions; woman has the right to mount the scaffold; she must equally have the right to mount the rostrum, provided that her demonstrations do not disturb the legally established public order.

Article XI

The free communication of thoughts and opinions is one of the most precious rights of woman, since that liberty assures the recognition of children by their fathers. Any female citizen thus may say freely, I am the mother of a child which belongs to you, without being forced by a barbarous prejudice to hide the truth; [an exception may be made] to respond to the abuse of this liberty in cases determined by the law.

Article XII

The guarantee of the rights of woman and the female citizen implies a major benefit; this guarantee must be instituted for the advantage of all, and not for the particular benefit of those to whom it is entrusted.

Article XIII

For the support of the public force and the expenses of administration, the contributions of woman and man are equal; she shares all the duties [*corvées*] and all the painful tasks; therefore, she must have the same share in the distribution of positions, employment, offices, honors, and jobs [*industrie*].

Article XIV

Female and male citizens have the right to verify, either by themselves or through their representatives, the necessity of the public contribution. This can only apply to women if they are granted an equal share, not only of wealth, but also of public administration, and in the

determination of the proportion, the base, the collection, and the duration of the tax.

Article XV

The collectivity of women, joined for tax purposes to the aggregate of
men, has the right to demand an accounting of his administration from
any public agent.

Article XVI

No society has a constitution without the guarantee of rights and the
separation of powers; the constitution is null if the majority of individuals comprising the nation have not cooperated in drafting it.

Article XVII

Property belongs to both sexes whether united or separate; for each it
is an inviolable and sacred right; no one can be deprived of it, since it is
the true patrimony of nature, unless the legally determined public need
obviously dictates it, and then only with a just and prior indemnity.

Postscript

Woman, wake up; the tocsin of reason is being heard throughout the
whole universe; discover your rights. The powerful empire of nature is
no longer surrounded by prejudice, fanaticism, superstition, and lies.
The flame of truth has dispersed all the clouds of folly and usurpation.
Enslaved man has multiplied his strength and needs recourse to yours to
break his chains. Having become free, he has become unjust to his
companion. Oh, women, women! When will you cease to be blind?
What advantage have you received from the Revolution? A more pronounced scorn, a more marked disdain. In the centuries of corruption
you ruled only over the weakness of men. The reclamation of your
patrimony, based on the wise decrees of nature—what have you to
dread from such a fine undertaking? The *bon mot* of the legislator of the
marriage of Cana? Do you fear that our French legislators, correctors of
that morality, long ensnared by political practices now out of date, will
only say again to you: women, what is there in common between you
and us? Everything, you will have to answer. If they persist in their
weakness in putting this non sequitur in contradiction to their principles, courageously oppose the force of reason to the empty pretentions
of superiority; unite yourselves beneath the standards of philosophy;
deploy all the energy of your character, and you will soon see these
haughty men, not groveling at your feet as servile adorers, but proud to

share with you the treasures of the Supreme Being. Regardless of what barriers confront you, it is in your power to free yourselves; you have only to want to. Let us pass now to the shocking tableau of what you have been in society; and since national education is in question at this moment, let us see whether our wise legislators will think judiciously about the education of women.

Women have done more harm than good. Constraint and dissimulation have been their lot. What force had robbed them of, ruse returned to them; they had recourse to all the resources of their charms, and the most irreproachable person did not resist them. Poison and the sword were both subject to them; they commanded in crime as in fortune. The French government, especially, depended throughout the centuries on the nocturnal administration of women; the cabinet kept no secret from their indiscretion; ambassadorial post, command, ministry, presidency, pontificate, college of cardinals; finally, anything which characterizes the folly of men, profane and sacred, all have been subject to the cupidity and ambition of this sex, formerly contemptible and respected, and since the revolution, respectable and scorned.

In this sort of contradictory situation, what remarks could I not make! I have but a moment to make them, but this moment will fix the attention of the remotest posterity. Under the Old Regime, all was vicious, all was guilty; but could not the amelioration of conditions be perceived even in the substance of vices? A woman only had to be beautiful or amiable; when she possessed these two advantages, she saw a hundred fortunes at her feet. If she did not profit from them, she had a bizarre character or a rare philosophy which made her scorn wealth; then she was deemed to be like a crazy woman; the most indecent made herself respected with gold; commerce in women was a kind of industry in the first class [of society], which, henceforth, will have no more credit. If it still had it, the revolution would be lost, and under the new relationships we would always be corrupted; however, reason can always be deceived [into believing] that any other road to fortune is closed to the woman whom a man buys, like the slave on the African coasts. The difference is great; that is known. The slave is commanded by the master; but if the master gives her liberty without recompense, and at an age when the slave has lost all her charms, what will become of this unfortunate woman? The victim of scorn, even the doors of charity are closed to her; she is poor and old, they say; why did she not know how to make her fortune? Reason finds other examples that are even more touching. A young, inexperienced woman, seduced by a man whom she loves, will abandon her parents to follow him; the ingrate will leave her after a few years, and the older she has become with him, the more inhuman is his inconstancy; if she has children, he will likewise abandon them. If he is rich, he will consider himself excused from sharing his fortune with his noble victims. If some involvement binds him to his duties, he will deny them, trusting that the laws will support him. If he is married, any other obligation loses its rights. Then what laws remain to extirpate vice all the way to its root? The law of dividing wealth and public administration between men and women. It can easily be seen that one who is born into a rich family gains very much from such equal sharing. But the one born into a poor family with merit and virtue— what is her lot? Poverty and opprobrium. If she does not precisely excel in music or painting, she cannot be admitted to any public function when she has all the capacity for it. I do not want to give only a sketch of things; I will go more deeply into this in the new edition of all my political writings, with notes, which I propose to give to the public in a few days.

I take up my text again on the subject of morals. Marriage is the tomb of trust and love. The married woman can with impunity give bastards to her husband, and also give them the wealth which does not belong to them. The woman who is unmarried has only one feeble right; ancient and inhuman laws refuse to her for her children the right to the name and the wealth of their father; no new laws have been made in this matter. If it is considered a paradox and an impossibility on my part to try to give my sex an honorable and just consistency, I leave it to men to attain glory for dealing with this matter; but while we wait, the way can be prepared through national education, the restoration of morals, and conjugal conventions.

Form for a Social Contract Between Man and Woman

We, _____ and _____, moved by our own will, unite ourselves for the duration of our lives, and for the duration of our mutual inclinations, under the following conditions: We intend and wish to make our wealth communal, meanwhile reserving to ourselves the right to divide it in favor of our children and of those toward whom we might have a particular inclination, mutually recognizing that our property belongs directly to our children, from whatever bed they come, and that all of them without distinction have the right to bear the name of the fathers and mothers who have acknowledged them, and we are charged to subscribe to the law which punishes the renunciation of one's own blood. We likewise obligate ourselves, in case of separation, to divide our wealth and to set aside in advance the portion the law indicates for our children, and in the event of a perfect union, the one who dies will divest himself of half his property in his children's favor, and if one dies childless, the survivor will inherit by right, unless the dying person has disposed of half the common property in favor of one whom he judged deserving.

That is approximately the formula for the marriage act I propose for execution. Upon reading this strange document, I see rising up against me the hypocrites, the prudes, the clergy, and the whole infernal sequence. But how it [my proposal] offers to the wise the moral means of achieving the perfection of a happy government! I am going to give in a few words the physical proof of it. The rich, childless Epicurean finds it very good to go to his poor neighbor to augment his family. When there is a law authorizing a poor man's wife to have a rich one adopt their children, the bonds of society will be strengthened and morals will be purer. This law will perhaps save the community's wealth and hold back the disorder which drives so many victims to the almshouses of shame, to a low station, and into degenerate human principles where nature has groaned for so long. May the detractors of wise philosophy then cease to cry out against primitive morals, or may they lose their point in the source of their citations.[1]

Moreover, I would like a law which would assist widows and young girls deceived by the false promises of a man to whom they were attached; I would like, I say, this law to force an inconstant man to hold to his obligations or at least [to pay] an indemnity equal to his wealth. Again, I would like this law to be rigorous against women, at least those who have the effrontery to have recourse to a law which they themselves had violated by their misconduct, if proof of that were given. At the same time, as I showed in *Le Bonheur primitif de l'homme,* in 1788, that prostitutes should be placed in designated quarters.* It is not prostitutes who contribute the most to the depravity of morals, it is the women of society. In regenerating the latter, the former are changed. This link of fraternal union will first bring disorder, but in consequence it will produce at the end a perfect harmony.

I offer a foolproof way to elevate the soul of women; it is to join them to all the activities of man; if man persists in finding this way impractical, let him share his fortune with woman, not at his caprice, but by the

---

[1]Abraham had some very legitimate children by Agar, the servant of his wife.

*See Olympe de Gouges, *Le Bonheur primitif de l'homme, ou les Rêveries patriotiques* (Amsterdam and Paris, 1789).

wisdom of laws. Prejudice falls, morals are purified, and nature regains all her rights. Add to this the marriage of priests and the strengthening of the king on his throne, and the French government cannot fail.

It would be very necessary to say a few words on the troubles which are said to be caused by the decree in favor of colored men in our islands. There is where nature shudders with horror; there is where reason and humanity have still not touched callous souls; there, especially, is where division and discord stir up their inhabitants. It is not difficult to divine the instigators of these incendiary fermentations; they are even in the midst of the National Assembly; they ignite the fire in Europe which must inflame America. Colonists make a claim to reign as despots over the men whose fathers and brothers they are; and, disowning the rights of nature, they trace the source of [their rule] to the scantiest tint of their blood. These inhuman colonists say: our blood flows in their veins, but we will shed it all if necessary to glut our greed or our blind ambition. It is in these places nearest to nature where the father scorns the son; deaf to the cries of blood, they stifle all its attraction; what can be hoped from the resistance opposed to them? To constrain [blood] violently is to render it terrible; to leave [blood] still enchained is to direct all calamities towards America. A divine hand seems to spread liberty abroad throughout the realms of man; only the law has the right to curb this liberty if it degenerates into license, but it must be equal for all; liberty must hold the National Assembly to its decree dictated by prudence and justice. May it act the same way for the state of France and render her as attentive to new abuses as she was to the ancient ones which each day become more dreadful. My opinion would be to reconcile the executive and legislative power, for it seems to me that the one is everything and the other is nothing—whence comes, unfortunately perhaps, the loss of the French Empire. I think that these two powers, like man and woman, should be united but equal in force and virtue to make a good household. . . .

11. WOMEN IN THE POPULAR PRESS: A LETTER FROM MÈRE DUCHÊNE, FALL, 1791

Source: *Cinquième lettre bougrement patriotique de la Mère Duchêne, où elle félicite les dames françoises sur leur amour pour leur patrie, où elle parle de leur influence sur la révolution, &c., &c.* (n.p., n.d.), in B.N., Lc² 2481.

In the fall of 1791 the Jacobin Hébert began publishing *Père Duchêne,* a journal written in the language of the common people and reflecting the gradual development of republican feeling in the sections and popular societies. *Mère Duchêne* soon followed. The true author is unknown. The satire reproduced here is noteworthy for its recognition of common women, although the journalist narrowly restricts the exercise of women's political rights to supporting and educating.

———— ◆ ————

Hercules spun at the feet of Omphale, and that wasn't what he did best. By thunder, French women would never have allowed it! They are too attached to the Revolution to scorn their husbands or lovers that much. For me, if Père Duchêne wanted to take my distaff and leave me his hammer, I would soon treat him as a bastard. Take my coiffure, my mobcap, my petticoat, and my pantaloons, cow bugger; myself, I'll take the helmet, the sword, and the musket.

Those are your feelings, ladies. When I see you walking with men wearing the national uniform, a grenadier's cap on their heads and a sword at their sides, when I see you walking like them with a firm step, I say to myself: There are the French women. There is their determined character. Soon I recall the taking of the Bastille, the *journées* of the fifth and sixth of October, the labors on the Champ de Mars, and the Fédération.

What satisfaction I take when I see my sex struggle with courage and intrepidity with men who used to abandon domestic concerns with disdain to women, who regard them almost as animals who must be confined in a zoo. No, damn it, no, women are not what they are thought to be. They can handle the distaff and the sword equally successfully. We will see the rebirth of Joan of Arcs, Jeanne Hachettes, and all those proud Amazons who were the glory and honor of our sex if the Fatherland is in danger, if the aristocracy wants to harm our liberty with arms at hand.

Ladies, not only are you prepared to spill your blood for liberty, to share all the perils with our brave warriors, [but] you still defend with the greatest zeal such a beautiful cause in your conversations and your [women's] circles. It's women, and I could name many if I wanted—it's women, I say, who will never yield to men in this matter. Good God! How you speak! How you reason! One word doesn't wait for another! You prefer to unstring your rosary rather than have your ideas disregarded. Moreover, you have a way about you which makes reason so weighty. Yes, my God! One would have to be unconscious to resist it.

What satisfaction I took on another occasion! An aristocrat was quarreling with a patriotic woman. He was overflowing with words and bad ideas. Partisan spirit had blinded him to the point that he kept falling into absurdities, contradictions, and false accusations. The woman, for her part, raised again your standard with an astonishing nerve and courage. The more heated he became, the more she bantered him. She persisted with finesse and unmatched nimbleness. Seeing that the laughter was at his expense, and becoming confused and rendered speechless, our former marquis abandoned the battlefield without saying good-bye to anybody. If *messieurs les aristocrates* aren't more agile handling their arms than handling ideas, they are damned bad fighters.

Although I am ignorant and not lettered, like former judges or the deputies, I don't lack a brain when it comes to political matters. Sometimes ideas come out of me which aren't whelp, which would even do honor to a legislator. Oh, it's too much, Mère Duchêne—it's not necessary to vaunt yourself like that! And why not, if it's the truth? Moreover, if it doesn't please you, you can go shove it. Can you believe in good faith that I would hesitate to stuff some good reasons up the noses of aristocrats?

In any event, since my arms are stronger than my head, I willingly leave the career of enlightenment to women who are more eloquent than I, and I offer my services to the nation as a warrior. I am naturally inclined to fist fighting, and I am used to boxing with my dear husband. At the first drumbeat I take up arms, I raise a squadron of Amazons, I put myself at their head, and, sword at hand, I thrust into the enemy battalions as if they were butter.

A certain much-revered author—I believe, as much as I can remember, that his name is Molière—a certain author, I say, doesn't want women to be taught. He wants them shut up with domestic duties. According to him, their spirit ought not to move past their needle. Are you bugging us, Mr. Poet? Wait, wait! I'm going to teach you that your horse Pegasus is a dumb animal. Nature made nothing useless; that's a law. I defy you to disagree. Women have imagination and penetration; they are fertile in resources and expedients. This talent wasn't given to them to string pearls. Women aren't doomed, damn it, to be geese. That's what you call an incontestable inspiration, and Mère Duchêne has a few more of the same cut and the same force in her brain.

Let's run down the historical record; let's stop especially at those great events which changed the face of empires. What a tone, Madame Duchêne! What airs! They'll take you for an orator! But don't be deceived; don't you know that my style ennobles, my ideas take flight, my genius grows when I have a sword at hand? Ah, to thrust like that!

Well, let's not digress. Thus we read in history that all those aroused and agitated men of spirit who have wished to bring about revolutions, whether in politics or religion, haven't regarded women as zeros. They have sought to put them by their sides, and they were right. Well they knew the female spirit. When women take sides, they don't yield; they are stubborn like mules, these hellions, and when they are angry it's worse—they don't give a damn. What makes them so especially necessary in revolutions is their talent for intrigue. How they twist and turn. How they know how to pull out of traps! They have the finesse and cleverness of a snake. They bend back and forth a thousand ways to reach their purpose. Yes, the devil, wily as he is, will yet be obliged to attend their school.

Without discussing other revolutions here, let's stick to ours. Although I am damned curious, I never stick my nose in other people's business. Thus I can say, in praise of French women, that their examples, their advice, their speeches have much influenced liberty. There are some who have thrust good advice at our deputies, and some who play such a brilliant role in the assembly that it is often indebted to the spirit of a woman. If they draw up their motions only inside their homes, then the ideas they communicate can contribute much to the development of those of men. The persuasive talents they possess to the highest degree once again give weight to their logic.

To prove the interest they take in the Revolution, and the influence they have on it, I need only cite their eagerness to follow the sessions of the assembly, the avidity with which they read all the pamphlets and all the newspapers. Damn it, do you see men showing such curiosity when some important event is announced? How they listen to you! How their eyes devour anything new!

Although these proofs I've just presented are powerful, there is another I must not forget, even more important than the others. That's the influence of women on education. If infants should drink in with their milk the principles of the constitution, who can and who should teach them their catechism in such circumstances? Who is there besides yourselves, ladies, who can make the love of liberty sprout in their yet tender hearts and spirits? If you rendered no other service than this to the nation, my God! —you would have done enough for the Revolution.

> Ladies, I am honored to be, with profound
> respect, your most humble and obedient servant,
> Pétronille Machefer,
> Wife of Père Duchêne

These letters appear on Tuesday and Saturday of each week.

12. THE PRESENTATION OF A DECORATED CHEST TO A
    SUPPORTER OF THE REVOLUTION: A SPEECH TO THE
    JACOBINS, DECEMBER 18, 1791

Source: [F.E.G.], *Discours des Citoyennes françoises, prononcé à la
Société des Amis de la Constitution, séante aux Jacobins, à Paris, 18
décembre 1791* (Paris, n.d.), in B.N., Lb⁴⁰ 653.

In the fall of 1791 women joined in the enthusiasm for the
Constitution. This is a speech made to the Jacobins as its author
presents a decorated chest to a Welchman who, as a priest, has
taken the oath of loyalty to the French constitution. Note her
statement that women's civic duties are quite ancillary to their
domestic responsibilities.

———————

Gentlemen:
    We are not Roman matrons; we bring no jewels, but rather a tribute
in recognition of the sentiments you have inspired in us.
    A few days ago an oath-taking Welch clergyman, an Englishman, a
brother, was the object of one of your sweetest embraces. What a
charming scene! Sensitive souls were touched, and our hearts were
moved.
    Today you give new joy to this brother, to yourselves; you hang three
flags in the Temple arch, one *American,* one *English,* one *French.*
    The union of three free peoples is to be cemented; please, gentlemen,
permit us to contribute something. Your pure sentiments make this our
duty. Accept a crown.
    English brother, accept another from the hands of innocence; it is the
work of fraternity. Friendship gives it to you.
    Good patriot, receive in the name of the French *citoyennes* here
gathered the ark of covenant [*l'arche d'alliance*] we bring for our brothers, the oath-taking Welchmen. On it is inscribed the map of France
divided into eighty-three Departments, the bonnet of liberty, the

French constitution, a civic crown, some stalks of wheat, the three flags, the national cockade, and these words in both languages: *vivre libre, ou mourir.*

May this immortal homage paid to liberty be, for the *English* and the *French,* the sacred pledge of their union. Do not forget to recite to our brothers how you received it, that it was deposited in the most fraternal of ceremonies. Invite all the English to participate in this familial act. May it be as precious to them as nature.

Say to your wives and repeat to your children that wise daughters, faithful wives, and tender mothers, having fulfilled their domestic duties and contributed to the happiness of their families and husbands, came to make this offering to the fatherland.

May a shout of joy reverberate over *Europe* and fly to *America* — listen! In the midst of echos, *Philadelphia* and surrounding counties repeat with us, *vive la liberté!*

Tyrants! Your crimes are known; peoples will no longer make war on one another; intimately united, they will command all tongues; henceforth [these tongues] will comprise but one, and strong in their liberty, they will be forever inseparable.

On behalf of the *citoyennes françois{es}, amies de la constitution,*

Signed

F.E.G.

III

The Escalation of Women's Protest: January, 1792, through February, 1793

THE PERIOD from January, 1792, through February, 1793, marked a crucial stage in the evolution of women's politics. The year was one of dramatic changes: war, the overthrow of the monarchy, renewed and intensified economic hardships, and the creation of two new revolutionary institutions: the National Convention and the clubs, about which the women would focus their organized activities. Women's petitions were concerned with the defense of Paris, divorce legislation, and other laws which would bring equal rights for women. The women of the people were once again mobilized by their concern with economic hardship. They moved decidedly to the left in one year, learning to coordinate their demands and protests, working with other political groups on the left, and presenting a potent threat to local and national authorities.

Within one year, support for the constitutional monarchy eroded, the military situation worsened, economic crises reappeared, the monarchy was overthrown and replaced by a republic, and Louis XVI was tried and executed. In the spring of 1792 the renewed republican campaign was conducted by the left wing of Paris politics, led by the Girondin faction in the Legislative Assembly and in the Jacobin Club. These groups collaborated with ardent provincial patriots known as *Fédérés*. They were strong advocates of war against all monarchical regimes, a popular position after the declaration of war against Austria in April.

In the summer of 1792 the French armies suffered losses, and tensions were heightened by evidence that the King was conspiring with French *emigrés* and foreign leaders. The Girondin left enlisted increasing support from the *sans-culottes* as it became more apparent that the King was disloyal and that the constitutional monarchists were unwilling to make the necessary sacrifices to save *la patrie en danger*. At the same time, increasing numbers of *sans-culottes* were asked to volunteer for the army. The people of Paris organized through the popular societies and the Section assemblies to cooperate with the *Fédérés* and plan a popular uprising to overthrow the disloyal monarch. On August 10, 1792, Parisians and provincial patriots defeated the royalist Swiss Guard at the Tuileries and ordered the imprisonment of the King at the Temple. Parisians began an intensive campaign to extirpate royalists from the capital, and election dates were set for a National Convention that would draft a constitution for the first French Republic.

New elections for the Paris Commune and the National Convention were held in September, and the Girondins emerged as the dominant political faction. The Girondin government began to formulate plans for a republican constitution and opened debates on the fate of the King. Louis XVI was executed on January 21, and within weeks England, Holland, and Prussia had joined Austria in war against France to prevent the infection of republicanism from spreading in Europe. To meet the military crisis, the National Convention called for a levy of three hundred thousand men, thus precipitating civil war in the Vendée between patriots and draft-resisting peasants.

Some of the women who had been politically active in the previous year continued to support women's interests as the political situation changed. Théroigne de Méricourt, who was a supporter of the Girondins, gave a speech at the Société fraternelle des patriotes de l'un et de l'autre sexe asking for a women's battalion, a company of Amazons. She also participated in the *journée* of August 10.[1] Etta Palm d'Aelders continued to press for her favorite issues of equal rights for women, education, and the right to divorce; we include in this chapter an account of a speech she made in April to the Legislative Assembly. Women also held festivals to demonstrate their support for the war, and they sewed for soldiers and rolled bandages.

Méricourt was not the only Amazon; women from the Hôtel de Ville Section petitioned the Assembly for the right to bear arms in the defense of the city. August 10 was a planned coup against the monarchy, coordinated by the male political leaders in positions of power in Paris, but women from the Sections took part. Three were listed among the wounded, including Louise-Reine Audu, a well-known participant in the October Days of 1789.[2] Pauline Léon would later document her joy at the outcome of the attack on the Tuileries.

---

[1]Marie Cerati, *Le Club des citoyennes républicaines révolutionnaires*.
[2]George Rudé, *The Crowd in the French Revolution*. p. 105.

This period of political crisis was also a time of economic hardship and disruption in the lives of ordinary Parisians, and it was this situation that occasioned the renewed political involvement of the common women. The outbreak of protest in January and February, 1792, is known as the Sugar Crisis. Civil war was raging between royalists and patriots in the colonies of the French West Indies. Speculators hoarded vast stores of colonial products such as sugar, coffee, and tea in expectation of future profits from depleted supplies. Hoarding in Paris made the supply of sugar unpredictable and had driven up the price considerably above 1790–91 levels.[3] Parisian women, most notably the laundresses and workers in the faubourgs, took petitions to the Commune and Legislative Assembly to express their dissatisfaction with the rising costs. When the Legislative Assembly ignored their complaints, the women resorted to direct action: *taxation populaire* in the faubourgs and central markets of Paris.

Between March and June, 1792, the Girondins in the Jacobin Society managed to silence the women's concerns about sugar by appealing to their patriotic instincts and asking people to abstain from colonial products for the duration of the military crisis. The women agreed and also supported Girondin efforts to gain ministerial posts since they believed that the Girondins would direct the nation to victory.

After the overthrow of the monarchy in August, the working people of Paris gradually withdrew their support from the Girondins and began to strengthen their political control in some of the Sections. Dissatisfaction with the Girondins was based on their continuation of the liberal economic program initiated during the constitutional monarchy. Discontented *sans-culottes* and poor women supported the radical Enragé, Jacques Roux. Roux spoke for the demands of the common people: political and economic terror against all enemies of the sovereign people, stringent laws against hoarding and speculation, and the immediate execution of the King, whose very existence they believed threatened the survival of the Republic.

Following the King's execution and the expansion of coalition armies in January, 1793, the Revolutionary Army was expanded as well. Increased military needs depleted the supply of grain for Paris, and yet the Girondin government refused to sacrifice its laissez-faire economic policies for a planned economic program which would assure equitable distribution to the civilian and military sectors. The women of Paris sent deputations to the Jacobin Society, the Paris Commune, and the Na-

[3]*Ibid.*, p. 96.

tional Convention to warn that they would interfere with the conscription of *sans-culottes* if no measures were taken to protect women's interests.

When the government tried to delay a decision on the economic crisis, the women of Paris on February 25 and 26 began expeditions of *taxation populaire* which were more widespread and better coordinated than those of the preceding winter. Moreover, the February women found sympathy, if not direction, from Jacques Roux, now a member of the General Council of the Paris Commune. Extensive property damage and anarchy in late February forced the National Convention to find an immediate solution to the grain shortage and to consider price controls on bread and government distribution of grain.

As these events indicate, the common women of Paris were acknowledged as a central political force during 1792. What is clear—and this phenomenon is critical for the lower classes and merits emphasis—is that common women were able to increase their political power steadily in 1792 and 1793 because political institutions in Paris were coming more and more under the control of the popular classes. Men were still the leaders, but now they were husbands, fathers, fellow members of the working and artisan classes. As the political institutions democratized, they also became more autonomous, no longer subservient to the middle-class Jacobins and deputies. The Paris Sections were the most important of these institutions. The Section assemblies, originally set up as forty-eight administrative bodies, took on deliberative functions to protect the interests of *sans-culottes* and their families. In July, 1792, they declared themselves *en permanence*. They admitted and enfranchised passive citizens, those who still could not meet national qualifications to vote. Women were admitted to the spectator galleries. Leadership in the Sections passed in 1793 from rich lawyers and merchants to small shopkeepers, revolutionary journalists, and the less wealthy lawyers and clerks, although the Sections were never led by the poorest *sans-culottes,* but by those who were literate and skilled in the speech making and petition drafting necessary for communicating with the Commune, the Jacobin Societies, and the National Convention. The Sections also could function as military units when the National Guard was reorganized along sectional lines. Now, the troops which had fired on the people on the Champ de Mars in 1791 were put under the control of the people themselves.

The fraternal societies changed along with the Sections. They now became truly popular societies which called upon women to take an active role in Paris politics. Expanding their educational functions, they became independent political bodies whose members debated issues, sent petitions, and championed the interests of war widows, soldiers, and needy citizens.

Finally, the Paris Commune was democratized. Many of its officials now came from the popular classes, and these men sensitized it to women's economic needs and demands.

In 1793 the women of Paris reached the zenith of their power to influence politics. Documents in the second part of this chapter, on the Sugar Crisis of 1792 and the February days of 1793, attest to the intense pressure that women protesters put on political leaders by threatening to disrupt public order any time their demands were not met. A comparison of these two events illustrates the evolution of their political skills. In 1792 journalists attributed the outbreak of food disturbances to royalist conspirators, and the Legislative Assembly ignored women's complaints about the subsistence issue. In 1793, however, merchants, journalists, and local authorities reported that women were instigating disruptions and that national deputies found it impossible to disregard their demands. The women of the people had learned to use newly democratic revolutionary institutions—Section assemblies and popular societies—to translate economic demands into potent political weapons, and they were combining activity within these institutions with organized acts of collective violence, *taxation populaire*. Middle-class radicals continued pressuring authorities for legislation to remove inequalities in other dimensions of women's lives. For six months in mid-1793 the women merged these concerns in a radical pressure group, the Society of Revolutionary Republican Women.

1. THE LIBERAL PRESS INTERPRETS THE SUGAR RIOTS OF JANUARY, 1792

The documents which follow are excerpted from the Girondin press and represent the liberals' stand in the face of episodes of *taxation populaire* in January, 1792. Popular violence was attributed to machinations by the Revolution's enemies and condemned as an attack on property.

———◆———

1*a*. Source: Report dated January 21, 1792, in *Patriote français,* January 22, 1792, as reprinted in P. J. B. Buchez and P. C. Roux, eds., *Histoire parlementaire de la Révolution française,* vol. XIII, p. 92.

Yesterday, the residents of the Faubourg Saint-Marceau forced open a warehouse that is rumored to belong to M. d'André,[1] and the sugar being hoarded there was sold at twenty-one *sous* a *livre.* All those who took it paid for it faithfully!

During the night, fire broke out in the prison of La Force and caused major damage. Although much of the prison was consumed in flame, no prisoners escaped. A clergyman has been accused of being responsible for the fire.

[1]M. d'André had been a representative in the Constituent Assembly. Upon finishing his term in the Assembly in September, 1791, M. d'André went into a wholesale grocery business and was execrated by the radical journalists for his indiscreet business activities. [Translators' note.]

———◆———

1*b*. Source: Gorsas, January 22 account, in *Le Courrier des 83
Départements,* as cited in Buchez and Roux, *Histoire parlementaire,*
vol. XIII, pp. 92–93.

A number of motives have been attributed to the incendiaries; some
allege that Abbé Bardi, [who has been] condemned to death, was responsible for this fire. The majority believe that some big wheel wanted
Sieur Lamotte, a prisoner, to perish in the flames. It seems probable,
however, that this disturbance was more widespread, because there was
a commotion at [the prison of] Bicêtre at the same time.

———

1*c*. Source: Report dated January 22, *Patriote français,* as cited in
Buchez and Roux, *Histoire parlementaire,* vol. XIII, pp. 93–94.

. . . These two events [the fire and the prison commotion], occurring
the same day in Faubourgs Saint-Marceau and Saint-Antoine, appear to
have been planned. Undoubtedly the aim was to divide the police forces
in two and to profit from their diversion. So it was that on February 28
they had the National Guard brought to Vincennes while the conspirators were meeting in the Tuileries. It is impossible to doubt that
the aims of the enemies of the Revolution were to incite a great uprising
in Paris for purposes of carrying out the plot we have exposed—or
another of the same kind. We are going to bring together a number of
facts which support [this thesis] and which were communicated to us by
trustworthy correspondents.

It seems certain that the gold and silver service and even the jewelry
at the Tuileries were hastily melted down. They were hatching a major
plot there. Several former servants, having stated their belief that the
King was a sincere friend of the Constitution, were retired without
delay, without compensation, and without pensions.

The Queen received unknown persons in her private chambers. It was
remarked that they left there with the air of people who believed they
had become important.

The young officers of the troops of the line stationed at the frontier
left their posts to join the King's Guard. In another *quartier* it was
noticed that impecunious soldiers employed at the Château circulated
among the merchants in Paris, took charge there, larded the tables of

these good people whom they flattered and whose secrets they pene-
trated, and made wholesale purchases which they paid for in cash.

Recently a merchant sold to a man staying at the Château his re-
mainders, which he had stocked in his store for twenty-five years. The
value of this purchase was more than 650,000 *livres.* From what the
buyer let slip out, it was discovered that he had drawn *assignats* from
the national treasury to pay for the purchase.

Whisperings at the Château are increasing and becoming concrete.
These whisperings concern the forthcoming abduction of the King,
which will be discovered only after a lapse of forty hours. . . .

One fact can be taken as certain. Suspect men, superzealous partisans
of the *ancien régime* are coming en masse into Paris. A former noble,
decorated with the Cross of the Order of Saint-Louis, stayed at M.
Blondeau's on the rue Croix-des-Petits-Champs, at the Hôtel du Dau-
phin. He had scarcely put his suitcase down in the hotel room when
another chevalier arrived who whispered something in his ear, then said
out loud: "I will not allow you to stay here; I have a lodging for you."
The traveling chevalier immediately took leave of the proprietor and
instructed the domestic at the hotel to take his suitcase and follow him.
The domestic obeyed, and where was he led? to what place? To the
Louvre in the small apartments below the sundial. And what did he see
there? Fifteen-to-twenty beds, fifteen-to-twenty chevaliers who were
squeezed into this hovel. . . . We leave to the reader the task of giving
these circumstances the attention they merit at this time.

———————

1*d.* Source: Gorsas, *Le Courrier des 83 Départements,* report of January
    23, 1792, as cited in Buchez and Roux, *Histoire parlementaire,*
    vol. XIII, pp. 94–95.

The expedition to the Faubourg Saint-Marceau has spread fear among
the hoarders and in the hearts of those who rent their warehouses to
them. The night before last, patrols were meeting up with wagons
coming from everywhere and loaded with sugar, with moist brown sugar
(we are copying) and coffee. In many warehouses only hoarded saltwort
was left.

What proves that the fire at La Force was the result of a plot is that a
bunch of libels were posted up all at the same time in all the corners of

the capital. One is entitled *Le Journal du peuple,* or rather the *Prospectus* for that journal, which bears the name of Boyer de Nîmes, who, fearing execution, fled this city and took refuge in Paris, in the arms of the despicable Tessier, Baron de Marguerites, saying he was the accomplice of all the horrors with which Tessier infected Nîmes. The other libel is titled *Address to the National Assembly* [and is] signed, it would seem, by unknown merchants and artisans claiming to be members of the citizen guard. The aim of this address is to stir the people up against the patriotic societies which are taken for brigands who infect the capital and who are accused of being the accomplices of thieves and assassins. . . .

2. A Jacobin Appeals to the Women of Paris to End
   the Sugar Crisis

Source: Speech by Louvet at a meeting of the Jacobin Society on
January 30, 1792, as reprinted in F.-A. Aulard, ed., *La Société
des Jacobins: Recueil de documents pour l'histoire du Club des Jacobins de
Paris,* vol. III, pp. 350–52.

On January 23, 1792, men and women from the Section des
Gobelins in the Faubourg Saint-Marceau took their grievances to
the Commune and to the National Assembly. Having been
ignored by the legislators and paternally admonished by the
Mayor of Paris, the people resumed their expeditions of *taxation
populaire.* They seized shops and stalls where essential foodstuffs
were sold; the confiscated items were distributed to the crowds at
the just price, *le prix juste,* which the people themselves set.
Sugar was the principal item seized in these operations. This first
wave of *taxation populaire* lasted almost a week. The Girondin
radicals in the Jacobin Society finally hit upon a solution: women
must refrain from purchasing sugar as a patriotic sacrifice.
Louvet, known for his persuasive eloquence, presented the
Jacobin line in a speech to the Jacobin Society on January 30,
1792. Louvet called attention to American patriots who, during
their own revolution, had abstained from using products from the
English colonies. Then he remarked:

. . . I know well that the privation I am going to speak about must fall
particularly hard upon our companions, but I also know that there is no
privation to which they are not ready to subject themselves out of regard
for the general interest. Already everything speaks for their efforts and
their sacrifices. At Versailles—France cannot forget it—they crowded
around the bar of the Constituent Assembly vying with one another to
deposit their jewels, their diamonds, ornaments so precious to beauty.

At the Champ-de-Mars they came in a crowd, their arms already all the more victorious, to raise up a consecrated earth. During the memorable *journée* of July 14, 1790, they smiled at the inclemency of cloud-filled skies; torrents of rain soaked them but could not drive them away. We heard them persist in singing with us the hymn of the Fédération. At our national celebrations I have seen some *citoyennes* beginning to reject a destructive luxury, encircled in modest grace; dressed simply, their hair adorned with only the tricolor ribbon, emblem of their civic virtue; more beautiful in charm than in adornment; apparently much less concerned already with pleasing through coquetry than with attracting by respect; and [less concerned] with charming the eye than with affecting the heart. I have seen and admired the progress of enlightenment, the happy effects of liberty. I have cried with joy, and I have said to myself: "The Revolution, which must regenerate our morals, has already had a powerful influence on those of our companions." One more effort now will hardly matter to those who have already supported us with such generous efforts. Certainly they will fortify, through their own resolves, the resolution we must take, but which can be effective only to the extent that they join with us. Certainly they will take it upon themselves to repeat continually and to prove to their husbands and children by their example that in Sybaris sugar might be considered an essential commodity, but in Sparta, threatened still more than ever before by a mob of enemies as audacious as they are perfidious, one must become habituated in advance to limiting oneself to the most ordinary food.

Gentlemen, I ask that we take a solemn oath not to use sugar with any of our food, except in case of illness, until the price has fallen. I am speaking not about some median price which most of us would be able to afford, but about a price low enough to allow the least fortunate to acquire it [sugar]. . . . Ah! who among us could find happiness in enjoyment when he knows that the largest and most precious segment of the people was deprived of it? I ask that we abstain from sugar until the price is not more than twenty or twenty-five *sols*, at the very most, [and] that this proscribed commodity no longer be seen on the table of the patriot, even the wealthiest, so that by this new deed the people can be informed that these much calumniated Jacobins are true patriots. Gentlemen, let us propose a formal motion to this effect in each of our Sections. This example [has] already been set by the citizens of [Section] Croix-Rouge, followed up immediately by our faithful friends in the Société fraternelle, and by the generous *citoyennes* of les Halles; this example, strengthened today by our resolutions, will be imitated—do not doubt it—throughout the capital and soon by all the Departments in the Empire. . . . [Louvet's motions were enthusiastically and unanimously adopted.] . . . Another member requested that the citizens and *citoyennes* in the spectator galleries be allowed to participate in the meetings of the Society and to offer, to France and to Europe, this new example of the generous sacrifices which Parisians continually make for the sake of conquering and safeguarding liberty. Immediately, the citizens and *citoyennes* in the galleries stood up and cried out with one voice: "Yes, yes, we make the same commitment."

Someone announced that several citizens and *citoyennes* from les Halles had already taken a civic oath to abstain from coffee and had substituted other foods for them.

The Society ordered that this patriotic act be given an honorable mention in the minutes. . . .

3. Parisian Women Protest via Taxation Populaire in February, 1792

Source: Jacques Godechot, ed., "Fragment des Mémoires de Charles-A. Alexandre," *Annales historiques de la Révolution française* 24 (1952):150–51, 155–58.

Alexandre's memoirs contain the most vivid surviving account of the Monnery sugar riots which broke out in February, 1792, in the Faubourg Saint Marceau. The women, who were the principal participants in these protests, demonstrated the effectiveness of violent direct action to secure their objective—provisioning.

———

[Alexandre, speaking in general terms about the events of February, 1792, in Paris, explains the motives of popular resentment and mobilization on the sugar issue:]

. . . The people were justified in complaining, but not in using threats and violence. The speculators, or rather, the hoarders—that is what the people called them—said, to exonerate themselves, that because sugar was a luxury product, the price was not and could not be frozen—that in truth it had and could have no other [price] than that dictated by the consumer's fancy. This sophism, born of cupidity, made no common sense, but that's the ordinary mode of reasoning [by greedy persons]. Surely in principle, and before our colonies reached the level of prosperity we witnessed at the time of the Revolution, sugar was a luxury item, but long ago it became an essential foodstuff. The people, who always think out of a sense of their needs, saw perfectly well that the goal of these hoarders was to force them to pay at least double the old price and to reduce them to this necessity or to deprive them of a product on which a part of their subsistence consumption depended, because it was their custom every morning to drink a large quantity of coffee, which kept them going until they returned from work around four or five in the afternoon and took a second meal, with which they ended the day; but the women, above all, were the most enraged at the hoarders, and the most threatening. Already, in the heart of Paris several fairly violent rows have taken place over this issue, and M. d'André, a former deputy in the Constituent [Assembly] who, following the first restoration, was minister of the general police for a brief time, was very compromised in his goods and in his person.

[Alexandre goes on to give his account of *événements* on the morning of the fourteenth of February, noting the tactics of *taxation populaire* invoked by the women to obtain "a kind of distributive justice, but one tainted in its principles by violence" (p. 154).]

. . . The people, all heated up, and delayed by what had occurred [disturbances which took place between seven and ten o'clock in the morning], abandoned their work and met in large numbers in the streets mentioned above; spirits were running high against the hoarders and hoarding; the most alarming measures were urged, nothing less [drastic] than breaking into the Monnery house, pillaging it, and even setting it on fire. I was being kept informed about all these discussions by some people who were less carried away than the others and who had some personal feeling for me.

It didn't take me long to become aware of these regrettable tendencies; in the space of several hours, different attempts were made to break into the house. I put up a suitable resistance, mixed with tact and civility. I went into the streets and chatted with the most inflamed attackers. I said, "Why are you allowing yourself such censurable excesses, which may well have equally unfortunate consequences?" "And you, our commander, why are you so determined to defend miserable hoarders who are trying to sell to us at the going price of gold a commodity they purchased at a low price and which is essential to us? And if only they were sugar dealers! But you can easily see that as they are dyers, their speculations should not extend beyond the chemicals necessary for working in this industry." The argument was a strong one, and there was little to be said.

"What do you want?" I replied, "I have been ordered by the authorities to protect this house; I promised to do it; I have to carry out my duty. You can pillage it, but I swear to you, you will have to pass over my dead body."

However, I gave the commander-general an account of my situation at the moment and of my fears. I asked him for help, and I observed that with the minimal offensive potential I had available, it would be impossible for me to sustain one more attack, if it were in the least bit serious.

In his reply [sent at] 3 P.M., he informed me that he was putting twenty cavalrymen at my service, twenty-five foot soldiers, and twenty-five light infantrymen, who arrived, not without difficulty, about 7 P.M., that is to say, when the mob had considerably decreased. In addition, he ordered me to take the necessary measures to place guards in the interior to keep the house and the warehouses safe from any damage.

The following night, we had a measure of calm, but the next day, the fifteenth, was a day of trouble and a very real agitation. . . .

[Alexandre describes the scene:]

However, the people, who had gathered in larger numbers and earlier than the previous day, were very menacing; threats led to action. I had to sustain a very heavy initial assault from their quarter, but it was unsuccessful. A second, which followed soon after, yielded better results: the entrance and the first-floor windows were forced open and broken. There was talk of setting the house on fire. I came out and spoke to the most excited [ones], who nonetheless never committed any violence against me. "Burn the house down, if you want to," I told them, "but the neighboring houses will burn down also, and the people they belong to haven't done you any harm or wrong." "You are right," was their reply, and they didn't burn anything. That was a major gain.

However, there was a third attack, very heavy, but which was sustained by the defenders without a shot and in such a way as to prevent the assailants from gaining entry into the house. But because they were throwing stones, several cavalrymen and foot soldiers were seriously injured. The commissioner of police, M. Junié, got through to us and was hit in the head [with a stone] which inflicted a major wound, but not a dangerous one, which seemed to make the attackers very angry. The commanding officer of the cavalry wanted to attack; I stopped him, and, in fact, both he and his cavalrymen would soon have been cut to shreds by the more than fifty thousand people who were surrounding us, and then everything would have been lost. The women above all, were the most excited. They were real furies. They wanted to go to the barracks, break in, and by main force take out the cannon of the battalion and put them to use against the Monnery house. I was informed about this in time and had such a heavy guard posted that the project failed.

Furious at having missed their chance, they took themselves off to the Eglise St.-Marcel, broke into the bell tower, and sounded the alarm which drew countless throngs from all the *quartiers* of Paris. In truth, I received an order from the municipality and the commander-general to use all possible means to stop the sounding of the alarm, but it was an easier [command] to issue than to execute.

I found myself in an extremely alarming situation . . . I didn't lose my head. I wrote to the Commander-General and to the Mayor to fill them in on the situation, and I added that if, in a few hours, they didn't come out with sufficient forces to relieve me, I would knuckle under and capitulate, because after all, I didn't see any need to let men who were under my orders be butchered and to start a civil war in Paris to support people as thoroughly despicable as Messieurs Auger and Monnery. I had a dispatch sent out via an orderly who got through only by leaping from garden to garden until he was beyond the line of attack. He brought back the verbal reply that I was going to receive help.

In truth, the rumor soon began spreading that a heavy column supported by six cannon, with the Mayor and the Commander-General at its head, was moving towards the Faubourg. When I went out into the street with my sword in hand, someone confirmed this news for me. Then a woman of the people, shoving her fist under my nose, said: "Oh shit! You sure have gotten us in deep!" "I!" I answered with a great deal of cool, "did I give you the advice to sound the alarm?" "No." "Okay then, it's your goddamned tocsin that got the police force mobilized and marching." "The swine! I think he's right."

Between four and five in the afternoon, the police force, the Mayor, and the Commander-General arrived, and to my great satisfaction I saw myself relieved; blocked in the way we had been since the preceding night, nothing could reach us, and we were dying of hunger—men and horses. My father, who was very worried and who was keeping a close watch on events, arrived as soon as he saw we had been relieved, bringing a lot of bread, meat, and wine. I had every bit of it delivered to the troops.

The sugar, whether it was the cause or the pretext of these disturbances, was removed and delivered safe and sound into the hands of its owners, along with the money collected from the sales of the first barrels which had been inopportunely pulled out; the crowds dispersed by themselves and with no violence. Calm was restored. In a word, it all appeared to be over. And nothing was, yet. . . .

4. AFTERMATH OF THE MONNERY DISTURBANCES: EXCUSES AND REPENTANCES

Following the Monnery riots, during which dozens of working men and women with families were arrested, citizens in the Section des Gobelins appealed to Section authorities as well as to the Legislative Assembly for the release of detained relatives and neighbors. Authorities on both the local and national levels, while understanding and supportive, were at the same time embarrassed by the violence and violations of property rights. They ended by urging clemency towards the participants in episodes of *taxation populaire* while charging outsiders with instigating the disturbances.

4*a*. Source: *Pétion {sic,* read *pétition} des citoyens de la Section des Gobelins* [February 26, 1792], in A.N., D III, 256 (4).

Legislators,

Afflicted citizens come in confidence to place in your paternal midst the tears of repentance and expressions of pain. Faithful to their duties, they have always distinguished themselves by their eagerness in fulfilling them. Must nearly three years' worth of obedience and sacrifice be eclipsed by a moment of blindness? Blindness, alas! all the more excusable because the cause is a recognized criminal machination which has had the effect of heightening activity because it works on misery and credulity.

The citizens of the Section des Gobelins, too credulous to suspect the existence of a trap, pushed too far not to fall into it, became aware of the danger only after their fall. They implore your indulgence as children await their father's forgiveness. Each minute a working citizen is taken from them, a precious mother; and this Section, previously the home of virtue and plainness, no longer offers anything other than a lugubrious scene of mourning and despair.

In the name of humanity and the peace that is so dear to them, legislators, cause their torment and their punishment to cease. Exercise over them the most beautiful of your prerogatives—clemency. Restore a father to his daily work, a mother to her large and innocent family. Involuntary playthings of a perfidious instigation, they moan in prisons. Pain and fear are consuming them there. Turn the blade of the law from above their heads; pardon the faults of aberration. Give these unfortunate people back their liberty, and henceforth their energies will be used only to bless you and to keep watch.

[petitioners' signatures appended]

4*b*. Source: [Probably a member of the Committee of Legislation of the Legislative Assembly], "Note demandée, servant d'éclaircissement à la pétition des citoyens de la Section des Gobelins du 26 Février 1792," in A.N., D III 256 (4).

Last November, some ill-willed persons came before the General Assembly of the Section [and] announced that there was a warehouse of hoarded sugar at Monsieur Monnery's house on the rue des Gobelins and that it would be necessary to go there. The citizens in the Section were opposed and didn't take any action.

Since this period, sugar has reached an exorbitant price. The laundresses, who comprised the largest number of citizens in this canton, were forced to stop using coffee, which they had been giving to their workers in the morning, and to substitute a glass of *eau de vie,* which was very bad for them.

The enemies of the public good profited from this discontent to stir up a riot, and about six weeks ago, when the occasion presented itself, a mob was assembled which went to the aforementioned Sieur Monnery's house, demanding that sugar be sold at twenty or thirty *sous.* Because of remonstrances by the *commissaire de police* in the Section, and then [a show] of public force, no distributions were in fact effected. And then a petition for the National Assembly was drawn up asking that means of preventing hoarding be legislated.

Subsequently, the proprietor of this sugar wanted to transport it to another place. He got several carriage loads out without danger. The evildoers, who were looking only to lead this Section's peaceful people astray, found a way to interrupt this transport, and the women laundresses and [women] workers of this *quartier* fell into the trap that was laid for them.

Once those who stirred up this riot succeeded in having the sugar taken and one portion of it paid for at the rate of twenty *sous,* they retreated and made a new appearance the next morning. They renewed their maneuvers. They themselves threw stones and got others to imitate their example, and they themselves were wily enough to escape justice.

The citizens and *citoyennes* of the Section des Gobelins who are domiciled there without having anything to do with the conspiracy have become the victims, as they are better known.

The correctional tribunal had many of them arrested. Several are at the *Concièrgerie*. All are fathers and mothers of large families which are languishing because of the detention of the authors [of their existence]. [They] live only from the earnings of their arduous labors, and . . . although [they are] in some sense guilty, [they] are [guilty] only from an alien impulse, being pure in heart and intention and, furthermore, very unfortunate.

4c. Source: "Extrait des Registres des délibérations de la Section des Gobelins, 25 avril, 1792, l'an IV de la liberté," in A.N., III 256 (4).

The General Assembly of the Section des Gobelins, convoked by drumbeat and by the sounding of the bell, composed of more than one hundred active citizens assembled at the habitual meeting place as a consequence of a petition signed by more than fifty active citizens for the purpose of discussing the issue of the men and women prisoners in the Oger and Monnery sugar affair.

Several members requested and obtained the floor, and after a long discussion, the assembly determined unanimously that it would name Messieurs Acloque, Desvogne, Junié, Gensi, Bertrand, and Baron for the purpose of taking all necessary measures, whether before the National Assembly, the Committee of Legislation, the Maison Commune, the tribunals, or anywhere it might be necessary to act for the purpose of obtaining justice promptly, along with the release of the men and women prisoners in this unfortunate affair.

One member stated and expressed his wish to see a number of women from the Section accompany the above-named commissioners in their work. The Assembly passed and adopted this motion unanimously and designated Mesdames Gerard, Lelu, Davesne, Dumounier, Colin, Boudin, asking *messieurs les commissaires* named above, to inform them.

{signatures of officers appended}

5. Etta Palm d'Aelders' Plea to the Legislative Assembly, April 1, 1792

Source: *Archives parlementaires*, vol. 41, pp. 63–64, April 1, 1792.

This is another of d'Aelders' radical pleas for complete equality between the sexes based on her belief that equality is a natural right.

———◆———

The former Baronne d'Aelders, a Dutch woman, accompanied by several other women, is admitted to the bar. After a long eulogy of feminine virtues, after having maintained that women equal men in courage and in talent, and almost always surpass them in imagination, she requests that the Assembly take into consideration the state of degradation to which women find themselves reduced as far as political rights are concerned, and reclaims on their behalf the full enjoyment of the natural rights of which they have been deprived by a protracted oppression. To attain this objective, she asks that women be admitted to civilian and military positions and that the education of young people of the feminine sex be set up on the same foundation as that of men. Women have shared the dangers of the Revolution; why shouldn't they participate in its advantages? Men are free at last, and women are the slaves of a thousand prejudices. They ask, therefore, (1) that the National Assembly accord a moral and national education to girls, (2) that they be declared of age at twenty-one, (3) that political liberty and equality of rights be common to both sexes, (4) that divorce be decreed.

The president answers the petitioners [telling them] that the Assembly will avoid, in the laws it is entrusted with making, everything that might provoke their regrets and their tears, and grants them the honors of the session. (The Assembly sends the petition to the joint Committees on Legislation and Education.)

6. WOMEN FROM THE HÔTEL DE VILLE SECTION OF PARIS ASK FOR ARMS, JULY 31, 1792

Source: *Archives parlementaires,* vol. 47, p. 322, July 31, 1792, at night.

———————————

Some *citoyennes* from the Section l'Hôtel de Ville are admitted to the bar.

One of them, after having placed before the Assembly a pike with a liberty cap on its tip, asks permission to arm herself and her companions for the defense of the capital.

The President answers the petitioners and grants them the honors of the session.

Monsieur Lecointe-Puyraveau. I ask that this be committed to the Military Committee.

Monsieur Thuriot. I oppose this transfer, and I ask that the Assembly proceed with the business of the day on the grounds that no law prohibits women from taking up arms.

(The Assembly proceeds with the business of the day on these grounds.)

7. The Journées of February, 1793

The *journées* of February, 1793, involved a wider geographical area than the previous year's episodes of *taxation populaire.* The participants combined assaults on what liberals defined as private property with specific requests, formulated by the popular societies and Section assemblies and presented to the National Convention, for fixed grain prices and harsh punishment for domestic and foreign enemies.

The documents indicate the gravity of the women's challenge and their tactical sense of the relative power of representative bodies. As in 1792, there was disruption in the Commune; more significantly, in 1793 the women brought their grievances to the National Convention. The laundresses acknowledged their irritation with the inflated prices of soap. When these women petitioners were asked to wait patiently for the government to make a decision, they took to the streets.

7a. A Deputation of Citoyennes at the Commune, February 24, 1793

Source: Report of February 24, 1793, in *Réimpression de l'Ancien Moniteur,* vol. XV, p. 555.

At the request of the interim Executive Council, the General Council of the Commune appoints two members who will arrange to join the mayor and the Procurator of the Commune to appear at sessions of the Executive Council in order to take effective measures to speed up recruitment for the army.

The Municipal Bureau, having received reports on the present state of subsistences in the city of Paris, and considering that emergency circumstances, need, and something of a rise in bread prices should call forth its full solicitude, orders administrators in the Department of Subsistence to take all measures which their wisdom and experience may suggest to provision the city of Paris so as to leave no pretexts from which our enemies can profit to disturb the public tranquility. The Municipal Bureau reserves for itself the responsibility of procuring the necessary funds so that payments for wheat and grain are not held up.

On the proposal of the Procurator of the Commune the municipal administration decrees that a proclamation be prepared for the citizens, urging them to fly to the defense of the Republic.

A large deputation of *citoyennes* appears before the municipal administration and asks for authorization to be introduced before the Convention to request a decrease in the price of foodstuffs and to denounce hoarders.

The mayor told this deputation that it need not request authorization to go the Convention; nevertheless, he requests that it [the deputation] return home quietly and rely on the solicitude of the people's magistrates who had already taken precautions in this domain by decreeing that an address would be presented in the National Convention to request a stringent law against hoarders. The *citoyennes* go away quietly.

7*b*. CITOYENNES AT THE JACOBIN SOCIETY, FEBRUARY 22, 1793

Source: *Procès-verbal* for the meeting of the Jacobin Society on February 22, 1793, as reprinted in F.-A. Aulard, ed., *La Société des Jacobins: Recueil de documents pour l'histoire du Club des Jacobins de Paris,* vol. V, pp. 37, 38.

. . . The President announced that a deputation of *citoyennes* from Section des Quatre-Nations requested the use of the Jacobins' meeting room for the following day at 4 P.M. to discuss hoarding. Desfieux pointed out that as the Jacobins' meeting room was already reserved every afternoon for the citizens of the eighty-four Departments, defenders of the Republic, the *citoyennes* could have it only during the morning. They might be offered the use of the hall of the Fraternal Society, which seated eight hundred.

(*Robespierre the Younger* objected that repeated discussions about foodstuffs would alarm the Republic. He was interrupted. He continued, and the Society set the motion aside.)

This decision increased the tumult. Spectators in the galleries cried out that right in the midst of the Society there were merchants, hoarders who enriched themselves on public misfortunes.

The President was forced to don his hat. Calm was not restored.

(The President explained that the Jacobins no longer were free to dispose of their meeting room during the day and were absolutely unable to offer it for use.

(*Dubois-Crancé* claimed that first liberty must be conquered, that afterwards foodstuffs would be cheap. He said that in his capacity as President of the Convention he would reject with horror any petition with the object of fixing prices on foodstuffs. The noise started up again.

(C . . . said that if the *citoyennes* were allowed to use this meeting room, thirty thousand women might foment disorder in Paris. *Jeanbon Saint-André* said that the solution would be to exclude from the popular societies any person who instigated discussion on this subject with the intention of breaking the peace. He concluded as follows:)

"This is not the time to get the people worked up over the question of subsistence. It [this question] is not on the agenda, and it compromises the calm and tranquility we must have. The Society must concern itself without distraction with an examination of the Constitution, and no other subject should be placed on the agenda before that one is exhausted."

(*Anthoine* reported on the work of the Committee on the Constitution of the Society. . . .)

7c. CITOYENNES AT THE NATIONAL CONVENTION, FEBRUARY
24, 1793

Source: Minutes for a session of the National Convention,
February 24, 1793, reprinted in P. B. Buchez and B. C. Roux,
eds., *Histoire parlementaire de la Révolution française, ou Journal des
Assemblées nationales depuis 1789 jusqu'au 1815,* vol. XXIV, pp.
328–33.

. . . *Lesage.* I ask for the floor to speak about a fact which concerns the
calm of Paris. Citizens, the city of Paris seems to be given over to the
most intensive anxiety; its fears appear to stem from lack of subsistence.

(Clamors are heard from the far left.)

Thuriot. I move a point of order; I ask that Lesage not be heard; I ask
that he leave.

Lesage: I ask to be heard.

Thuriot: In committee.

Lesage: It is a personal matter.

Deville: You are not the administrator of Paris. You want to stir up
trouble in this city and in the Convention.

Thuriot and Tallien come to the center of the room and demand
heatedly that Lesage be denied the right to speak. . . . . . . [*sic*]

The President: I will consult the assembly to find out whether Lesage
will be permitted to continue speaking.

The assembly decrees that Lesage be heard.

Lesage: I thought that the facts I had knowledge of should be communicated to the Assembly. I said that the bakers of Paris did not seem
to have enough bread for all citizens and that the citizens were panicked,
that feelings were worked up. . . . . . [*sic*] It seems hard [to believe]
that Paris, which is surrounded by Departments where there is an
abundance of grain, is itself lacking [grain].

Several voices: There isn't any shortage [of grain].

[Lesage:] One thing is certain; it is that right now, as I am speaking to
you, they are fighting over bread at the bakers' doors. I ask whether
anyone can charge evil intentions to my informing the Convention about
these facts; I ask you whether it isn't important for the Convention to
know whether Paris lacks subsistences; I ask, and here I conclude, that
the Mayor and the Procurator of the Commune be immediately mandated to make a report on the state of subsistences for Paris.

Thuriot: As I have followed all the revolutions that have taken place
in Paris, I can attest that of all the weapons used by aristocrats, subsist-

ences has been the principal one. I was alarmed, as Lesage [was] by the rumors being spread; I ran around everywhere trying to determine what truth there was in them. Even today I went to see the Minister of the Interior; I conclude that it is highly imprudent to announce before this body that unrest is spreading over subsistences for Paris. It is in the committees that concerted action must be taken concerning provisionment in order to avoid presenting the people with an alarming picture which isn't accurate. Paris has the necessary grain; there are some difficulties, perhaps, in the administration; malicious people profit from this to spread alarm; those who need only two loaves of bread take four.

(Several voices from the left: it's a fact.)

This is a means used by all the friends of the King to incite uprisings, to cause a commotion, and to crush the people, but it's useless for them to do that; we will save it [the people].

(Yes, yes, come the cries from all over the room. The speaker turns to the right.)

[Thuriot:] All right! Since you want to save it [the people], take the useful measure that has been suggested, advance a sum of money to Paris; if you do not, I will say that your panicking is [meant] only to second the counterrevolutionaries.

(Some violent clamoring is heard on the right. Yes, yes, exclaim a few members on the left.)

[Thuriot:] I request that the Committees of General Security and Commerce work together with the Municipality of Paris and the Minister of the Interior on provisionments for Paris and that they give us a report on the state of subsistences for this city.

Lasource: I ask for the floor to report on the facts. You have been told that the citizens of Paris wanted a fixed price on foodstuffs.

(Several voices: it's false.)

You have been told that there was agitation in Paris.

(The same voices: no, no.)

Here is the fact. At the door of the hall [of the Convention] I found about three hundred *citoyennes;* they said they had come to present a petition; I asked them what its purpose was. It is to ask you for a report on the decree which permits the sale of silver. They agreed with me that a fixed price for subsistences would starve Paris. They are disposed. . . .

Tallien: I have some important facts to communicate to the assembly. In the last few days some men have been circulating in the faubourgs and announcing that Paris is going to be without bread; that is why more people are at the bakers' doors than is usual; someone wants an uprising, and I have proofs. The day before yesterday I introduced myself to a group of women; they had gotten together to present a petition to you with the objective of obtaining a fixed price on soap. I tried to discourage them from their plan, but I could not make any progress with them. It was not difficult for me to figure out that they were not patriotic women but instruments whom the aristocrats were manipulating. I wrote to the Mayor of Paris; he recalled to me what often happened. To provoke trouble, women are placed in the front ranks; they are pushed into crying out, then the men appear who instigate the uprising. "They are preparing one," the Mayor told me, "I see it, I am convinced of it." This morning I saw the Mayor. I spoke to the Committee on Subsistences; I was assured that the unrest over subsistences was ill-founded. One fact which the Convention must know about is that since Pache was elected Mayor of Paris, there has been no end to the insults heaped upon him; that is because the same people who forced him out of the Ministry are still after him.

(Several voices on the right: prove the fact.)

I am asked for proofs, here they are. At a meeting of the General Council a man whom I had long considered a patriot moved that Pache could not occupy the office of Mayor before having turned in his reports, and this man is connected with those who have constantly shown themselves to be Pache's enemies, who persecuted him the entire time he was in the Ministry. Another fact: I was awakened this morning at 7 A.M. I was told that there had been an uprising in the Faubourg Saint-Antoine. Yesterday the blind in Section de Quinze-Vingts decided to present a petition to you, and at that moment the administrators of this establishment [for the blind] had the blind lined up in two lines and had them say, "We are going to the Convention to ask for bread." Be careful, Citizens, lest administrators whom you are told are such patriots have their petition presented at the very moment you are told there is no bread at the bakeries. I ask that you adopt Thuriot's proposal and that the gallery no longer resound with words of *famine, lack of bread:* all that can have only a very bad effect.

The President: I have just received a letter in which some *citoyennes* ask to be heard in order to express their alarms about subsistences in the heart of the Convention.

Mathieu: I ask that the petitioners be admitted. I have word from a baker to whom I sent [for news] that he made two batches more than usual, and if bread is in short supply, that is because people who usually take four *livres* took eight this morning. The principal cause of this apparent shortage is ill-founded misgivings that have been spread about.

The assembly closes discussion.

Thuriot's proposal is adopted as follows: The National Convention decrees that the Committees of Agriculture, and General Security, and Finances will meet immediately [and] will hear the Minister of the Interior, the Administrators of the Department, and the Mayor and Procurator of the Commune of Paris concerning the state of subsistences for this city and concerning measures taken to assure that [Paris] will not be lacking [in subsistences], and orders them to report on this to the Convention. . . .

A deputation of *citoyenne* laundresses of Paris is admitted to the bar.

One of the secretaries reads their petition, as follows: "Legislators, the laundresses of Paris have come into this sacred sanctuary of the laws and justice to set forth their concerns. Not only are all essential foodstuffs being sold at excessive prices, but also the price of the raw materials used in bleaching have gotten so high that soon the least fortunate class of people will be unable to have white underwear, which it cannot do without. It is not that the materials are lacking; they are abundant; it is hoarding and speculation which drive up the price. You have made the head of the tyrant fall under the blade of the laws, let the blade of the laws bear down on the heads of these public bloodsuckers. We ask the death penalty for hoarders and speculators."

The President: *Citoyennes,* the Convention will occupy itself with the object of your concern, but one of the ways of driving up the price of goods is to scare away commerce by constantly crying "hoarding," etc. The assembly invites you to remain for the duration of this session.

Some Parisian *citoyennes* meeting as a fraternal society in the locale of the former Jacobins request, via the intermediary of a deputation, as a means of forcing down the prices of subsistences, the report on the law which makes silver negotiable.[1]

Duhem: The Committees of Commerce, Agriculture, and Finances have been concerned with means of diminishing the price of absolutely essential foodstuffs. They are presently in conference with the Minister of Public Contributions and the administrative bodies. I ask that they deliver their report tomorrow.

This proposal is adopted.

The President tells them [the members of the deputation] that the assembly is currently taking up in its committees the subject of subsistences. He extends the honors of the session to the deputation.

[1]Probably a reference to the women who registered as Société révolutionnaire républicaine before the Commune on May 10, 1793 (see chapter four, document 1). [Translators' note.]

7*d*. THE WOMEN OF PARIS RESPOND TO THE DELAYING
TACTICS OF THE NATIONAL CONVENTION, FEBRUARY 25,
1793

Source: Prud'homme, *Révolutions de Paris,* vol. CXC, no. 190
(February 23–March 2, 1793), reprinted in Buchez and Roux,
Histoire parlementaire, vol. XXIV, pp. 333–35.

The *journée* of February 25 has just brought on new storms; it presages
still greater ones. Constitutive acts and armies are not the issue right
now. Alas! other cares force us into a cruel diversion and engross the full
attention of the friends of the country and liberty.

For several days symptoms of a frightening nature were threatening us
with a fateful occurrence; an artificial shortage, similar to the one of
1789, had been under way in Paris for several days. The sale of bread
was subject to delays, and difficulties in obtaining it had already cost
more than one *citoyenne* many tears. Soap, which could still be obtained a
month ago at fourteen to sixteen *sous* rose to thirty-two *sous,* and already
several laundresses were wailing about the lack of work and the impossibility of continuing in their profession. Already, bitter complaints
were being heard in the spectator galleries of the General Council of the
Commune. It [the Council] replied: "Go take your complaints to the bar
of the Convention."

The advice was heeded. Sunday, among the petitioners, several cried
out: "Bread and soap!" These cries were supported outside the hall by
large and very agitated groups. The Convention took all that in with
considerable coolness and adjourned until Tuesday, when the matter was
to be taken up. Far from calming and satisfying [them], this resolution
embittered them still more, and upon leaving the bar [of the Conven-
tion] the women in the corridors said aloud, to whoever was willing to
listen: "We are adjourned until Tuesday; but as for us, we adjourn
ourselves until Monday. When our children ask us for milk, we don't
adjourn them until the day after tomorrow."

8. Police Reports on the Journées of February, 1793

Police reports on episodes of *taxation populaire* during the
February days of 1793 provide important evidence of women's
central role as instigators, leaders, and supporters of a form of
protest which custom legitimated and which experience had
shown to be effective. Police agents filing their reports wavered
between sympathy for the condition and even the tactics of the
female-dominated crowds on the one hand and sensitivity to the
rights of proprietors and the principles of law and order on
the other.

8*a*. Source: *Commissaire*'s report on damages committed at the
warehouse of Citizen Commard, February 26, 1793, Section des
Gardes Françaises, in Archives de la Préfecture de Police de
Paris, AA 153, nos. 78ff.

Section des Gardes Françaises
Police

February 26 and March 6, 1793.

Procès-verbal on damages committed on February 25, 1793, at Citizen
Commard's place. . . .

In the year 1793, the second [year] of the Republic, on Tuesday, the
twenty-sixth of February, at 11 A.M., before us, Jean-Baptiste-Jacques
Varangue, *commissaire de police* of the Section des Gardes Françaises,
assisted by the secretary-clerk, appeared Citizen Laurent Commard, a
licensed wholesaler at 412, rue des Bourdonnais, operating as Commard, Sons, and Company.

He told us that yesterday, about 3:30 or 4 P.M., a considerable
number of men and a larger number of women appeared at the door of
his house. First, several of these women asked him whether he had any
soap, to which he replied no. Seeing that a portion of them were taking
a stand against him personally, he went back in. Neighbors and other

good citizens approached these women. They assured them that there
wasn't any soap, and in fact, he hasn't had any at his place for a year.
One of these women, letting it be seen that she was pregnant by slap-
ping her stomach, said, "I need sugar for my little one." Immediately all
the women said, "We must have sugar." These women were denied
entry to the warehouse.

Then two children, about twelve or thirteen years of age, dragged
two empty barrels in front of the door of the warehouse. They stood up
on them, and, kicking with their *sabots,* they broke a paned-glass window frame above the door. Then there appeared an individual, about
five feet, four inches tall, wearing a bronze-colored jacket, with a round
hat, and a white apron around him, like a butcher boy. [He was]
twenty-two to twenty-four years old. Using a piece of hooping, he
completed the job of breaking the aforementioned window-frame.
Climbing over it, the two children and another individual got into the
warehouse. With the aid of a hammer and other tools they found in the
aforementioned warehouse, they broke the lock on the aforementioned
door, which opened immediately. Then all the women streamed into
the warehouse and seized the sugar, brown sugar, and coffee that was
stored there. Several insisted on paying, as follows: twenty *sous* a *livre* for
sugar; ten *sous* a *livre* for brown sugar; and twenty *sous* a *livre* for coffee.
And as it is in the declarant's interest to obtain a certified report of
violations of his property, he requests that we come to his house and
warehouse. . . .

Consequently, we, the aforementioned *commissaire de police,* assisted as
above, went with Citizen Command to his house, located on rue des
Bourdonnais, no. 412, which is owned by Dame de Sainsey. In the
presence of Citizens Joseph Tellier, *marchand parfumeur,* living at rue des
Bourdonnais, no. 412, and Michel Ballet, *marchand tailleur,* also living
at rue des Bourdonnais, no. 412, we went through a first courtyard, at
the far end of which, on the ground floor, is a warehouse with its entry
via the aforementioned courtyard. We found the door closed, and above
it a paned window frame containing twelve panes, of which six were
broken, the aforementioned window frame being about four feet high by
three and one-half feet wide. The traverse beam to the right of the
aforementioned window frame was broken. We had the door to the
warehouse opened by pushing it hard, because it had been closed from
the inside only by several barrels and boards which had been placed there
to close it as best one could. This door having been opened, we saw that
the screws on the lock, and the lock itself, had been forced and broken
with a hammer or other tool, to the point that the lock was held by one

screw, which was entirely forced and which was easily detached on the spot.

In this warehouse there is a little office for writing on the left, facing the aforementioned large courtyard, the said office enclosed in glass. And of twenty-four panes, twenty-one were broken. To the right of this office is another [office] which serves as well for writing, which looks out onto a small courtyard at the back of the aforementioned house, and which receives light from a casement window containing six panes, one of which was broken. We noted in this office that the books were all in disarray, covered with ink and mud, and that a very small amount of mocha coffee was spilled on the table. Having returned to the warehouse, we saw that there had been a wooden cupboard about five feet high going all around the aforementioned warehouse and through the little offices previously mentioned. We found no merchandise in this cupboard. We did find there four old hats, which the aforementioned Sieur Commard told us belonged to the people who broke into his place, all of whom climbed up on the aforementioned cupboard to take the merchandise that was there.

Underneath the aforementioned cupboard we found a cask of coffee, two-thirds full; a barrel of brown sugar, from which one-sixth of the contents had been removed; the above-mentioned barrel damaged on its side; another undamaged barrel; in addition, another, broken on the side, of which one-fifth of the contents were missing; another barrel which had been placed bottom up and which had been smashed in on top, from which one-eighth of the contents seems to have been removed; lastly, another barrel on its side, smashed in on the bottom, from which one-tenth [of the contents] were taken; and finally, ten barrels of English sugar and a barrel of Orleans sugar, emptied.

After we made the certified report, as above, the aforementioned Sieur Commard told us that on Sunday, the twenty-fourth of this month, they had in storage five barrels of brown sugar, of which two were delivered the following day, Monday, to Sieur Patureaux. In addition, they had a barrel of coffee from Martinique, containing 801 *livres*. The five barrels of brown sugar, for which they do not yet have the bill from Sieur Labbé, their supplier, who lives on rue St. Denis at the corner of rue des Lombards, weighed altogether 7,836 *livres* net, as recorded on their scale. They had, in addition, a barrel of Orleans sugar, a shipment from Sieurs Hubert Husson of the aforementioned establishment—net weight, 1,131 *livres*. In addition, they estimate that they had about 500 *livres* of sugar powder and brown sugar in their warehouse, gathered here and there from the deliveries they made to their customers. On the same day, Sunday, the twenty-fourth of this month, they received from Rouen, in a shipment from Sieur Tarbé, six barrels of English sugar.

He produced for us the consignment note dated Rouen, the twentieth of this month of February, stating that the driver was obliged to deliver within five days, or forfeit one-third [the value] of the [contents] of the carriage. The next day, Monday, at 10 A.M., they also received four other barrels of the same kind of sugar in a shipment from Citizen Tarbé, once again, following a consignment note dated this month, stating likewise that the driver was obliged to deliver these ten barrels weighing 8,358 *livres* under the same conditions as those which applied for the consignment note discussed in detail above.

Citizen Command estimates that the merchandise mentioned above, and which was pillaged, adds up to this sum, as follows, namely:

1/3 of the 801 *livres* which the cask of coffee weighed, making	
267# [*livres*] of coffee missing at 220 per hundred	587.8 s
1,244 *livres* brown sugar following the estimate made for what was emptied from 5 barrels, at 220# per hundred	2,736.16
1,131 *livres* Orleans sugar at 280# per hundred	3,166.16
500 *livres* sugar powder at 150# per hundred	750.
10 barrels English sugar, weighing: Ort 8,358, from which, subtract for depreciation 1,190 remaining net 7,168 at 275# per hundred	19,712.
The Mocha coffee was in a paper bag. There was about	
30 *livres* which amounts in cash to	90.
Total losses which Citizens Command estimate they sustained during the pillage that took place at their establishment	27,043.
On which Citizens Command received back, in *assignats,* placed in a briefcase handed over to them by the individuals in charge of receipts	1,158.4
	25,884.16

The wife of Citizen Guillaume Cherouze, a coal
carrier [who is] their neighbor, who was in their
house at the time the pillage took place, made an
unbelievable effort to oppose [what was taking
place], but seeing the futility of it, she decided to
enter the warehouse in several trips and brought out
and hid in their kitchen six loaf sugars and two
pieces weighing altogether 102 *livres.*

Citizen LeTellier, *parfumeur,* and likewise a
neighbor, who in the same way tried to prevent the
breaking into the warehouse, also salvaged from
pillage three loaf sugars and a piece weighing
altogether 53 *livres,* these two items making up the
sum of   426.05

total loss   25,458.11

Concerning all of which Citizen Command makes the present declaration. . . .

8*b*. Source: *Commissaire's* report on events of February 24, 25, 26,
1793, Section de l'Arsenal, in Archives de la Préfecture de
Police de Paris, AA 69, nos. 296–97.

In Year Two of the French Republic, on February 24, at 8 A.M., in
1793, we, Silvain Guillaume Boula [?], *commissaire de police,* assisted by
André Lirey [?] Caillouet, secretary-registrar for the Section de l'Arsenal, as a result of remarks that were being heard everywhere, went
through the streets of our arrondissement. We heard nothing but assurances concerning goods of prime necessity. Having made this round
several times, we saw nothing openly contrary to public order. We
received a letter from the police administration relative to bread. We
believed we ought to hold off executing it after we conferred with the
Committee. Recorded at 7 P.M., same day, same month noted above.
    And we signed [secretary's and *commissaire's* signatures appended]
    And the following day, the twenty-fifth of the same month, same

year, at 7 A.M., we went, still assisted by the citizen-secretary-registrar, to the doors of the bakers in our Section to see whether bread deliveries were being made without incident and to take remedial action, if possible. We had the satisfaction of seeing that the measures we had taken the night before, in joint action with the Committee, had produced the full effect we were hoping for. Consequently, we returned to the Committee to find out whether there wasn't some new order, and finding none, we returned to our arrondissement.

There wasn't what you would call a tumult, but [rather] small groupings of citizens and *citoyennes* at intervals. In some [of these groups] it was being said, "The bakers were rascals and deserved to be worked over." In others, "The grocers deserved the same, because they were hoarders," and finally, in others, "The majority of those who were directing the Republic were also rascals." And among others [there was] a drunk citizen who made himself conspicuous by saying, "We used to have only one king, and now there are thirty or forty of them." We did everything we could to restore calm in these groups. We succeeded in some; it was impossible in others; and lastly, it was folly in still others. All this [was happening] without our being able to arrest any of the leaders, who were absolutely unknown to us and not from this Section.

We returned to the Committee at 1 P.M. after having spent the whole morning on the business detailed above.

But at about 2 P.M. word reached us that a crowd was on the way to Citizen Rousseau's shop on the Quai des Armes. We went there at once, still accompanied by the citizen-secretary, and notwithstanding the crowding, we got through to the counter. We climbed up onto it, and having called for silence in the name of the law, we got it. We took advantage of this to recall the oath to protect the safety of persons and properties. We couldn't keep this up, because we were interrupted by cries and apostrophes of all kinds, as much against us as against Citizen Rousseau and his grocery boy, who, at the beginning, had been imprudent enough to brutally push back a pregnant woman, even threatening to string her up from a beam. Five citizens from the Guards arrived. They could not do anything, not even speak. *This was a dangerous moment.* We supported for the moment a demand to inspect the house made by citizens and *citoyennes* designated for this purpose. That was the business of the moment. We were even forced to accompany them. This inspection was made calmly enough, except for a few remarks. They wanted to inspect Citizen Arnoult's place as well, on the pretext that the aforementioned Rousseau had hidden his merchandise there. This inspection was agreed to by Citoyenne Arnoult. When we returned, we saw an officer, Citizen Colmet, arrive, accompanied by several armed citizens, who tried in vain to restore order. They retreated shortly afterwards.

And finally, there was a woman of fairly good appearance, unknown to me but whom we would recognize perfectly. She was about five feet, one inch tall, thirty years old, with blond hair, white skin, and slightly red eyes. She wore her hair in a demibonnet to which a rose-colored ribbon was attached. She was dressed in a *déshabillé* made out of linen with a blue background and a standard design on it. She wore a mantlet of black taffeta and a gold watch on a steel chain. The way we knew she had one [a watch] was that when she emerged from the crowd and came over to the counter, she looked for her watch, [and] drew it out, saying, "I thought it had been taken." This woman did everything in her power to add to the sedition. She had gone on the inspection. And once they returned, it was she who set the price for soap at twelve *sous* per *livre;* and for sugar at eighteen. After that, the aforementioned merchandise on hand at the aforementioned Rousseau's place was handed over with an unbelievable impetuosity. Everyone wanted to pay, to be waited on, and to get out, all at the same time. We were compelled to take in the cash in order to prevent a total loss. The aforementioned woman took the aforementioned goods, for which she paid us, and we barely had the time to take in the money, hand over the goods, and put the money in the drawer. In this crowd of citizens and *citoyennes* we couldn't observe everyone attentively enough to be able to point out anyone except for the woman described above. We clearly recognized some of the *citoyennes* from our Section, but it would be impossible for us to recall the faces and descriptions except for Citizen Jolly, captain of the company in this Section, who is known to be a good patriot, whom we saw near the aforementioned counter and who, like everyone else, was paying the prices noted above, and who took some soap. We didn't hear him say anything relevant to the circumstance. And we believe absolutely that he was there only because of the perfidious advice of some enemies of the public good, whom he took for patriots and who, knowing how to wrap themselves in this cloak, could address themselves only to citizens whose pure hearts dictated that they would be unable to uncover the foulness of which they [these enemies of the people] are capable.

Several citizens having signaled us to get out fast, we left and went to the shop of Citizen Blauguernon [?], also a grocer, on the rue de l'Etoile, where we had the good luck to calm the people. On demand we went to the shop of Citizen Cain, also a grocer, on the rue St. Antoine, where, again, notwithstanding the numbers, we reached the counter.

Our call and entreaty got us a hearing, which allowed us to recall the most recent oath, but in vain, the tumult and the cries indicating [?] that the time for oaths had passed and that what was necessary was the goods. Once again we believed it was our duty to call for the necessary calm and order. We were heard, and we spoke for about five minutes. We were listened to with pleasure, and calm was restored.

We left, and it might have been about five o'clock when we were asked once again to go the Quai des Armes, given that there was a new crowd of citizens there. We went there immediately. And once there, we saw what we were told we would see. But we had brought along with us many armed citizens who dispersed this mob. We saw there a *citoyenne,* well dressed, who was influencing people and stirring up trouble. Having listened to her during a period allowed for this moment, we apprehended her, calling upon constituted armed force for support. [There followed] *another perilous moment,* given that the people were opposed to her being taken away.

Finally we brought her before the Committee, where we drew up a *procès-verbal,* and we sent this *citoyenne* to the *commissaire de police* of the Section de la Maison Commune so that whatever the laws dictate might be done.

Once this business had been attended to, we left, and seeing a tumult at the door of Citizen Houllier's shop, we once again restored calm, having called in advance for a cavalry patrol to carry out our orders, which they did. And then we went to the shops of Citizens Cain, Lessard, and Prévot, also grocers on the rue St. Antoine, where the tumult was almost over, and having called upon all these citizens to close their shops at nine o'clock, having even handed them over, under consignment, to Captain Roquet, we returned at last to the Committee at 8 P.M. without any notable incidents, and we were fully convinced that the People is always good. It has been tricked for hundreds of years now, but it has lost neither heart nor its love for the general good. It requires only to be educated and it will do and sacrifice even everything once it is led along a route where it will see an end to its misfortunes, and the hope of attaining happiness, if only for its posterity.

Drawn up and concluded on the day, month, and year indicated above. We signed   [signatures of secretary and *commissaire* appended]

And the twenty-sixth of the same month and year indicated above, still accompanied by the citizen-secretary-registrar, we toured, during the course of the day, all the streets in the Section, and as a large proportion of the citizens were under arms, and as successive patrols were set up, nothing noteworthy occurred. We can offer assurances that things were quiet during the night.

Consequently, we drew up the present [report] to serve and be of value, as reason dictates.

Terminated at 8 P.M. same day and year as indicated above. And we signed   [signatures of secretary and *commissaire* appended]

IV

Organized Feminine Political Power: Spring through October, 1793

FROM FEBRUARY TO OCTOBER, 1793, Parisian women came to enjoy their greatest organized power in a political club exclusively for women, the Society of Revolutionary Republican Women.

Attempts in 1790 and 1791 by de Gouges, Méricourt, d'Aelders, and others to found women's groups were largely failures because their appeal was principally to bourgeois women who may have been put off by the leaders' marginal status. Furthermore, middle-class women felt they had access to the power centers of revolutionary politics when they sat in the galleries of the national legislature and the political clubs.[1]

The Républicaines-révolutionnaires were active at the height of the power struggle in Paris between the Girondins and Jacobins, when there was an obvious opportunity for political influence. Merging issues of interest to the radical middle classes and the Parisian poor, the Républicaines-révolutionnaires sponsored programs of penal reform and occupational training for girls, spoke up frequently on matters involving public morality, and advocated the politics of subsistence and the use of terror as an instrument of political purification. Their association with the radical left wing of Enragés and their affiliations within the Sections, popular societies, assemblies, and clubs brought them prominence and protection as long as the Jacobin leaders needed their support in their struggle for political control. Once victory over the Girondins was consolidated, the Jacobins moved to co-opt key *sans-culottes* programs while silencing their leaders and dissolving or deactivating their political institutions.

In 1792 radical Jacobin deputies had worked closely with Parisian radicals in the Cordeliers and the Commune to discredit the monarchy

[1]See Marie Cerati, *Le Club des citoyennes républicaines révolutionnaires*, p. 20.

and popularize republican ideals. Radical deputies and Jacobin members, the Montagnards, allied with the *sans-culottes* in the Sections and campaigned for a more democratic constitution, price controls, harsh laws against political enemies, and economic legislation to assist the needy. Their opponents, the Girondins, felt that paying such attention to working-class problems in Paris could deflect energies and money from the vigorous prosecution of the war against the Coalition, and they remained committed to a free market.

Once the Republic was a reality, the power struggle centered on the question of whether the Parisian *sans-culottes* could push the Convention further to the left. The key issues were the economic grievances of the common people, rejection of a free-market economy in favor of price controls and the regulation of supply, and terror—how far the government should go in arresting and executing its suspected enemies.

The Society of Revolutionary Republican Women brought together militant women who kept pushing the Montagnards for economic legislation. In February a deputation of women from the Section des Quatre Nations had requested the Jacobin meeting hall to discuss measures against hoarding and scarcity. The request was denied, and Jacobin Society members expressed the fear of a massive women's protest that could lead to "disorder in Paris."[2]

Between February and May, when the Républicaines-révolutionnaires registered their Society with authorities at the Commune, the women kept up the pressure. We have evidence that members of the Society continued their affiliation with the principal revolutionary leaders and organizations. One of the Society's future presidents, Pauline Léon, a native Parisian known in her Section, had been attending sessions of the Cordeliers Club since February, 1791.[3] Claire Lacombe, another president, was a provincial actress who did not arrive in Paris until the summer of 1792. Her quarters were on the Right Bank within a short distance of the Legislative Assembly, the Jacobin Society, and the Hôtel de Ville. She played a role in the *journée* of August 10, and in the winter of 1792–93 she attended popular societies and spoke occasionally at meetings of the Jacobin Society.[4]

Contemporaries commented that many of the women in the Society

<hr />

[2]F.-A. Aulard, *La Société des Jacobins*, vol. V, pp. 37–38.

[3]See document 6, chapter 4, and also Cerati, *Le Club des citoyennes républicaines révolutionnaires*, chap. 5.

[4]Aulard, *La Société des Jacobins*, vol. V, p. 123; Margaret George, "The 'World Historical Defeat' of the Républicaines-Révolutionnaires," *Science and Society* 40, no. 4 (Winter, 1976–77):410–37.

had contacts in the Sections which allowed them to communicate effectively with the *sans-culotte* population.[5] They were also allied with the Enragés, the most extreme spokesmen on the left for the interests of the Parisian *sans-culottes*. Both Léon and Lacombe had liaisons with one of the leading Enragés, Théophile Leclerc, whom Léon married in November, 1793. The alliance formed between the Républicaines-révolutionnaires and the Enragés in the summer of 1793 would prove to be a tactical advantage at first, but ultimately it became a disastrous handicap for the women's relations with the Montagnards.

During the last two weeks of May, 1793, these ardent female patriots supported the Montagnards at the climax of their struggle with the Girondins for domination of the Convention. Garbed in red pantaloons and red woolen bonnets of liberty, they heckled Girondins at their meetings and in the streets; they encouraged women in the popular societies to take whatever measures were necessary to expel moderates from their midst. They joined with the Cordeliers in a deputation to the Convention on May 19 to demand the passage and enforcement of a harsh law against suspects.

Between May 31 and June 2, thirty-one Girondin deputies in the Convention were ousted in a coup which consolidated the Montagnards in power—a planned insurrection coordinated by the Sections, the National Guard, the Jacobin organization, the popular societies, and the Enragés. The Society of Revolutionary Republican Women played prominent roles in these events. They stood guard at the doors of the Convention, refusing to admit Girondins and pursuing those who fled; they were present at the Hôtel de Ville and requested permission to deliberate with the Revolutionary Council of the Commune.

Immediately following the Montagnard victory, the Républicaines-révolutionnaires enjoyed their greatest prestige in the Montagnard Republic. They believed the Montagnards would honor their promises to the people. The women had not yet moved as far left as the Enragés, who attacked the new Montagnard Constitution unveiled to the public in early June. The Enragés were critical of the omission from the Constitution of sanctions against hoarders and speculators, but the Revolutionary Republican Women were enthusiastic about the Constitution, and on July 1 they approved a speech denouncing the Enragé leader, Jacques Roux, as an opportunist.[6]

---

[5]*Moniteur*, September 19, 1793, as cited by George, "'World Historical Defeat,'" pp. 428–29.

[6]Cerati, *Le Club des citoyennes républicaines révolutionnaires*, pp. 75–77.

In July a rift opened between the Society and the Montagnards, and the Society moved closer to the Enragés. The Revolutionary Republican Women learned that the Montagnards were unable or unwilling to satisfy the material demands of the Parisian working poor and *femmes sans-culottes*. The Montagnards assigned highest priorities to winning back the support of as many Girondins as possible in order to establish domestic tranquility. They hesitated to enact laws involving political and economic terror which would alienate the middle class. Charlotte Corday's assassination of the radical journalist Marat on July 15 served as a warning to the Revolutionary Republican Women that the Montagnard government had been too tolerant of Girondins. Militant revolutionaries believed that Corday had been a tool of exiled Girondins. She became the target of the Revolutionary Republican Women's particular hatred.

The Society of Revolutionary Republican Women completely cut off all support for the Montagnards in August, 1793. From their perspective the Montagnard government was incompetent. In the midst of deepening economic and military crises in the summer months, the Montagnards were still trying to modify their policies to bring about a compromise with the moderate republicans. The Montagnard constitution, promulgated in the first week of July, contained no concessions to the Enragés' criticisms; it omitted promises of economic controls and a political terror. Instead, it emphasized education, democratic manhood suffrage, and assurances to the peasants that they would not have to pay compensations for feudal dues to former nobles.

The Revolutionary Republican Women moved their headquarters from the library of the Jacobin Society to the former church of Saint-Eustache in the central market area. They also strengthened their alliance with the Enragés Jacques Roux, Jean Varlet, and Théophile Leclerc. On August 1, when the government called for a *levée en masse* to save the fatherland, a deputation of Revolutionary Republican Women appeared at the National Convention demanding as the condition for Parisian women's support that the Convention pass legislation to protect the civilian population.

The women's Society had reached the apex of its strength by September, 1793. Several hundred members met in their club. They campaigned for a law compelling all women to wear the tricolor cockade as a symbol of their republican loyalties. They circulated petitions to popular societies and the National Convention for the immediate implementation of price controls and the Law of Suspects. Along with other groups on the extreme left, including the Enragés, they exerted massive political pressure in the Sections, the popular societies, and the Jacobin Club and among Convention deputies. This pressure brought about legislation in September. On the fifth, legal terror was decreed the order of the day; on the ninth an *armée révolutionnaire* was created; on the seventeenth the Law of Suspects was passed; and on the twenty-ninth uniform price controls on necessities were established by the Law of the General Maximum. The Convention decreed on September 21 that all women must wear the cockade in public. Once these laws were passed, the women pressed for their vigorous enforcement.

In September the growing hostility both of other women and of left-wing male Montagnards brought about the ultimate defeat of the Society. The Revolutionary Republican Women's organization could not overcome opposition among other Parisian women. Market women, former servants, and religious women adamantly opposed price controls and severe punishments for suspect aristocrats and former clergy. To the Society of Revolutionary Republican Women and their followers in popular societies such women were as much "aristocrats" as those of noble lineage, and thus a threat. The struggle between the Society and market women over the issue of the tricolor cockade illustrates the deep divisions among women. Second, the Montagnards were beginning to identify the Revolutionary Republican Women as dangerous rabble-rousers, and they denigrated the Society's leaders in Jacobin meetings and warned popular societies against supporting their "seditious and aristocratic" petitions. (See document 13, chapter four.) On September 16, Claire Lacombe was denounced by the Jacobin Society before the Committee of General Security, and she was seized and briefly detained.

By October the Montagnards had consolidated power in Paris and the Departments and had established the Jacobin government. They had imprisoned Enragé leaders Varlet and Roux, convinced that their persistence in pursuing radically democratic grass-roots policies threatened Jacobin control of the national government.

At precisely this time the Society of Revolutionary Republican Women stepped up their opposition to Jacobin policies and their exposure of the Jacobins' unfulfilled constitutional promises. They presented petitions to the Commune and the Convention asking that prostitutes be rehabilitated, that the Law of the General Maximum be enforced, that merchants be placed under revolutionary surveillance, and that *sans-culottes'* power be wielded vigilantly to check and control government officials.[7]

---

[7]George, "'World Historical Defeat,'" citing *Moniteur*, September 18, October 9, 27, 1793; and Alexandre Tuetey, *Répertoire général des sources manuscrites de l'histoire de Paris pendant la Révolution française*, vol. IX, p. 1388.

They tried to force all women to adopt their costume and obey the law on the cockade. With even more vigor than in September, market women reacted in violent street disputes. On October 30 the market women petitioned the Convention for the abolition of the Society, contending that the members threatened their commerce and harrassed them. The Convention seized the opportunity to dissolve the Society of Revolutionary Republican Women. On October 30 the government decreed that henceforth all women's clubs and associations were illegal. Appeals by leading members of the Society for reconsideration of the decree were ignored by the National Convention, and the members of the Commune of Paris sternly reminded women that their primary responsibilities were in the home and not in public places.

The successes of the Society of Revolutionary Republican Women had come at a time of uncertain political control in Paris. The members depended on alliances with radical men in the Jacobins, the Convention, the Commune, the Cordeliers, the popular societies, Section assemblies, and the Enragés. Success also hinged to a degree upon the existence of a common interest among other women. When conditions favoring their bid for influence changed, the Society could not survive.

1. THE SOCIETY OF REVOLUTIONARY REPUBLICAN WOMEN REGISTERS WITH AUTHORITIES AT THE COMMUNE

Source: *Réimpression de l'Ancien Moniteur,* vol. XVI, pp. 361–62.

———————

Commune of Paris, May 10. . . .

Several *citoyennes* presented themselves to the secretariat of the municipality and in conformity with the law concerning municipal regulations declared their intention of assembling and forming a society which admits only women. This society has for its objective deliberation on the means of frustrating the projects of the republic's enemies. It will bear the name of Revolutionary Republican Society and will meet in the library of the Jacobins, rue Saint-Honoré.

2. The Society of Revolutionary Republican Women Joins the Cordeliers to Denounce Traitors

Source: F.-A. Aulard, *La Société des Jacobins: Recueil de documents pour l'histoire du Club des Jacobins de Paris,* vol. V, pp. 198–99.

In the first weeks following the formation of the Society of Revolutionary Republican Women, the Society's members cemented advantageous working alliances with well-established, influential revolutionary organizations which shared their demand for a systematic politics of terror against enemies of the Republic—Girondins, aristocrats, hoarders, speculators. Exploiting its members' earlier affiliations with the Cordeliers Club, delegates joined forces with members of that club and formed a joint deputation to the all-powerful Jacobin Society. In this way, nine days after its formation, the Society was able to publicize its petition recapitulating the tactics and goals of terror.

———

Session of Sunday, May 19, 1793.
. . . A deputation from the Cordeliers Club and the *citoyennes* of the Revolutionary Society of Women is admitted. The *orator* announces a petition drawn up by the members of these two societies joined together and reads this petition, the substance of which is as follows:
"Representatives of the people, the country is in the most imminent danger; if you want to save it, the most energetic measures must be taken. . . ." (*Noise.*)
"I demand," the orator cries out, "the fullest attention."
Calm is restored.
He continues: If not, the people will save themselves. You are not unaware that the conspirators are awaiting only the departure of the volunteers, who are going to fight our enemies in the Vendée, to immolate the patriots and everything they cherish most. To prevent the execution of these horrible projects, hasten to decree that suspect men

will be placed under arrest immediately, that revolutionary tribunals will be set up in all the Departments and in the Sections of Paris.

For a long while the Brissots, the Gaudets, the Vergniauds, the Gensonnés, the Buzots, the Barbarouxes, etc., have been pointed out as being the general staff of the counterrevolutionary army. Why do you hesitate to issue charges against them? Criminals are not sacred anywhere.

Legislators, you cannot refuse the French people this great act of justice. That would be to declare yourselves their accomplices; that would be to prove that several among you fear the light which the trial investigation of these suspect members would cause to flash.

We ask that you establish in every city revolutionary armies composed of *sans-culottes,* proportional in size to the population; that the army of Paris be increased to forty thousand men, paid at the expense of the rich at a rate of forty *sous* a day. We ask that in all public places workshops be set up where iron be converted into all kinds of weapons.

Legislators, strike out at the speculators, the hoarders, and the ego-istical merchants. A horrible plot exists to cause the people to die of hunger by setting an enormous price on goods. At the head of this plot is the mercantile aristocracy of an insolent caste, which wants to assimi-late itself to royalty and to hoard all riches by forcing up the price of goods of prime necessity in order to satisfy its cupidity. Exterminate all these scoundrels; the Fatherland will be rich enough if it is left with the *sans-culottes* and their virtues. Legislators! Come to the aid of all unfor-tunate people. This is the call of nature; this is the vow of true patriots. Our heart is torn by the spectacle of public misery. Our intention is to raise men up again; we do not want a single unfortunate person in the Republic. Purify the Executive Council; expel a Gohier, a Garat, a Le Brun, etc.; renew the directory of the postal service and all corrupted administrations, etc.

A large number of people, the orator cries out, must bear this address to the Convention. What! Patriots are still sleeping and are busy with insignificant discussions while perfidious journals openly provoke the people! We will see whether our enemies will dare show themselves opposed to measures on which the happiness of a republic depends.

The President. The Society hears with the keenest satisfaction the accents of the most ardent patriotism; it will second your efforts with all its courage, for it has the same principles, and it has evinced the same opinion. Whatever the means and the efforts of our enemies, liberty will not perish because there will remain forever in the heart of Frenchmen this sentiment that insurrection is the ultimate reason of the people. (Applauded.)

3. Women in the Section de Montblanc Protest Their
   Exclusion from Meetings of the General Assembly

Source: A.N., F⁷ 4704, case of Fielval.

The testimony printed below is extracted from the dossier of
Pierre Fielval, accused by members of his Section of unpatriotic
behavior. It relates to the record of a complaint which Fielval
filed with the *commissaire de police* of the Section against irate
women who held him responsible for their exclusion from
Assembly meetings and who retaliated with harrassment and
threats.

Section de Montblanc.
Second year of the Republic, 1793, Thursday, May 30, 2 P.M.

Before us, Louis-François Beffara, *commissaire de police* in the Section de
Montblanc, Pierre Fielval appeared, citizen captain of the Ninth Company of the Section [de l'Homme] Armée, living on rue Taitbout,
Maison Descaussenac [?]. He stated that yesterday at ten o'clock, as he
left Section headquarters at the close of the General Assembly over
which he had just presided, he found himself assailed, attacked,
threatened, and insulted in the most outrageous fashion by some *citoyennes* who were gathered at the entrance to headquarters and who
alleged that it was on the basis of his motion that the Assembly ordered
that *citoyennes* could not be present at meetings due to a lack of space in
the hall. Among them was one *citoyenne* who said she was the wife of
Citizen La Croix, a carpenter on rue Lazare, opposite [rue] St. Georges,
[and] who approached him, saying he was a rogue and a scoundrel, and
the wife of Citizen Langlois, living on rue ———— [?] who was making
the same remarks. And both of them, among others, threatened to pull
off his epaulettes and even to hang him.

Concerning which facts, he felt he had an obligation to make the
present declaration before us, using the contents of which he files com-

plaint against the aforementioned *citoyennes,* noting that several citizens were witnesses to the aforementioned facts and are in a position to make their declarations concerning them.

The same day, at 6 P.M., before us, the *commissaire* named above, there appeared Pierre Diacon, lieutenant in the Ninth Company of the Section [de l'Homme] Armée, residing on rue LePeletier, who told us that last night, about 10:30, after the session was over, being on duty at the *corps de garde,* he saw several *citoyennes* who were assembled in front of the *corps de garde* and who were making a lot of noise, complaining that they were no longer able to enter the assembly hall. Several among them asked him whether he was a patriot, to which he replied that that wasn't their business, that he didn't have to give any accounting to them, that his civic behavior was known, and that they would do better to mind their households than to gather information on who was and who wasn't a patriot. Several of these *citoyennes,* while speaking to him, even exclaimed, "Yes, yes, this is a patriot." A minute later, as he wanted to leave in order to go eat, Citizen Prat told him that Captain Fielval was in danger and threatened. He sent him to remain there and lend him armed assistance, if necessary, which he did, and concerning which he made the present declaration. . . .

Charles Croüen, a carpenter, living on rue Taitbout, no. 18, also appeared. He declared that yesterday, while he was on guard at Section headquarters, about 10 P.M., he saw several *citoyennes* who were gathered in a crowd in front of the [illegible] [and] who were making a lot of noise and complaining that they were being excluded from the assemblies. There was a commotion, and at that moment the women ran over to the rue [Ste.] Catherine [?]; then it was said that they were running after Citizen Fielval, who had just come out, concerning which he makes the present declaration. . . .

4. Gorsas' Account of the Forcible Removal of the Girondin Deputies from the National Convention, May, 1793

Source: [A.-J. Gorsas], *Précis rapide des événements qui ont eu lieu à Paris dans les journées des 30 et 31 mai, premier et 2 juin 1793* (n.p., n.d.), B.N., Lb⁴¹ 666.

The first two documents in this chapter describe reactions of two men who were targets of politically radicalized women in May and June, 1793.

Gorsas was one of thirty-one proscribed Girondins forced out of the Convention by the victorious Montagnard faction, abetted by militants from the Commune and Paris Sections and members of the Society of Republican Revolutionary Women. In the excerpted pamphlet, Gorsas assumes that the women are led by radical Montagnards. His horror at their behavior is reminiscent of conservative deputies' reactions to the October women in 1789. For him, the women's activism is evidence of the collapse of the Revolution into anarchy.

. . . A muffled fermentation, moreover, prevails in Paris. Some women meet, undoubtedly excited by the furies; they are armed with pistols and daggers; they make declarations and rush to all the public places in the city, bearing before them the standard of license. In vain is this crime denounced to the Commune; in vain does one wish to escape dangerous consequences. Pache answers that there is nothing to fear. What, I say! These drunken bacchanalians have been received in the midst of the General Council; there they have been greeted, feted, and given the fraternal accolade.[1] And what do they want, what do they demand?

[1] The "drunken bacchanalians" are the members of the Society of Revolutionary Republican Women. [Translators' note.]

They want to "put an end to it"; they want to "purge the Convention, to make heads roll, and to get themselves drunk with blood." . . .

While these events took place [preparations for the sections to march to the Convention], the National Convention was engaged in the most distressing debates; it was besieged by a crowd of shameless men and women; [the Convention] deliberated amidst booing[2] and the most insulting provocations, and these boos and provocations were carried to such an extreme that many members of the Mountain believed, at least for political reasons, that they should rise up against these excesses. One of them even demanded that the Convention form itself into a Committee of the Whole. Finally, Lacroix, yielding to a movement he had wanted to withdraw from, wrote "No! the Convention is not free!" . . .

---

[2] Armed women held the deputies captive lest they display a prearranged signal; one of them [the deputies], pursued by five or six of these shrews, was forced to jump from a casement window.

5. Lacombe's Demand for the Replacement of Lafayette as French Chief of Staff

Source: Claire Lacombe, *Discours prononcé à la barre de l'Assemblée nationale, par Madame Lacombe, le 25 juillet 1792, l'an 4e, de la liberté* (Paris, n.d.), B.N., 8° Le[33] x (63).

In the following two documents, Claire Lacombe and Pauline Léon, presidents of the Society of Revolutionary Republican Women, offer brief accounts of their backgrounds and political careers.

Lacombe, who is knowledgeable about military policy and issues involving national leadership, presents the Legislative Assembly with a demand for Lafayette's removal. Interestingly, she sets herself apart from women who are mothers; they must still put their domestic responsibilities first.

———————————◆———————————

A Frenchwoman, an artist without a position: that's what I am. However, Legislators, what might be the object of my despair instead fills my soul with purest joy. Unable to make pecuniary sacrifices to aid my Fatherland, which you have declared in danger, I come to pay it homage with my person. Born with the courage of a Roman and with the hatred of tyrants, I would consider myself fortunate to contribute to their destruction. May the last despot perish! Intriguers, vile slaves of Nero and Caligula, may I be able to annihilate you all! And you, mothers of families, whom I would blame for abandoning your children to follow my example, while I do my duty combating the enemies of the Fatherland, you do yours instilling in your children the sentiments that all Frenchmen should have at birth—the love of liberty and the horror of despots. Never forget that without the virtues of Vesturia, Rome would have been deprived of the great Coriolanus.

Legislators, you have proclaimed the Fatherland in danger, but that is not enough; dismiss from office those who alone have created the danger and sworn the destruction of France. Can you leave in command of our armies the perfidious Cataline {Lafayette}, pardonable only in the eyes of those whose infamous projects he wished to serve? Why do you delay in flinging a decree of indictment at him? Are you waiting until the enemies, to whom every day he delivers our cities, arrive in the Senate to destroy it with hatchet and fire? You have only to maintain this guilty silence for a few days and you will soon see them in your midst. Legislators, there is still time; rise to your proper height; appoint leaders to whom we can give our confidence; speak a word, a single word, and the enemies will disappear.

Signed,
F. Lacombe

The President's Response.
Madame,

Made more for softening tyrants than for struggle against them, you offer to bear arms for liberty. The National Assembly applauds your patriotism and accords you the honors of the session.

6. Anne Pauline Léon, Femme Leclerc, Reconciles Her
   Political Behavior with Radical Revolutionary
   Principles and Policies

Source: A.N., F⁷ 4774⁹, dossier Leclerc.

Pauline Léon and her husband, the Enragé Théophile Leclerc,
were arrested on 14 Germinal, Year II [April 3, 1794]. Léon
made this statement in prison on July 4, 1794. She denied
questionable political affiliations and involvement in any crime
and reviewed the highlights of her revolutionary career.

———————————◆———————————

Précis of the revolutionary comportment of Anne Pauline Léon, Femme
Leclerc. Born in Paris on September 28, 1758, of Pierre-Paul Léon, a
manufacturer of chocolate, and Mathurine Télohan, his wife, I was left
at the time of the Revolution with my mother—a widow for the last
five years. I [had] to keep up her business and raise her family, composed
of five children, and consequently I was given bed and board with her.
That lasted until the time of my marriage, that is to say, until 29
Brumaire of the second republican year, when she turned over to me the
direction of her affairs, which forced me to be in attendance in the
house.

My father was a philosopher. He raised us following his principles,
and if his modest means did not permit him to give us a very distinguished education, at least he did not leave us with any prejudices.

On those memorable days when the Bastille was taken, and on the
following [days], I experienced the liveliest enthusiasm, and although I
was a woman, I did not remain idle. From morning till evening I could
be seen inciting citizens against the partisans of tyranny, [urging them]
to despise and brave aristocrats, barricading streets, and inciting the
cowardly to leave their homes to come to the aid of the Fatherland in
danger. The traitor Lafayette seemed suspect to me from the time he was
installed as general, and my suspicions were confirmed on October 5 and

6. Since that time I have sworn myself to eternal hatred of him, and I have used all possible means to unmask him.

In the month of February, 1791, I went with several citizens and patriots, my friends, to Fréron's house, where we broke and threw out of the windows the bust of Lafayette which was in the apartment. About that time I was introduced to the Société des Cordeliers, which I have been attending without interruption ever since then, and [to] the Fraternal Society of [the Section] de Mutius Scaevola.

The day of the tyrant's flight to Varennes, I raised my voice against this infamous treason. I and my mother and a friend were almost assassinated at the former Palais Royal by a group of bodyguards and *mouchards* of Lafayette. We owed our safety only to some *sans-culottes* who took the risk of defending us and who succeeded, by dint of their courage, in snatching us from the hands of these monsters.

On July 17 of this same year [1791] we went to the Champ de Mars to sign the petition. We almost lost our lives because of the fury of those among Lafayette's soldiers who had escaped the carnage. On returning home, we were insulted and mistreated by our neighbors, brought before our respective Sections, threatened with imprisonment, and, finally, drenched in abuses.

On August 10, 1792, after having spent part of the preceding night at the Section de la Fontaine de Grenelle, I went out the next morning, armed with my pike, into the ranks of the citizens of this Section to fight the tyrant and his satellites. Only after almost all these patriots implored me did I agree to surrender my arms to a *sans-culotte*. I did so, however, only after I admonished him to make good use of them in my place.

My signature is found at the bottom of a printed address which called for the death of Louis Capet, and on a large number of patriotic petitions.

All patriots are aware of my conduct on May 31 and of my actions both in forming the Société révolutionnaire, which I believed was appropriate for hastening this glorious era, and in directing its [the Society's] endeavors toward that end. Finally, everyone knows what my political views are. In the popular societies, under the gaze of an immense crowd, I manifested my love for the Fatherland, propagated the principles of a sweet equality, and supported the unity and indivisibility of the Republic. It is there that I vowed to execrate the scoundrels Roland and Brissot and the whole gang of federalists and where, finally, I undertook the defense of all persecuted patriots such as Robespierre, Marat, etc. In the Sections of the Faubourgs Saint Antoine and Saint Marceau, at the central club, in the presence of *commissaires* from all the

Sections and popular societies I preached, with all the energy I am capable of summoning up, the holy insurrection which, by delivering the Mountain from its shackles, necessarily would give birth to the Republican Constitution. On the Champs Elysées, in the presence of the people's representatives, and its magistrates, I urged citizens to fly to the defense of their Fatherland. Finally, in the heart of the National Convention, I expressed, on behalf of the *citoyennes* of my Section, their joy and satisfaction over the completion of the Constitution.

Since that time, having married a poor and persecuted patriot, and my husband having been called to the defense of the country, I bore this separation not only with resignation but with complete devotion. Circumstances at that time provided me with other distractions. I devoted myself altogether to the care of my household, and I set an example of the conjugal love and domestic virtues which are the foundation for love of the Fatherland.

At the beginning of Germinal (Year II), a natural sentiment and an irresistible one for young married persons led me to *La Fère* to embrace my husband one last time before he went off to fight the enemies of our Fatherland. To afford me this satisfaction, my mother took charge of the care of my household during the brief interval of my trip. It was in this town that my husband and I were arrested on 14 Germinal and by order of the Committee of General Security. Having arrived at the Luxembourg [prison] on the seventeenth, we have been waiting since then, with resignation, for justice to give us back our liberty, Fatherland, and family. I will only point out that we are absolutely ignorant of the reasons for our arrest. Free from crimes, we are [free] of fears. We have made all kinds of sacrifices for our Fatherland. We have served it out of regard for its needs and with the most complete disinterest. We are poor, indebted, and absolutely isolated from all those who are, or have been, public officials.

Statement made in the Luxembourg prison, 16 Messidor, Year Two of the Republic, One, Indivisible, and Indestructible,

[signed] A. P. Léon, Femme Leclerc

7. THE REGULATIONS OF THE SOCIETY OF REVOLUTIONARY REPUBLICAN WOMEN

Source: *Règlement de la Société des citoyennes républicaines révolutionnaires de Paris* (n.p., n.d.), in Bibliothèque historique de la Ville de Paris, 958939.

The Girondins accused the Revolutionary Republican Women of favoring anarchy, but within the club the members made serious efforts to conduct their affairs in an orderly fashion. They had their regulations printed, and therein they set down strict procedures for meetings, election of officers, membership, and correspondence and deputations.

———————

Convinced that there is no liberty without customs and principles, and that one must recognize one's social duties in order to fulfill one's domestic duties adequately, the Revolutionary Republican *citoyennes* have formed a Society to instruct themselves, to learn well the Constitution and laws of the Republic, to attend to public affairs, to succor suffering humanity, and to defend all human beings who become victims of any arbitrary acts whatever. They want to banish all selfishness, jealousies, rivalry, and envy and to make good their [Society's] name.

But besides the spirit and principle of a Society, there still must be a particular rule which lays down all the conditions of the Society; consequently they [the Revolutionary Republican *citoyennes*] have drawn up the following regulations:

Article I
The Society's purpose is to be armed to rush to the defense of the Fatherland; *citoyennes* are nonetheless free to arm themselves or not.

II
The Society shall have a President, a Vice-President, and four Secretaries, who will be changed on the first Sunday of every month; they

can be reelected only after two months. The functions of the President are to preside over the Society, to respond to deputations, and to assure that the regulations are observed.

III

The functions of the Secretaries are to maintain a register of all the deliberations of the Society and to keep up its correspondence under the President's direction; in addition to these regular functions they will keep a register of the members of the Society and the names of affiliated societies—a catalog of these will be exhibited in the meeting room.

IV

Two monitors will be appointed by acclamation. One will be at the entrance to the room to make all persons who enter show their cards, and the other will be in the meeting room to maintain order. They will be changed with the officers.

V

The President will wear the bonnet of liberty, and the two monitors will wear a ribbon of the nation on their left arm. When the President is unable to establish order with the bell, she will take off her bonnet; then all the *citoyennes* will rise and remain standing until she puts her bonnet on again.

VI

There will be a Treasurer and two Assistant Treasurers who will be responsible for one another. Their nominations will be made the second Sunday of the month, and they will remain in office for three months.

VII

The Treasurer will report every month to the administrative committee, and this committee will report to the Society. There will be no expenditures that the Society has not approved.

VIII

There will be an Archivist and an Assistant Archivist; they will be responsible for one another. Their functions are limited to putting the papers of the Society in the best order. They will retain their posts for three months. All the papers will be numbered. At the end of their tenure they will give to the administrative committee an account of the papers they have received; the committee will give them a receipt if they are in order, and if not, will make a report of it.

IX

There will be three committees: Administration, Relief, and Correspondence. Each committee will have twelve members, of whom six will leave at the end of three months and will be replaced by the Society.

X

All the elections, above mentioned, will be by roll-call vote, and the others, as for commissioners, will be made by the officers.

XI

The Society, considering it important to save the acts and proceedings of its sessions, has decreed that minutes be kept for all sessions and that they be signed by the President and at least two of the Secretaries.

XII

The Society, believing that people should join together only for mutual honor, support, and encouragement in virtue, has decreed that it will receive in its midst only those *citoyennes* of good habits; it has made this the most essential condition for admission and has resolved that the lack of good habits is one of the principal reasons for exclusion.

XIII

Citoyennes who seek admission to the Society are to be presented by one member and supported by two others. At the following meeting their names will be proclaimed and posted. They will be admitted if no one raises objections; if any objections are raised, their admission will be postponed. The committee of correspondence will listen to the various objections and present its report to the Society, which in its wisdom will judge the denunciations made by certain *citoyennes* who will be directed to sign them.

XIV

When the list of members-elect has been announced, posted, and put to a vote in the Society, the Secretaries will deliver a card to the person admitted, inscribing her on the register of the Society's members.

XV

All newly received *citoyennes* will be summoned by the President, in the name of the Society, to take the following oath: "I swear to live for the Republic or die for it; I promise to be faithful to the Rule of the Society as long as it exists."

XVI

Those *citoyennes* who are to take the oath will place themselves in the order in which they were called before the Secretaries' desk; then the President, in the name of the Society, will read them the formula of the oath while they hold up their right hands; at the end they will speak out, into the respectful silence which should prevail at that moment, "I swear it."

XVII

All packets sent to the Society are only to be opened by the President or, if she is absent, by her substitute, who can only be a former President or a Secretary then holding office.

XVIII

All correspondence will be signed by the President and the Secretaries with the seal of the Society, and the Committee of Correspondence is responsible for sending the decrees that the Society deems proper to be circulated to affiliated societies or any other places.

XIX

All the members of the Society make up a family of sisters, and since an arbitrary act against one of its members must attack the whole Society, the one who suffered the violation of the laws is urged to inform the Society, which will obtain justice for her.

XX

No member may borrow the card of anyone whatever, under penalty of exclusion from the Society for one month and even loss of her rights of entry if she repeats the violation.

XXI

No *citoyennes* may place themselves on the dais, not even those who left their place, unless they are called there by the President.

XXII

No collection will be made unless the Committee on Relief has reported on a request it received and has determined whether the petitioners have rights to the charity of the Society.

XXIII

No deputation can be admitted unless it has first shown its authorization to the President, who will sign it along with two of the Secretaries.

XXIV

Out of respect for the Societies represented by the deputations, they will be heard as soon as they are introduced and will be suitably seated opposite the President in a place always kept vacant. The monitors are charged not to allow members of the Society to occupy that place.

XXV

No one may occupy any seat unless she has been a member of the Society for at least three months; the monitors, who are not considered seated, are exempt from the above formalities.

XXVI

Believing that no member can be denied the right to speak and that young *citoyennes* could, with the best of intentions, compromise the Society with ill-considered motions, the Society decrees that one must be eighteen years old to be received as a member; however, mothers may bring children younger than eighteen, but they will have no right to deliberate.

XXVII

The Society, considering that at times some *citoyennes* would want to attend, although they were not members, decrees that a *citoyenne* requesting entry may be admitted if she is supported by two other members of the Society, provided no objections are raised.

The Society, having heard the above regulations, approved them on July 9, Year II of the Republic.

Signed:

Rousaud,　　　　President

Potheau

L. Monier

Dubreuil　　　}Secretaries

Pauline Léon

8. ACCOUNT OF A SESSION OF THE SOCIETY OF
   REVOLUTIONARY REPUBLICAN WOMEN

Source: Pierre Joseph Alexis Roussel, *Le Château des Tuileries,* 2
vols. (Paris: Legouge, 1802), vol. 2, pp. 34–46.

This derisive account of a session of the Society in the fall of
1793 appears to be based on notes taken by Roussel and his
English guest, Lord Bedford. It is the only full record we have of
a regular meeting of the Society.

———

. . . The session of this female society was held in a vaulted room,
formerly used as an ossuary. The president and the secretaries were
placed opposite the entrance. Two rows of benches on each side were for
the members of the Society; I counted sixty-seven of them. No galleries;
the curious placed themselves at the far end of the room and were
separated from the club members only by a simple breast-high bar.
When we came in, the session had just begun. Before describing it I will
say that some of these women covered their heads with red caps, in
particular the president and the secretaries. This grotesque spectacle
almost choked us, because we felt constrained not to let ourselves burst
out laughing. This session seemed so comical to us that we each made a
separate record of it when we left, while our memories were still filled
with these details. All I am doing is copying our notes.

Session of the Society of Women, Meeting in the Ossuary
of the Church of Saint-Eustache
Presidency of Citoyenne Lacombe
After the reading of the minutes and of the correspondence, the
president recalled that the order of the day concerned the utility of
women in a republican government, and she invited the sisters who had

worked on this subject to share their research with the Society. Sister Monic[5] was given the floor and read what follows:

> From the famous Deborah, who succeeded Moses and Joshua, to the two Frei sisters, who fought so valiantly in our republican armies, not a single century has passed which has not produced a woman warrior. See how Thomyris, queen of the Scythians, battles and conquers the great Cyrus; the Marullus girl chases the Turks from [Stylimène]. Catherine Lisse saves the city of Amiens; the wife of Dubarry defends Leucate against Henry III; Joan of Arc, who forced the English to flee before her, shamed them into raising the siege of Orléans, and the name of that city is added to hers.
>
> Without my having to cite for you the individual names of these courageous female warriors, which would only serve to throw into greater relief the timidity of our sex by these rare examples of the courage of a few of them, I will remind you of the virile and warriorlike vigor of that colony of Amazons whose existence has been cast into doubt because of people's jealousy of women; I will tell you danger didn't frighten these new Roman women, who cast themselves in the midst of the cutting edge of arms, justly avenging their late husbands; I will cite for you the women of Aquileia, who strung their defenders' bows and garbed their horses for battle; finally, I call your attention to the *citoyennes* of Lille, who, at this moment, are braving the rage of assailants and, while laughing, are defusing the bombs being cast into the city. What do all these examples prove, if not that women can form battalions, command armies, battle, and conquer as well as men? If any doubt remained, I would cite Panthee, Ingonde, Clotilde, Isabelle, Margueritte, etc., etc.
>
> But I will not stop here, and I will say to these men who think they are our masters: Who delivered Judea and Syria from the tyranny of Holofernes? Judith. To whom did Rome owe her liberty and the Republic? To two women. Who were those who gave the final lesson in courage to the Spartans? Mothers and wives, who, in

---

[5]*La femme Monic* at that time kept a small haberdashery shop, on the little street of Rempart, and today directs one of the taverns at the end of the Champs-Elysées. She served as spy for the Committee of Public Safety and director of the knitters at the Jacobins. Her speech, which we give, is not an invention; it had been given to her by the deputy Basire, who told it to me. We shall have occasion to speak again of this woman.

handing them their shields, said only these words: Return home borne upon your shield or bearing it.

I do not know why I am burying myself in the dust of history to search for traces of the courage and sacrifice of women, since we have them in our revolution and right before our eyes. In 1788, during the siege of the Palais, women exposed themselves to the brutality of soldiers hired by the court, in order to hail stones down upon them. At the storming of the Bastille, women familiar only with fireworks exposed themselves to cannon and musket fire on the ramparts to bring ammunition to the assailants. It was a battalion of women, commanded by the brave Reine Audu, who went to seek the despot at Versailles and led him triumphantly back to Paris, after having battled the arms of the *gardes-du-corps* and made them put them down. In spite of the modesty of our president, I will say that on August 10 she marched valiantly against the château, at the head of a corps of Fédérés; she still bears the marks of that day.[6]

If women are suited for combat, they are no less suited for government. How many of them have governed with glory! My only problem is how to select examples. Theodelinda, queen of Lombardy, brought down Agilulf and extinguished the wars of religion which were blazing in her territories. Everyone knows that Semiramis was a dove in the cabinet and an eagle in the field. Isabelle of Spain governed with glory. Here again is a woman who supported the discovery of the New World. In our times Catherine of Russia achieved what Peter only outlined. But I will go further still and maintain that when the reins of government are held by men, women alone move and direct them. Exceptions are rarer than examples. Augustus proposed nothing to the Roman Senate without consulting Livia. Without searching the histories of other people, let us keep to ours. *La Belle Ferronnière* directed Francis I, Henry II. Charles IX and Henry III ruled only by the counsels of Catherine of Medici; the fair Gabrielle was behind Henry IV's mistakes; Madame de Pompadour governed the governor of France; finally, the courtesan Dubarry, who was herself a doll, made a

---

[6]This fact is true. Mademoiselle Lacombe, a very pretty girl, abandoned herself to all the excesses of the revolution; she left the theater, came to Paris, got to know the most hotheaded patriots, and lived with one of them. On August 10 she appeared as an Amazon and demanded from Westerman that he allow her to serve; she was put at the head of some men, and she received a dagger wound. During the revolution, she could be seen everywhere at the Assembly and at the Jacobins. She founded and directed the female Society in question.

marionette out of Louis XV. Thus one can prove that women have always directed governments. Thus one can conclude that they deserve to govern. I would almost say, better than men. Under the despotism of kings these reflections are not permitted, but in a republican regime it is a different story. I will not draw any further conclusions; I ask that the Society in its wisdom consider what rank women should have in a republic, and whether they should still be excluded from all positions and from administration.

This discourse, often interrupted, was crowned, when it was over, by violent applause. Nothing seemed more comical to us than to hear passages of history declaimed by a woman who murdered the language with an assurance difficult to describe. The applause was followed by a long period of murmuring through which one could make out a few words and proposals, each one more ridiculous than the last. One called for the raising of an army of 30,000 women to go into battle against enemies, with all prostitutes being forced to march. Another proposed that women be admitted into all branches of administration. Finally, after a half-hour of debate, all proposals were condensed into a petition to present to the Convention, calling for a decree obliging women to wear the national cockade. We were going to leave when we heard one of the club members ask for the floor, to make a new proposal. Let us remain, Lord Bedford said to me, I am too much amused to leave . . . [in text]. Olympe de Gouges spoke as follows: "While admiring what sister Monic has just said, I believe she has left out essential proposals that I am merely going to point out to you. Not only are empires governed through women's ascendancy, but one can maintain, without being refuted, that they are the force behind everything. Who fuels or extinguishes the warrior's courage? Regard Omphale, Delilah, Armida. If the Supreme Being created the soul of man, he left to woman the task of animating it. Watch the young girl dictating to her lover whatever laws please her. At her will, she makes of him a hero or a coward, a criminal or a virtuous man. Isolated, man is our slave; it is only when reunited in a mass that they overwhelm us in their pride. The greatest fault of our sex has been to submit to this unsuitable custom which puts man in the ascendancy; but let us profit from the difference in dress to arrive at some distinction. Here is what I have thought up: If there are no longer any processions, there will have to be public festivals; confide the direction and regulation of them to us. A lovely woman at the head of a crowd of citizens, charged, for example, with inciting young men to fly to the defense of the Fatherland, would say to one of them: Depart, and upon your return, the hand of your mistress will be the reward for your exploits. Whoever hesitates to fight the enemy will hear her voice speaking these words to him: Stay, you cowardly soul; but never count on being united with your lover; she has sworn to reject the desires of a man who is useless to his country. The art we possess to move the souls of men would produce the salutary effect of enflaming all spirits. Nothing can resist our seductive organ. The warrior would be happy to receive laurels from the hand of beauty; young husbands would believe their chains more fitting if they were forged by the hand of a woman. Let us request the direction of festivals and marriages, and that we be the only ones charged with the education of youth. This is all the more easily done, as the priests, whose privilege this used to be (for reasons I cannot fathom), are no longer here. It is up to us to replace them, and to found the religion of the true sans-culottes."

This last proposition occasioned bursts of laughter. Discussion of these interesting matters was postponed until another session, and we left with the crowd.

The Englishman said to me: —Confess that these extravagances are very amusing. —I confess, but when I think about it, the delirium of these women frightens me. If their brains are overheated, you know the obstinacy of this sex; they are capable of committing certain excesses.

—Your nation possesses the remedy: the weapon of ridicule and banter, which it knows so well how to wield, will destroy these comical pretentions. Among the follies we have just heard, one can find nothing based in reason. It is, of course, certain that our customs give women much influence over the State. It cannot be denied that they are the most active force in society, the common center to which all the passions of men are attracted, and that they hold together honor, interest, love, taste, and opinion. It is thus a manifest contradiction not to count them for anything in our code of laws. —I grant this contradiction; but you will also admit that it is fully justified by this universal and consequently dangerous ascendancy that you recognize in the sex.

—That is true. However it seems to me that instead of forgetting women in their households, one could use them. For example, if they were made the reward for great actions, I do not think there would be any effort men would not make to merit their esteem and their favors.

—I think as you do. But we are old stick-in-the-muds, and we forget them in our new laws, only because the first lawgivers of nations have not mentioned them, and because habit, stronger than reason, makes innovations too difficult in this delicate area. Besides, who is the man bold enough to innovate in this matter?

—Of course, your revolution changes the object of political speculations.

—It is precisely this upheaval which will prevent the true philosopher from casting out a new subject of discord, by presenting some project to give women credit in government. They are strong enough with their ascendancy over us. Let us leave them with the empire of grace and beauty.

9. PETITION FROM THE REVOLUTIONARY REPUBLICAN
   WOMEN TO THE NATIONAL CONVENTION ON THE
   LEADERSHIP OF THE ARMIES AND THE LAW OF SUSPECTS

Source: Champion, *Pétition des citoyennes républicaines révolutionnaires lue à la barre de la Convention nationale* (n.p., n.d.), in B.N., Lb[40] 2412.

On July 15, 1793, Charlotte Corday stabbed Marat, hoping to spare France from the political terror he advocated in his journal. Her act alerted the Revolutionary Republican Women to the omnipresent danger from Girondins and other moderates; the women made Corday the symbol of moderation and the target of their wrath. Throughout the summer of 1793, Revolutionary Republican Women campaigned actively for the punishment of political enemies, especially suspected hoarders and speculators.

By August even the Montagnards seemed too lenient to defend the nation, and the women moved into closer association with the Enragés—Roux, Varlet, and Leclerc. In this address Champion, the president of the Society, adopts Leclerc's ideas on national defense and insists on rigorous enforcement of the Law of Suspects.

Legislators:

Justly indignant at the numerous lies coming from the Ministry, notably from the Ministry of the Interior, whose minister got away with abandoning his post by resigning from it, we come to demand that you execute the constitutional laws; we were not the first to accept this Constitution just to have anarchy and the reign of intriguers continue without end. The calculated war has lasted long enough: it is time at last that the children of liberty be sacrificed for their Fatherland and not to the ambition and pride of a pile of scoundrels who lead our armies. Show by dismissing all nobles that their defenders are not among you; above

all, hasten to prove to all of France that the envoys of a great people have
not been made to come at great expense from all corners of the republic
simply to enjoy a pathetic scene at the Champ de Mars. Show us that
this Constitution, which we believed we should accept, exists and
should make for our happiness; for it is not sufficient to tell people that
their happiness is in the offing—they must experience its effects, and
the experience of four years of misfortune has taught people to distrust
the beautiful promises that are ceaselessly being made. People are indignant that men gorged on their gold and fattened on the purest of
their blood preach sobriety and patience to them.

Believe us, Legislators, four years of misfortunes have taught us
enough to know how to discern ambition even under the mask of
patriotism; we no longer believe in the virtue of these men who are
reduced to praising themselves; finally, more than words are necessary if
we are to believe that ambition does not rule your committees; organize
the government according to the Constitution. In vain are we told that
France will be lost by this measure; she could not be lost if responsibility
were no longer an empty word, or if the lying minister knew for certain
that he would carry his head to the scaffold. Finally, we see only the loss
of intriguers in a country where the laws are strictly observed. Do you
want us to believe that the enemies of the Fatherland have no obliging
defenders in your midst? Ruin all the nobles without exception; if there
are any of good faith among them, they will give proof of it by volun-
tarily sacrificing themselves to the good fortune of their Fatherland; do
not fear to disorganize the army; the more talent a general has, the worse
his intentions, and the more urgent it is to replace him; do not do
injustice to patriots by believing there are no men among them worthy
of commanding our armies; take some of these brave soldiers whose
talent and merit have been sacrificed to the ambition and pride of the
formerly privileged caste.

If under the rule of despotism crime obtains preference, virtues
should have it under the rule of liberty. You have passed a decree under
which all suspects are to be arrested, but I ask you—isn't this law
ridiculous when it is the suspects themselves who are to execute it? Oh,
Legislators, thus are the people toyed with; see this equality which was
to have been the foundation of their happiness; there is the recompense
for the incalculable troubles they have so patiently suffered. No, it will
not be said that the people, reduced to despair, were obliged to do
justice themselves; you are going to give it to them by ruining all guilty
administrators and by creating extraordinary tribunals in sufficient
number so that patriots will say, as they leave for the front: "We are

calm about the fate of our wives and children; we have seen all internal conspirators perish under the sword of the law." Decree these great measures and the general mobilization—you will have saved the Fatherland.

10. LECLERC'S EXHORTATION TO THE REVOLUTIONARY
    REPUBLICAN WOMEN ON THE ARMÉE RÉVOLUTIONNAIRE

Source: Théophile Leclerc, *L'Ami du peuple,* no. VII (August 4, 1793), in B.N., Lc² 704.

Throughout August the Enragé Théophile Leclerc, editor of the radical *L'Ami du peuple,* called attention to activities of the Revolutionary Republican Women and solicited their support for an *armée révolutionnaire* to arrest former nobles, priests, magistrates, and speculators. Note that Leclerc implies that the women have a much broader political role than the *citoyennes* of the Section des Droits de l'homme assigned them in the fall (see document 11, this chapter).

. . . It is your special duty to warn of [the ambitions of hoarders and aristocrats], Republican Revolutionary Women, generous women truly above all praise for the courage and energy you have developed; your sex, gifted with a much greater sensibility than ours, will feel more vividly the misfortunes of our country, and your tender solicitude for the fate of your husbands, brothers, and children will make you adopt this infallible measure for public safety. [You are] inaccessible to outside influences, as there are among you neither places to give nor receive; a base interest has not suffocated in your souls the sentiments of nature; your spirit is hers, and believe me, it well deserves the academic phrases of all our erudite men. Go—by your example and your speech awaken republican energy and reanimate patriotism in lukewarm hearts! Yours is the task of ringing the tocsin of liberty! Time is short, the peril extreme! You have deserved first place, fly, glory awaits you! . . .

11. A LAUDATORY ADDRESS TO THE REVOLUTIONARY REPUBLICAN WOMEN

Source: *Discours prononcé à la Société des citoyennes républicaines révolutionnaires, par les citoyennes de la Section des Droits de l'homme, en lui donnant un guidon sur lequel est la Déclaration des droits de l'homme* (n.p., n.d.), in B.N., Lb^{40} 2411.

This speech was made as the *citoyennes* of the Section des Droits de l'homme presented a martial standard to the Society of Revolutionary Republican Women.

———————

Your Society is one of the elements of society, and it is not the least essential; liberty finds a new school here; mothers, wives, and children come here to be instructed and to be inspired together to practice social virtues.

You have broken one of the links in the chain of prejudices; for you that prejudice no longer exists which made passive and isolated beings out of half the individuals by relegating women to the confined sphere of their households.

You want to keep your place in the social order; neutrality offends and humiliates you. In vain they try to distract you from the great interests of the country which have moved your souls, and henceforth you will contribute to the common interest.

Public spirit will be more fully felt, and good manners can be reborn, if the wives of *sans-culottes,* desirous of knowing their duties well in order to fulfill them better, give to the little mistresses the example of an association of which the salutary aim is vigilance and instruction.

And why should women, gifted with the faculty of feeling and explaining their thoughts, see themselves excluded from public affairs?

The Declaration of Rights is common to both sexes, and the difference consists in duties; there are public ones and private ones. Men particularly are called to fulfill the former; nature herself indicates the preference—she has imparted to them a robust constitution, strong organs, [and] all the means able to sustain laborious work. Whether in the armies or the Senate or public assemblies, they occupy such positions preferentially; reason, valuing convenience, must yield to this.

Women, on the contrary, have as their first obligation private duties; the sweet functions of wives and mothers are entrusted to them, a thousand details carry them away and consume a great part of their time, and their leisure is less frequent; nevertheless, it is possible to reconcile what nature imperiously requires with what love of the public good commands. After they have attended to their indispensable occupations, there are still some moments of leisure, and *les femmes citoyennes* in the fraternal societies who consecrate them to surveillance and to instruction have the sweet satisfaction of seeing themselves doubly useful.

Citoyennes, the clamors of petty spirits whom novelties astonish, the buzzings of the envious, already want to put shackles on your institution; answer with scorn, and courageously pursue your task; liberty smiles on your laudable aspirations and understands them as the most favorable omen. Already she sees you under her banner propagating her principles. Your apostolic missions prepared the memorable revolution of May 31;[1] in the midst of this last triumph, [you were] vigilant sentinels, stationed at important posts—you occupied them with firmness and intrepidity. Your mission was delicate; there were certain proprieties to observe, and your zeal, which knew how to restrain itself within just measures, facilitated our success. Courage! Perseverance, brave Republican women! Make your patriotic actions more frequent!

May this standard guide your steps everywhere egotism and indifference carry off the citizens of the Fatherland; carry in your deputations this expressive emblem of equality; let the eye of its enemies be often struck by it. Under its beneficent shadow come all of you to marshal yourselves for public ceremonies; at the first signal of danger, let this revolutionary standard mingle with the tricolor flags; let it lead to victory devoted Republican women who strip off the weakness of their sex before the obvious perils the country. Finally, place it on its altar, and there, taking the Creator of Liberty as witness of your prowess, swear respect to good laws in the outpouring of the most fraternal union; [swear] implacable hatred of tyrants; swear also to raise your children in the principles of liberty and equality and to teach them early that without love of the Fatherland there is for them no virtue and no prosperity.

[1]"May 31" is a reference to the ouster of the Girondins from the Convention. [Translators' note.]

12. Claire Lacombe's Associates in the Société des Citoyennes Républicaines Révolutionnaires Testify Against Her

Source: A.N., F⁷ 4756, dossier 2 (Claire Lacombe).

As the Jacobins consolidated power, the Revolutionary Republican Women became hopelessly divided. Their more moderate members sided with the Jacobins and disassociated themselves from the more militant members like Claire Lacombe and Pauline Léon, who decried the tyranny and hypocrisy of Jacobins. In these testimonials Lacombe's associates accuse her of disloyalty to the Jacobins.

———————————————

Ninth Prairial, Year Two
Memorandum by Citoyenne Jobé, in the month of August, 1793.

The person cited, Citoyenne Lacombe, said, at the speaker's rostrum during the Citoyennes révolutionnaires' meeting at the Ossuary, "You are infatuated with and enthusiastic about Robespierre, whom I regard as only an ordinary citizen." When she learned that this had reached the ears of good patriots, she denied this fact, and at the following meeting she used her general staff, composed of several women [who] supported her, as usual, and who were deployed throughout the room, in order to put pressure on the Society. Citoyenne Jobé was asked to sign and said she didn't know how to write.

Another memorandum by Citoyennes Lemoce and Hérouart, concerning the decree of the National Convention, which declared the Republic revolutionary until the peace: The aforementioned Lacombe, cited above, made the following remarks at the aforementioned speaker's rostrum: "This decree was good only for getting the people to revolt incessantly [and] for driving them to bloodshed and pillage and undoubtedly leading them to make a second assault on the prisons, renewing horrors already committed there. When there were laws, they should be followed, and promptly executed."

[signed] Lemoce, Hérouart

At the same speaker's rostrum, Citoyenne Lemoce heard the afore-mentioned Lacombe disapprove of the victories we were scoring over the Lyons rebels at the time of the commune's revolt, saying that French blood had been spilled by the French and Pavie [illegible] to discourage the people—a heart-rending and terrible tableau of the death of inno-cent people during this siege. In imitation of Hébert, nicknamed Père Duchêne, she made some very energetic sallies against the merchants of Paris, saying that the grave diggers and coffin makers would be very busy.

[signed] Lemoce

Again, Citoyennes Lemoce and Hérouart knew that the aforemen-tioned Lacombe kept at her home one Clair d'Oze, known as Leclerc, a known intriguer who wanted to have it believed that he was being pursued by the Commission of Twelve, but rather [he] was suspected of being one of its principal agents. Moreover, the aforementioned La-combe has shown how immoral this man was by maintaining before the Jacobins as well as [before] the electors, and at the rostrum of the Citoyennes républicaines that she had never kept any man at her house, that is to say, for the last eighteen months, not even Leclerc. However, she acknowledged this when she was accused by Léon, afterwards Le-clerc's wife, and this was in front of the whole Society, of actually having slept with the latter [Leclerc].

[signed] Lemoce, Hérouart

The aforementioned Lacombe, returning from a visit she had made to the Jacobins, complained bitterly about the little success she had had and about the indifference with which she had been greeted. To this the named *citoyenne* Plébmy answered, "And what the devil were you doing at your fucking Jacobins?" This indecent language was the occasion for considerable tumult in the Société des Citoyennes, and decided Ci-toyenne Hérouart to call for her expulsion, but no action was taken on her motion.

[signed] Lemoce

One day, the same (Lacombe) told Citoyenne Lemoce that she often went to the Committee of General Security and that the members of the

Committee asked her how many *citoyennes* were members of the Society of Republican Women. She answered that there were three to four thousand. Lemoce asked her why she had lied so impudently, because she was one of the most recently accepted into the society, [and] her number was only 170, or something like that. "Good," answered Lacombe, "we must make those white beaks grow pale and tremble."

[signed] Lemoce

The request by the Sections of Paris for the National Convention to take the necessary measures to assure subsistence to this Commune gave rise to a discourse delivered by Barère, representative of the people, on behalf of the Committee of Public Safety, in which it was shown that there still existed intriguers and new Cordays who were using all possible means to sow discontent among the people and drive them to fear famine. These words and this designation greatly annoyed Citoyenne Lacombe. She insinuated to other *citoyennes* that it might be they whom the Committee was designating as new Cordays; she persuaded them to appoint a deputation to go to the aforementioned Committee to question it about this.

The aforementioned Lacombe, Citoyenne Lemoce, and two other *citoyennes* were appointed for this mission. They went to the Committee of Public Safety. Citizen Robespierre assured them that as this applied only to bad *citoyennes,* the Committee had not at all meant to single out their Society in particular, and they left, satisfied with their mission.

Citoyenne Lemoce, having seen the members of the Committee of Public Safety only at the speaker's rostrum at the Convention and at the Jacobins, found them fatter [looking] in the Committee where she had just seen them; she communicated this reflection to the named Lacombe without pointing out that in an immense room like that at the Convention the more distant observation point necessarily would make objects appear smaller. Shortly afterwards, the aforementioned Citoyenne Lemoce did reason in this manner but the aforementioned Lacombe had already answered her, "Eh! It's since these Gentlemen have been courting deputies that they've gotten fat."

Citoyenne Lemoce pretended not to understand a thing and answered, "Undoubtedly, because the country air is healthier and the food is fresher; it is not surprising that they are heftier."

"Good," Lacombe replied. "You do not seem to understand that it is about the *Bourse* that I'm speaking." "But," said Citoyenne Lemoce, "Robespierre has never been there." "Oh! as for him, he is too cowardly and too scared for his life. Did you notice how pale he was when I spoke to him? Fear was painted on his face."

"My word!" Citoyenne Lemoce replied, "if such a thing is true, it doesn't do you any honor; and as for the cowardice you accuse him of, I am convinced that is not the case, and that if he doesn't leave on mission, his usefulness in the midst of the Convention is the only reason."

These answers shut her up.

[signed] Lemoce

Names of the members of the aforementioned Lacombe's General Staff:

Fleury	Barré
Dubois[1]	Two cake sellers from Nanterre
Mounier	Pléby
Martin	Captains, and others whose names escaped her

The aforementioned Léon, wife of Leclerc, both of whom are mentioned in the interrogations, proposed to the Society of Republican Women that the forty-eight Sections of Paris must be solicited to ask for new elections to the Convention; that it had been for long enough now that its members had been lagging in their seats; and that, as Jean-Jacques Rousseau said, the prolongation of power was often the tomb of liberty. Undoubtedly, Rousseau had not meant to speak of a time of revolution.

[signed] Lemoce

[1]The aforementioned Dubois is the same one who said, about a week before the appointment [?] of Collot d'Herbois, that they were working on establishing a case against Robespierre.

[signed] Lemoce

13. THE JACOBINS DENOUNCE THE SOCIETY OF
REVOLUTIONARY REPUBLICAN WOMEN

Source: F.-A. Aulard, *La Société des Jacobins: Recueil de documents
pour l'histoire du Club des Jacobins de Paris,* vol. V, pp. 406–9.

The following two descriptions of a meeting of the Jacobin
Society on September 16, 1793, both document an irreparable
split between the Society of Revolutionary Republican Women
and the Jacobins. In these minutes the Jacobins expose Claire
Lacombe's association with the Enragé Leclerc as well as the
Society women's scornful treatment of Robespierre and in
general the provocative and incendiary behavior of women in
the Sections. They propose that Lacombe be apprehended for
questioning by the Committee of General Security and that
local authorities in Paris arrange for the arrest of other suspect
women.

———————

Session of Monday, September 16, 1793
Léonard Bourdon as President
(*A secretary* announces that the Society of Revolutionary Women took
the side of Leclerc, friend of Jacques Roux; Citoyenne Lacombe, President of this Society, wrote to Citoyenne Govin, Leclerc's denouncer, to
summon her to come to explain her conduct. *Chabot* declares that
Citoyenne Lacombe came to pester him in order to beg him to take
action before the Committee of General Security to obtain the release of
Monsieur de Rey, former Mayor of Toulouse, among the most suspect
aristocrats. *Basire* reports that a deputation from the Society of Revolutionary Women went before the Committee of General Security to
reclaim the liberty of Semandy, detained at Saint-Pélagie. On the
denunciation of the deputies from the primary assemblies of Bouches-
du-Rhône, the speaker told them it was impossible to give them satis-

faction. With respect to this issue they went to the home of Moyse Bayle, who gave them the same answer as Basire. Basire asserts, as Chabot already had, that these women spoke with scorn of "Monsieur Robespierre, who dared to treat them as counterrevolutionaries.")

A citizen begins by attributing to women all the disorders which have occurred in Paris. The galleries complain, but he ends by asking for the arrest of *muscadines* as well as *muscadins*. The entire Society applauds.

Taschereau says that Citoyenne Lacombe meddles everywhere; at an assembly where the speaker was present, she asked first for the constitution, the whole constitution, only the constitution, and you will note in passing this hypocritical and Feuillant language; after that she wanted to sap the foundation of the constitution and overturn all kinds of constituted authorities.

N . . . —The woman who is denounced before you is very dangerous in that she is very eloquent; she speaks well at first and then attacks the constituted authorities. In a speech I heard she fired a red-hot broadside into the Jacobins and the Convention.

A citizen who read today's issue of Leclerc [his journal] cites a passage he believes merits the severest punishment. Leclerc says that if they wanted to arrest him, he would stab both the person who issued the arrest warrant and the person who executed it. Durosoy and Royou did not use a different language when they paid with their heads the penalty of their madness and their villainy.

Citoyenne Lacombe appears at this point in one of the galleries and seems to be asking for the floor. The tumult and the disorder become so great that the President dons his hat; it is only at the end of a considerable period that calm returns.

The President points out to her that this is how she provides proof for the declarations that have just been made against her, and that a real crime, when patriotism is in question, is to cause disorder or to prolong it in an assembly of people who need to deliberate calmly concerning the interests of the people. These two propositions are put to the vote: (1) to write to the Revolutionary Women to engage them to rid themselves by a purifying vote of the suspect women who control the Society; (2) to send [word] to the Committee of General Security to commit it to having suspect women arrested. (Decided unanimously.) This amendment is made: that Citoyenne Lacombe be taken immediately before the Committee of General Security. (There is applause.) There is also [an amendment] to ask the Committee for Leclerc's arrest.

CHABOT. You cannot indict just any citizen before the Committee of

General Security, but you may ask the Committee of General Security to summon the Lacombe woman, because I do not have any doubt that she is the instrument of counterrevolution.

BASIRE. To propose that the Committee of General Security arrest suspect women is to fall short of one's objective, because in a huge city like Paris it is very difficult for the Committee to discover their residence and very easy for the latter to get away. But the Society will do better to write to all the revolutionary committees of Sections which have a better knowledge of the suspect women in their arrondissements and which will have them arrested with greater certainty and ease.

RENAUDIN. That would be useless on the Society's part. It is better for the Committee of General Security to write to all the revolutionary committees, engaging them to take this measure on its behalf; the committees will not refuse.

DESFIEUX. The measure you took with Custine serves you perfectly. I ask that you use it. Leclerc is a counterrevolutionary; you want to arrest him as well as the Lacombe woman; send a deputation of members from your midst. Let the Committee of General Security, when it has all these individuals arrested, have seals placed on the papers of both, where, I have no doubt, proofs of counterrevolution will be found.

CHABOT. This motion is insidious, because if Lacombe happened to deny everything she told me, that would be the most certain way of justifying herself; but I have proofs and witnesses that she spoke to me in this language; she will not deny it; and if she admits it, one can, on that very point, convict her of counterrevolution.

They accuse us, these counterrevolutionary women, of having oppressed the people and sworn to thwart the nation's interest. Have we become wealthier since this period?

I will cite facts against the Revolutionary Women, against Lacombe. Let them cite them against me. Doubtless they have the right to accuse me, but this must be done only on legitimate grounds.

A citizen denounces the note taker from the *Journal de la Montagne* as living regularly with Leclerc. He asks that these relations be clarified. (There is applause.)

DESFIEUX. I have just been told, as I came into the room, that Citoyenne Lacombe asked for me. I declare that I have not had any kind of relation with her whatever; I have never spoken with her except in public places. Likewise, I have no kind of relations with Leclerc, Jacques Roux, or other denounced persons who have just been discussed. One need only read Leclerc's issues to convince oneself; I am denounced there, insulted; but such acts do me honor, and the only shame that could fall upon me would be to be praised by such a man.

(. . . Various denunciations are made against the editor of the *Journal de la Montagne*. Committed to the *comité de présentation* to rule concerning all these facts.

(Desfieux reproduces the denunciation made concerning the liaison of the notetaker from the *Journal de la Montagne* with Leclerc. He asks that it be committed to the *comité de présentation*.)

The session was adjourned at ten o'clock.

14. CITOYENNE LACOMBE'S REPORT TO THE SOCIETY OF
    REVOLUTIONARY REPUBLICAN WOMEN CONCERNING
    WHAT TOOK PLACE SEPTEMBER 16 AT THE JACOBIN
    SOCIETY

Source: *Rapport fait par la Citoyenne Lacombe à la Société des
républicaines révolutionaires [sic] de ce qui s'est passé le 16 septembre à
la Société des Jacobins concernant celle des Républicaines révolutionaires
[sic], séante à S. Eustache; et les dénonciations faites contre la
Citoyenne Lacombe personnellement* (n.p., n.d.), in B.N., 4° Fm
35160.

In this pamphlet, an account of the meeting of the Jacobin
Society on September 16, 1793, Lacombe presents her own
version of the reactions and reprisals which the Society's radical
democratic activities provoked from Jacobins and
Robespierrists—revolutionary leaders who, only a few months
earlier, had offered the Society's members a meeting hall,
welcomed their deputations, and endorsed their policies on
terror and subsistence. In September, when members were
acting independently and autonomously to support these same
policies, the Jacobins hesitated to cast aspersions on the market
women, food suppliers to Paris. Rather than confronting the
Society with their dilemma, they instead tried to discredit its
members with chauvinistic and paternalistic polemic.

———————————

I transport my readers to the Jacobins' meeting hall, and I begin. A
secretary speaks: The Society of Revolutionary Republican Women has
always given evidence of a first-rate patriotism, and you gave it all due
credit. However, just today it faltered, removing a good republican
woman, Citoyenne Gobin, from its membership list because she in-
vested her full energy in denouncing the man named Leclerc.

I answer that what the secretary alleges is false because he has the letter which the president wrote to Citoyenne Gobin in conformity with the will of the Society [and] which conveyed not that she was stricken [from the membership list] but that she would have to provide the Society with the proofs she had of charges made against Citizen Leclerc, so that the latter could be prosecuted as a counterrevolutionary. If she failed to produce the proofs of what she alleged, she would be removed from the Society and billed everywhere as a calumniator. And so, to prove that she was not one at all, she had us denounced before the Jacobin Society.

Chabot: ". . . [in text] This is the moment to tell the whole truth about these allegedly revolutionary women. I'm going to lay bare for you the intrigues that stir them up, and I promise you'll be shocked. I know what risks you run when you embitter a woman, and all the more so when you embitter a large number of them, but I'm not afraid of their intrigue or their remarks or their threats.

A few days ago I was summoned by the head of these women, Citoyenne Lacombe, who asked me what we had in mind for the former Mayor of Toulouse. I answered that I was shocked that she would petition on behalf of a former noble, a man who had had patriots thrown into prison. She retorted that he gave bread to the poor. Ah, I replied—but that's how counterrevolution is hatched. Finally, she threatened me with the full censorship of the Revolutionary Women if I, along with the Committee of General Security, didn't order his release. I admit that I let out a swear word, and I left.

The next day she appeared at my house again to repeat what she said the day before, the same thing. Madame Lacombe—I just can't consider her a *citoyenne*—confessed to me that she wasn't so much concerned about Monsieur de Ray [the Mayor of Toulouse] as about his nephew. I—who am accused of allowing myself to be led about by women—told her: "I will never do for them [women] what men make you do, and all the women in the world will never get me to do anything but what I want to do for the Republic." Madame Lacombe then treated me to the most reactionary [Feuillant] remarks. She claimed that one didn't keep men in prison like that; that Revolution or no Revolution, they had to be questioned within twenty-four hours, released if they were innocent, and sent to the guillotine at once if they were guilty—in short, all the remarks that you hear aristocrats mouthing all the time when we arrest one of their friends. It's because I like women that I don't want them to be forming a body apart and calumniating even virtue. They've dared attack Robespierre, calling him Monsieur Robespierre [aristocratic form]. I ask that you take forceful measures against the Revolutionary

Women to check this crazy mania that's seized them. I ask that they purge themselves of all the schemers they're protecting in their midst and that they be mandated by letter to do it."

I answered the most patriotic Monsieur Chabot. First of all it is true that I had him called out of the Jacobins on Friday, the thirteenth of this month. Here is the speech I held forth with; it is a bit different from the one which he put into my mouth.

"Chabot, I am here to ask you to do a favor to yourself, to yourself . . . [in text], not me. What's at issue is the Mayor of Toulouse, whom you removed from office three months ago along with two administrators. I have learned that these latter two have been ordered back in, and as the Mayor was removed on the same grounds, I was surprised to learn that this was a victim whom you reserved the right to sacrifice. Therefore, I am here to ask you, for yourself, to give him the same justice that his colleagues obtained. Either he is guilty along with them, or, along with them, he is innocent."

"He is guilty," Chabot answered. "He had patriots imprisoned, seventeen of them in Toulouse." "I will not believe it," I said, "until you give me palpable proofs." "Besides," he said, "he is rich enough to live in Paris." "I know," I told him, "that his having a fortune is charged against him as a crime, but it is true nonetheless that he has used it only to succor the unfortunate since the Revolution. He is cherished by all the people of Toulouse. That is how the aristocrats behave to deceive the people. They do them good."

"Besides," he retorted, raising his voice, "he is a nobleman." "There is the best proof you could give me of his innocence," I told him, "because as he was not removed on account of his nobility, you are making a big war horse out of him. I say to you, as a true Republican Woman, that if you do not give him the justice that is due him, I will go to the bar of the National Convention to obtain it for him."

I do not know what Monsieur Chabot calls his curse word. I know that as I spoke my last [word], he turned on his heel.

The next day I went to his house to say that I was not there to pay court to him—as I didn't do that for anyone—but to ask him whether he was better disposed than the day before to give justice to the Mayor of Toulouse. He told me that this Mayor was a counterrevolutionary. "Well, you must prove it, and have him guillotined." Trying to dodge the question, he told me that we were a Society of women who allowed ourselves to be led around. I told him: "Chabot, neither cajolery nor *assignats* have tempted the Revolutionary Women, and besides, I'm telling you I know the Mayor of Toulouse only indirectly. I'm taking an interest in him only because I have inside knowledge of his innocence. I know, having collected information from the best patriots of Toulouse, that his only crime was to have wounded your vanity when you were sent as *commissaire* to his Department. He was forced to deal harshly with one of your agents who had been denounced before the commune for having touted principles that were hardly revolutionary."

Monsieur Chabot became angry and protested that he would never allow this report to be made to the Committee. I asked him why administrators who had been removed along with the Mayor had been ordered back in preference to the latter. Monsieur Chabot answered that he had been willing to pardon, and notably [to pardon] Dardignac, President of the Directory, who in this capacity had signed all the orders. I expressed my surprise that he arrogated to himself the right to pardon. I told him we didn't get rid of the tyrant [Louis XVI] in order to replace him with others.

He said, "Denounce me; have me dragged before the Revolutionary Tribunal, it's all the same to me." "It's really amazing," I told him, "that someone who professes himself a patriot, is really so unlike one in his actions."

"You are a women's Society," he replied, "which wants to get involved in [public] affairs, and you're being misled." I repeated my first answer, that "neither cajoleries nor *assignats* would ever tempt the Revolutionary Women. We are interested only in the oppressed, and I look upon the Mayor as a victim you felt like sacrificing. That is so true that you have had offers made to his nephew, whom you know is a fine patriot and who, from the time of his uncle's disgrace, has not left him for a single instant. I tell you that in order to destroy the uncle all the more easily, you have had positions offered to him [the nephew] three times in order to get him away from Paris and in this way deprive the uncle of the only consolation left to him. Is this the way men should comport themselves towards their fellows? I dare to assure you that if you don't give the Mayor the justice he has a right to expect, I'll argue for it myself at the bar of the Convention, and we'll see whether you have the right—you powerless dictator—to sacrifice patriots while you give preferential treatment to counterrevolutionaries every day. I warn you that if I go before the bar [of the Convention] I will tell some truths that will not be to your advantage."

At that point Monsieur Chabot composed himself, turning towards me with his hypocritical air, and fixing me with his cockroach eyes, he said: "Do you want that? Okay, I'll have the report drawn up tonight, and tomorrow the Mayor can leave, only he'll no longer be Mayor. We'll send him to his place of residence, because if we send him to Toulouse, the people would reelect him. I can't deny that he accomplished an infinite amount of good for the people, and besides, he has some excellent qualities, but he has too much influence at Toulouse. He mustn't go back there."

I leave it to the reader to give this passage the consideration it merits.

Monsieur Chabot told me, still looking directly at me, that he was never able to refuse anything to women. I answered that it made me mad that he was a public figure; that I pitied my country because the counterrevolutionaries also had women, and it wouldn't be difficult for them to obtain pardons by sending [their] women to him. This is the truth about what took place between Monsieur Chabot and me. He said he had witnesses. I owe it to myself to point them out. When I came into his house, I saw, first of all, the vile companion of his disordered life. Once I was inside his salon, I saw on a couch a woman scented with musk and a man dressed in a reddish-orange frock coat with a very large silver braid at the collar. These are the people Monsieur Chabot could produce for me {as witnesses}.

I continue with the meeting of the Jacobins . . . [in text] Bazire says: . . . [in text] "And I also, all sickly, as you see me here, I have tangled with the Revolutionary Women." (There is laughter.) Renaudin says, "Do not laugh, this can turn out to be more serious than you think." Bazire: "I will explain myself. The other day, seven to eight Revolutionary Women came to the Committee of General Security to demand the liberty of a man named Sémandy, detained at Sainte Pélagie [the prison], whom they claimed had been wrongly arrested. We told them that a Section-based counterrevolution was being planned in Paris such as that which took place in Lyons, Marseilles, Bordeaux, etc., etc. Sémandy had been exposed to us by the deputies of the Bouches du Rhône as having played one of the principal roles in the [counter-revolutionary plot] in Marseilles." I answered Monsieur Bazire. And I do not hesitate to say that he was being deceptive when he said that the deputation [of the women's Society] had demanded the release of Sémandy. It [the deputation] was informing itself concerning the reasons for his detention so that if he were not guilty, justice might be obtained by having him released by the Tribunal, which must take cognizance of [this situation]—all of which is quite different [from what Bazire alleged]. He lies when he dares to say that our *commissaires* asked him for permission to visit all the prisons in order to inform themselves about the reasons for the prisoners' arrests so as to be able to force their release should they deem this appropriate . . . [in text]. The Revolutionary Women know the LAW, and it is only in conformity with it [the law] that we would have come to the aid of oppressed patriots . . . [in text]. He lies with the shameless audacity natural to him when he says that our *commissaires* called him a sucker. The Revolutionary Women know the meaning of words too well to have addressed such an insignificant one to Monsieur Bazire. I would like to believe that he latched onto it out of modesty.

You lie, Monsieur Bazire, when you dare to say that our *commissaires* called Robespierre "Monsieur." We keep watch over all public figures. And far be it from us to confuse Citizen Robespierre with the Bazires of the day. Be careful, Robespierre. I noticed that those accused of having lied believe they can sidestep the denunciation by accusing those who denounce them of having spoken ill of you. Be careful lest those who are forced to wrap themselves in your virtues also pull you with them over the precipice. As for you, Monsieur Bazire, the big war horse which you've built out of the word "Monsieur" Robespierre, which you've placed in the mouths of our *commissaires,* proves nothing except that you are a miserable liar.

Renaudin: "*Citoyenne* Lacombe, or Madame Lacombe, who likes nobles so much, is sheltering a noble in her house. I have just been informed that she is lodging in her house the former Monsieur Leclerc, a well-known counterrevolutionary."

I declare on my own behalf that I do not know anything about the person who denounced me—nor do I know the reasons that led him to do it—but his assertion is so stupid, and at the same time so false, that my only answer is to send him to the Hôtel de Bretagne, rue Croix des Petits Champs, where I have lived for twenty-two months. He will be completely free to convince himself that it is often the case that when one speaks on the basis of what others say, one does nothing more than echo an idiot.

I noted that I had arrived at the public gallery where I habitually went just as this Renaudin was denouncing me. I came down immediately, and because it is in my nature always to confront my enemies face to face, I went to the door that led into the [meeting] hall. I told the guard at the door, "I am being denounced. I must get in to answer my denouncers." The guard said to me, "I cannot take it upon myself to let you in. But go to the Secretariat. Write to the President. I will deliver your note." I followed his advice. I wrote to the President, who was Sijas (that I had just heard myself being denounced as I came into the public gallery; that I flattered myself that the friends of liberty and equality who had heard my denouncers would be willing to give me the right to be present at the meeting to justify myself; that I was ready to appear). The guard at the door took my note to the President. This latter took it upon himself, without consulting the Society [the Jacobins], to send me off with the humiliating reply that I could not be admitted. Indignant—as I had a right to be—I went back up into the public gallery, and right at the very moment when the President was about to have a resolution passed which would have dishonored it [the Jacobin Society]. I asked for the floor. I said that before voting, the friends of liberty and equality owed it to themselves to listen to me.

Here it would be difficult for me to describe the effects which my justifiable request produced. The women in the gallery I was in, most of them rising up, cried out: "The intriguer." "Down with the new Corday." "Get out, miserable woman, or we will tear you to pieces." Now imagine at the same time a large number of self-styled members leaving their places to gather around the gallery where I was in order to hold forth in the same language as these distraught or perfidious women. Behold the galleries—a majority—applauding this senseless gesture in an outburst of feeling, and you will tremble for my life.

Be reassured, friends of liberty. I will hold firm in the face of this horde led only by passion. Consider that they are out to fight against a free woman who is only calumniated and not guilty; who, notwithstanding the danger which surrounds her, maintains the *sangfroid* of innocence—a terrible weapon which will fell those who were out to get her.

I replied to those who, with cries of rage, were ordering me to leave that I would not go, that they could assassinate me, that here was an action worthy of their courage, but that they would never have the power to send me away. "Here I will perish, or I will be heard. Is it in this cowardly way that you show yourselves to be the friends of justice, by strangling truth?" Here there was a movement—as much on the women's part as on the part of those who were instigating them—to fall upon me. And then, assuming this pride and courage worthy of a Republican Woman, I told them: "The first one of you who dares to come forward, I am going to show you what a free woman can do." No sooner was this last word spoken than, as the cries and gesturing flagged, I heard one of them pronounce this terrible word which taught me what cowards might dare do to overwhelm weakness and which caused me to see at the same time the full extent of the danger I had run. Would you believe it, citizens? A man, seeing that I was determined to sell my life at a high price, dared to say, "Take care! This G. [epithet] is always armed." Therefore, as I had taken the precaution of carrying them for self-defense, the game was up for me. Ah! consider on my behalf the sorrowful reflections to which this passage lends itself; or rather, let us join in believing that for the honor of humanity and liberty there are not enough of them. These monsters, who are strong only when they oppress the weak, seeing at last that it was impossible for them to send me away, contented themselves with giving me a guard to impose silence on me if I had the urge to tell the truth. Once order was restored, the President upbraided me, telling me that it didn't help my cause to stir up trouble like this by asking for the floor from the public gallery where I was sitting. Citizens, would you have anticipated that the same President who had just sent back my note would dare to answer me this way? The denunciations continue, as much against me as against the Society. All the ills that are befalling Paris are attributed to us. We are accused of having pillaged sugar—which happened two months prior to our existence as a *société populaire*—of having [pillaged] soap. And the constituted authorities convened in the Department of Paris voted a statement in which they declare that we deserved well of the Fatherland for having prevented pillaging.

And finally, we are accused of being counterrevolutionaries. The request is made that I be brought before the Committee of General Security. Following several motions, one more extravagant than the other, to destroy the Society of Revolutionary Women—because it must be destroyed, no matter what the price—the proposal was made that the papers at my house be sealed. But Monsieur Chabot, who until then had treated me as one of the chiefs of the counterrevolutionaries, was so convinced that he had been nothing more than a base calumniator that he didn't hesitate to say that this last proposition was a trap set for the Jacobin Society; that if, when the seals were lifted, they found only patriotic papers at my place, it would be easier for me to justify myself; but that he held me to be a counterrevolutionary and that it was necessary that I be imprisoned immediately. The orders of Monsieur Chabot were not followed point by point, but three guards were sent to me in the gallery—all the more indecent, as there were only women in this gallery. So there I was, seated in the middle of them, placed under arrest in the presence of four thousand people. I told one of the guards that if he had orders to take me somewhere, he could let me know; that I was ready to submit to the laws. He told me that it was not time yet; that we had to stay there. As I had nothing to reproach myself with, it was not surprising that my face showed the calm of innocence. Who will believe it? This very calm attracted the grossest insults. I heard someone say, "Look at this new Corday. What a front she puts up; nothing can unsettle such people." To console me, one of the guards said to me, "It's sad to sleep in prison." "Why sadder for me than for others? I will add but one more to their number."

Finally, at 9:30 my guards enjoined me to follow them. I obeyed. We went down the stairs, and as we went out into the courtyards, I was more than a little surprised to see them filled by a huge crowd which was awaiting the departure of the one person who knew nothing of her crime. It was not without having given me—several times over—the hope of seeing myself led to the guillotine that we got out of the courtyards. We were followed by countless numbers of persons who lavished the most odious names upon me. Friends of liberty, I swear that if my soul were capable of fear, the [fear] of becoming the victim of a distraught people would be the only one capable of shaking me up. It seemed—so great were the numbers—as if Pitt or Cobourg had fallen into our hands.

Finally I arrived at the Committee of General Security without the slightest incident. After we had been forced to wait in the antechamber two hours, a gendarme told the person guarding me—because of the three guards, only one was left with me, the other two having gotten tired of waiting—that he could come in. When we passed the first room, a deputy, running after my guard, told him he couldn't enter; that no one was there. Then the one who was guarding me said, "*Citoyenne,* I am indignant about the way you have been treated. This is an arbitrariness without example. It seems to me that the Committee is not disposed to hear you. I will escort you back to your house."

Having arrived at the door, I asked him whether he had orders to guard me at my place during the night. He told me no. I assured him that if he received any the following day, he could come in complete security; that he would find me at home. As I prepared to go upstairs, the caretaker of the house told me I could not do so, given that there were seals on my door. I went back into the street, and calling to the guard, who had not gone away, I requested that he take me to the Section to attest that as I had spent two hours at the Committee of General Security, I was unable to be present at my place. Having arrived at the Section, I asked the members of the Committee if it would be possible for them to remove the seals on my door to place them on my papers. A member told me that would be impossible until the following day. I observed that it was late at night and that it was very inconvenient for a single woman to be forced to look for a bed at this hour. In a time of revolution, if someone came by on an inspection of my house and found that I was bedded down somewhere other than in my own house, what answer could I give so as not to appear suspect? "You will say that your place had been sealed," I was told.

As I left, I met two members of the Revolutionary Society who, having had the kindness to take an interest in me, had decided to spend the night making the rounds in order to learn what had become of me. After they expressed the satisfaction they felt at seeing me, I told them about my distress. Immediately, the sister of our archivist said to me, "Come sleep at my place. My husband is at the frontiers. Come. We will sleep together." At the same time, turning towards the person who accompanied me, she said, "Citizen, I answer for Citoyenne Lacombe. I live in such a street, at such a number. If you receive orders, you can come there to get her." I must be fair to the citizen guard. He very politely had offered to have a bed given to me at his place, but when this obliging *citoyenne,* whom I will call my guardian angel, offered to share her [bed], I accepted with all the more pleasure, as it would have been painful for me to be obliged to someone I knew only under such disagreeable circumstances. So ended an evening during which the Society of Revolutionary Republican Women, this Society which, since its creation, has not held a single meeting without giving proofs of its patriotism and humanity, suffered the cruelest outrage in the person of its President—she who, having had the honor of meriting its confidence, dares to challenge all enemies of the Fatherland to come forward with a single proof that all her proceedings haven't tended towards the happiness of the republic.

But, even given the few outrages we have received, we will render justice to the truth . . . [in text]. No, Citizens, it is not the friends of liberty and equality who have oppressed us, it cannot be those who have saved the Fatherland three times and who are capable of saving it once again who would have been driven to excesses against those whose happiness consisted of sharing their dangers. No, the true Jacobins were not at their ordinary meeting place on this day. Intrigue alone took possession of their meeting place, or if there were a few friends of liberty and justice in this crowd of intriguers, we dare flatter ourselves that indignation alone prevented them from taking the floor.

Extract of the procès-verbal of the removal of the seals at Citoyenne Lacombe's house.

The Committee of Surveillance of the Section of the Halle au Bled, in the year seventeen hundred and ninety three, second [year] of the French Republic, one and indivisible, the sixteenth of September, on the basis of a denunciation made before our Committee: we the *commissaires* of the said Committee went to Citoyenne Lacombe's place on rue Croix des

Petits Champs, to the house called the Hôtel de Bretagne, in order to examine papers there and to place seals there, if necessary. Having found the *citoyenne* not at home, placed seals on the door of her apartment in the presence of Citizen Jacques Perdriau, living at the Invalides, and Citizen François le Gris, and the Citoyenne Alexandrine Briu, Marguarite Charler, wife of Citizen Courteil, chief tenant; and they signed: Femme Courteil, Perdriau, le Gris, Filion and Brunet, both *commissaires.*

On the seventeenth of the month, Citoyenne Lacombe, having presented herself to the Committee of Surveillance of the said Section to request that we proceed with the lifting of the seals placed on the door of her apartment: having noted that the seals were in good condition, we, *commissaires,* made the most scrupulous examination of all these papers. We found nothing suspect. On the contrary, we found nothing but correspondence of fraternal societies, which breathes the purest patriotism, and different personal letters where the public good and patriotism were beautifully expressed. We, *commissaires,* on the requisition of the aforementioned *citoyenne,* have ordered that a copy be delivered to her to serve and be used as may be thought proper. This September 17, 1793, Year Two of the French Republic, one and indivisible.

And signed: Filion and Brunet, *commissaires,*

Femmes Lacombe, President

Sibon, Vice-President

Potheau and Martel, Secretary.

15. Decree of the National Convention Requiring the Wearing of the Tricolor Cockade

Source: *Décret de la Convention nationale, du 21 septembre 1793, l'an 2 de la République françoise, une & indivisible, qui enjoint aux femmes de porter la cocarde tricolore* (Chaalons [*sic*], n.d.), in Bibliothèque historique de la Ville de Paris, 19779.

The Society of Revolutionary Republican Women alienated not only the Jacobins but the market women as well. The sharpest antagonisms revolved around the issue of price controls, which the market women viewed as harmful to trade. The whole question was disputed in marketplace squabbles over the wearing of the tricolor cockade. The Revolutionary Republican Women tried to force women to wear it, and market women retaliated, hurling balls of mud and rotten fruit at their opponents. The Convention passed this decree.

———————◆———————

The National Convention, on the motion of a member, decrees that women who do not wear the tricolor cockade will be punished with eight days' imprisonment for the first offense; in case of a repetition, they will be deemed suspect; those who tear a national cockade away from another person or desecrate it will be punished with six years of confinement.

Endorsed by the Inspector
Signed, Blaux

In the name of the Republic, the provisional Executive Council mandates and orders all administrative bodies and courts to record the present law in their registers and to read, publish, post, and execute it in their Departments and respective jurisdictions. In witness whereof we have affixed our signature and the seal of the Republic. Paris, September 21, 1793, the second year of the French Republic, one and indivisible.

Signed, Bouchotte.

Countersigned, Gohier, and sealed with the seal of the Republic.

16. Police Reports on Marketplace Disturbances over the Cockade

Source: Pierre Caron, ed. *Paris pendant la Terreur: Rapports des agents secrets du Ministre de l'Intérieur,* vol. II. Documents taken from A.N., F⁷ 3688³.

These police reports make it clear that the authorities feared the women as a threat to their control and were well aware that the marketplaces were key locations for potentially dangerous disturbances.

Report of Roubaud, September 21. [P. 160]
A group of women at Les Halles near Saint-Eustache complain in coarse terms about the shortage of necessities and announce that that cannot last much longer, that they must have provisions at the prices of 1789, and that they will impose a tax since the Convention has no regard for their misery.[1]

Report of Rousseville, September 21. [P. 161]
Yesterday's order[2] concerning *citoyennes* who insult the national cockade has stirred up very violent reclamations, and if there had not been some patriots gathered at the entrance of the rue des Petits-Champs on the side of the place des Victoires, many patriotic *citoyennes* would again have been mistreated; some dandies [*muscadins*] were there to encourage ill-willed women, but they escaped when we approached.

Report of Latour-Lamontagne, September 21. [Pp. 154, 155]
The same fermentation on the subject of the cockade, especially among the women of Les Halles. It is a new apple of discord which the

[1]This is a threat to provoke an incident of *taxation populaire.* [Translators' note.]
[2]This was Henriot's order of the day inviting patriots to see that "agitators" were arrested. Caron, *Paris pendant la Terreur,* p. 161 fn. 3. [Translators' note.]

evildoers have thrown among us; they inspire in women the desire to share the political rights of men. When they have the cockade, they say, they will demand civic cards, want to vote in our assemblies, share administrative positions with us—and from this conflict of interests and opinions there will result a disorder favorable to our projects. One must, however, give justice to these women; generally they evince the most profound respect for the national representation; they refuse to wear the cockade because the law does not order it. "Let the Convention speak," they say, "and we shall execute whatever decree it issues."

It seems that singular rumors are spread in this regard; I heard some women say that people wanted to have them wear the cockade only in order to make them leave next for the front, because there were not enough men to defend them.

Report of Rolin, September 21. [P. 158]

These days, in the quarter of the place Maubert, many disputes flare up among the women, the fishwives of the place not wanting women to wear the cockade; they have snatched them from many women, and even injured them and thrown their bonnets in the mud.

Report of Latour-Lamontagne, September 22. [P. 164]

The cockade issue always divides the women, and it appears that the decree rendered on this matter by the National Convention has not produced the promised effect. Those with evil intentions, disconcerted by such a wise measure, are at this moment drawing up new batteries. These enemies of public tranquillity flatter the pride of women, seeking to persuade them that they have as many rights as men in the government of their country; that the right to vote in elections is a natural right they should demand; that in a state where law consecrates equality, women may claim all civilian and military employment; that things would doubtless go much better if affairs were conducted by good republican women; that one could cite a thousand examples of women who are celebrated in the science of government, just as in military arts; etc. That is the summary of a very long and most carefully worked out discourse which yesterday was spouted by a young dandy, disguised in the costume of a *sans-culotte,* in the presence of some women in the Jardin-Égalité. But he lost the whole fruit of his anarchic eloquence; they listened to him nearly as one would listen to a charlatan who dispensed his balm, and they withdrew before anyone appeared to try to put his prescription to use. Nonetheless, the incident proves that people with bad intentions use all sorts of maneuvers to sow discord among us.

. . . The decree on the cockade excites great rumors in the markets of Paris. Doubtless bribed by people with bad intentions whose maneuverings this wise measure has disrupted, some women complain in an outburst which only betrays the disorderly spirit that moves them. Except for that, it can be said the decree is generally accepted.

[Translators' note: The reports continue to mention such market disturbances until September 30.]

17. A Self-Declared Aristocrat Opposes the Requirement to Wear the Cockade

Source: A.N., F⁷ 4735, case of Marie-Scolastique Guerin.

Dozens of interrogations were made by the revolutionary authorities of women unwilling to observe the cockade decree during Year II.

———————————

Appearance before the Comité de surveillance et révolutionnaire of the Section de Brutus.

On the twenty-third of the first month of Year Two of the French Republic, One and Indivisible, Citizen Jean-François Henry Houlleau, Justice of the Peace for the Section de l'Homme Armée, declares that, having seen some citizens without cockades, and having invited them to adorn themselves with them, they bought them immediately.

Addressing himself to another *citoyenne* who did not have one on, he went over to her and asked her whether she was a Republican Woman, and [he said that if] she was, she should have the national cockade. To this the *citoyenne* replied that she was not a Republican Woman, but very much an aristocrat. As the declarant was insistent, in order to commit the *citoyenne* to acting in conformity with the law, she went over to a woman seller who was displaying on the Boulevard Montmartre, near the former Hôtel Mantolon. She got a cockade there and fastened it to her bonnet, but [she did so] saying that she would never betray her own way of thinking and that she was an aristocrat.

The declarant told her in loud tones that up until now he had spoken to her as a citizen, but that in his capacity as public functionary he was going to speak to her in the name of the law and decorate himself with his badge of justice of the peace, which he did. As this *citoyenne* continued making her remarks, he told her that he would not be able to avoid arresting her if she kept this up—and he did, with the aid of a patrol which he met up with on rue Montmartre, opposite the former residence of [illegible]. In the presence of the aforementioned patrol she repeated the remarks reported above.

[signed] Houlleau.

Citizen Pierre De la Ruelle, sergeant of the Revolutionary Company, [Section] Poissonnière, commanding the patrol mentioned above, declares that he heard the remarks noted above by Citizen Houlleau, Justice of the Peace, and he signed: De la Ruelle.

In addition, the citizens composing the aforementioned patrol declare that they heard the remarks reported above, and signed,

[signatures appended.]

The *citoyenne* was questioned by us concerning her rank, residence, and profession.

A. Marie-Scolastique Guerin, living on rue de l'Echéquier, no. 12, Section Poissonnière, a *rentière* with twelve thousand *livres* in income . . . drawn on the Bank of LaFarge and the former Chevalier Ségur.

Q. Why did she say she was not a Republican Woman at all, but very much an aristocrat?

A. She said that this was her way of thinking and that she would never change.

Q. What did she understand "being an aristocrat" to mean?

A. Not doing evil to anyone, living off her revenue, doing good when she was able to, and bearing everything they might want her to bear.

Q. Where was she born?

A. At Menery, in the District de Corbeil.

Q. Who was her father?

A. A merchant at Menery—a grocer and haberdasher.

Q. How long had she been living in Paris?

A. For sixteen years.

Q. How come she had been able to have twelve thousand *livres* in *rentes* for the duration of her residence in Paris?

A. Her father had provided her with the sum of twelve thousand *livres* when she came to Paris.

Q. How had her father obtained such a situation for her?

A. By means of his personal fortune, and her father had provided a brother and five other sisters with the same means.

Q. What was the foundation of her father's wealth?

A. Lands, vineyards, and houses.
Q. Where are these holdings?
A. At Menery.
Q. Are all her father's holdings at Menery?
A. Yes, except for what she has in Paris, in an account with Ségur, LaFarge, and Laville of Paris.

And at this point, Citizen Bucaille, a member of the civil committee of the Section Poissonnière, living on rue de l'Echéquier, no. 12, and Cantin, owner of this same house, were brought in [and] declared that they looked upon Citoyenne Guerin as having fallen into a kind of madness, that for the past three weeks she had been showing signs of it daily, and they signed: Bucaille, Quentin [*sic*].

[Translators' note: Citoyenne Guerin's case was referred by the Committee in the Section de Brutus to the Committee in the Section Poissonnière for a hearing. The latter ordered Citoyenne Guerin held in the Mandelonnette Prison for questioning; seals were placed on the doors of her apartment. On 26 Vendemiaire, Year II, Citoyenne Guerin was ordered released on grounds of mental illness.]

18. WOMEN WEARING BONNETS ROUGES* ENCOUNTER
    RESISTANCE FROM THE AUTHORITIES AND FROM
    MODERATE PATRIOTIC WOMEN

Source: A.N., F⁷ 4774, dossier 1, case of LeSage-Landry.

The following incident occurred in Brumaire, Year II, amidst
rumors that the Society of Revolutionary Republican Women
planned to compel all women to wear the red woolen bonnets
of liberty. Authorities considered these *bonnets rouges*—referred
to also as *bonnets de police* in this document—as a source of
renewed public disorder, while Femme Sacriste looked upon the
red liberty cap as improper dress for female patriots.

*The revolutionary cockade, required by the law of September 21, was a tricolor ribbon. The
bonnet rouge was a cap knit of red wool traditionally worn by men but now adopted by members of
the Society as a symbol of revolutionary patriotism. [Translators' note.]

Comité de surveillance révolutionnaire of the regenerated Section, formerly [Section] du Mail, now Guillaume Tell.
                Seventh day of the second month of 1793, Year Two of
                the French Republic, one and indivisible, 5 P.M.
Procès-verbal concerning three women who stirred up trouble when
two of them wore one *bonnet de police* each on their heads while making
fun of women who were not wearing them. October 28, 1793.
        Citoyenne Marie-Françoise Dorlet, wife of Citizen Pierre Sacriste, a
brazier, living on rue du Bout du Monde in the house of the carriage
maker, appeared before the Committee.
        She told the Committee that a quarter of an hour ago, as she stood in
front of her door, she saw two women passing by with two *bonnets de
police* on their heads. These two women insulted her as they passed by.
Then she, the deponent, took it upon herself to remove their caps,
saying "Off with *les bonnets rouges* [red caps], because they are only for
men to wear." These two women answered this person, saying: "Off

with your cockade, because you've removed our bonnets," which led the deponent to tell them: "If you have the right to wear *bonnets rouges,* we'll go to the Committee to see about it." And they came with her to hear the ruling of the Committee concerning this matter which is within its jurisdiction.

And she stated that she was unable to sign her name.

Citizen Jacques Bounin, merchant on rue Pavée St.-Sauveur, no. 2, also appeared. He stated that a quarter of an hour ago, as he was walking on rue des Fossés-Montmartre, he saw Citoyenne Femme Sacriste, named above, snatch the *bonnets de police* from the heads of the two women whom the above-mentioned Femme Sacriste designated above. These two women told her, "Off with your cockade." The aforementioned Femme Sacriste retorted: "It is appropriate for me to wear it." With these remarks and the arguing that was taking place among them on the subject, they ended up by saying, "Let's go to the *corps de garde* to find out who's right." He, the deponent, followed them to protect the safety of the cockade, which the two women wearing the *bonnets de police* wanted to take away from the aforementioned Femme Sacriste. [His statement] was read back to him. [He] said it contained the truth and signed: Bounin.

Citoyenne Elizabeth Poulain, a cook for Citizen Mougue, a merchant-bookseller living on rue Croix-des-Petits-Champs, no. 65 [?], also appeared. She stated that a quarter of an hour ago, as she was walking along rue des Fossés-Montmartre, she saw two women, each of whom had a *bonnet de police* on her head, having an argument with Femme Sacriste, who pulled off the aforementioned bonnets. These two women said to Femme Sacriste, "Off with your cockade." The aforementioned Femme Sacriste retorted, "I will wear the cockade, and you will not wear the bonnets." Then she, the deponent, seeing that they were going to the Committee, followed them. She said that was all she knew. [Her statement] was read back to her. [She] said it contained the truth. She adhered [to her testimony]. [She] said she was unable to sign her name. . . .

Whereupon the Committee called upon one of the women designated above as having had a *bonnet de police* on her head. She said her name was Louise Elizabeth Charlot, wife of Citizen François Marie LeSage, a worker in gauze, living on rue des Marias, Faubourg St. Martin, no. 35, in the house of the *commissaire de police.*

She said that while walking with her two comrades along the rue des Fossés-Montmartre, Femme Sacriste started running after them, and having caught up with them, she snatched away her *bonnet de police,* that of Femme LeSage, and threw insults at them, calling them, among other things, bitches and prostitutes and saying that they were doubtless being paid off to wear *bonnets de police*. Then she, Femme LeSage, told the aforementioned Femme Sacriste that they were as free to wear *bonnets de police* as cockades, and that there wasn't any greater harm in wearing *bonnets de police* than cockades. The aforementioned Femme Sacriste reproached them with having said that women's hair would have to be cut. The aforementioned Femme Sacriste made a big disturbance and was responsible for a gathering of men around the aforementioned Femme LeSage as well as her two companions. These men loudly applauded the aforementioned Femme Sacriste, saying, "Well done, it's only men who should wear *bonnets de police*," and then the aforementioned Femme Sacriste forced them to go with her to the Committee to await its decision concerning this matter. [Her statement] was read back. [She] said it contained the truth, adhered to it, and stated that she was unable to sign her name. . . .

The second woman designated above as wearing a *bonnet de police* also appeared. She declared that her name was Catherine Cristophe, wife of Pierre Landry, a shoemaker, residing at rue Faubourg St. Martin, no. 99. She stated that while she was walking with the aforementioned LeSage and another of her comrades along the rue des Fossés-Montmartre, Femme Sacriste ran over to her and pulled off her *bonnet de police,* after having done the same thing to the aforementioned Femme LeSage. She made indecent remarks to them which she [Landry] doesn't dare repeat. The aforementioned Femme Sacriste grabbed her by the arm to force her to come to the Committee, repeatedly pulling off her *bonnet de police.* She, Femme Landry, advised her to respect the cockade which was attached to her *bonnet de police,* and notwithstanding this, the aforementioned Femme LeSage [*sic*—Sacriste is meant here] threw the aforementioned bonnet into the mud. [Her statement] was read back to her. [She] said it contained the truth, and stated that she was unable to sign her name.

Marie-Jeanne Luisan, wife of Jean-Jacques Malcauze, a carpenter on rue du Marais, no. 46, also appeared, and stated that while she was with the aforementioned Femmes LeSage and Landry, her two friends, and as they were walking along on rue des Fossés-Montmartre in order to return home, having come from the Champ de Mars, she saw Citoyenne Sacriste accost them and pull off their *bonnets de police* while insulting them. And she, Femme Malcauze, noted that they had been surrounded by many men, who were calling out, "Pull off their *bonnets de police,* because the only people who have them are prostitutes and women paid

off by the aristocracy to wear them," and [these men said] they were
Jacobines. She, Femme Malcauze, seeing that they were being insulted
and harrassed, had the idea of coming before the Committee to avoid
any scandal. [Her statement] was read back. [She] said it contained the
truth, and signed: Marie-Jeanne Luisan, Femme Malcauze.

Given the above account, and furthermore, considering that the row
in question was responsible for large crowds forming and for a lot of
trouble, not only in the place des Victoires-nationales but in the Sections du Contract social and Halle aux bleds as well; given that in the
unfortunate situation public affairs are in, the greatest surveillance is
called for relative to everything that might disturb security; and [con-
sidering] that this recent habit of women wearing *bonnets de police* can be
regarded as a rallying sign or as an occasion for disorder:

The Committee orders that the three *citoyennes,* named Femmes Le-
Sage, Landry, and Malcauze, who say they are from the Section de
Bondé, will be taken before the Revolutionary Committee of the aforementioned Section for purposes of identification and so that their conduct might be examined. . . .

19. REVOLUTIONARY REPUBLICAN WOMEN IN A SHOWDOWN
WITH THE MARKET WOMEN AND REVOLUTIONARY
OFFICIALS

Source: Prudhomme, *Révolutions de Paris,* vol. XVII, no. 215 .
("du tridi 23 Brumaire, au decadi 30, an deuxième de la
République française, une et indivisible"), pp. 207–10.

Bickering over the issue of the red bonnets exploded into
pandemonium at a meeting of the Society of Revolutionary
Republican Women on 7 Brumaire. Unsympathetic Section
authorities were quick to realize that the disorder could be
exploited to rout and discredit the Society. On their side,
members of the Society held their ground and insisted on their
rights.

———————◆———————

Procès-verbal concerning what happened to the Revolutionary Republican
Women at their usual meeting place beneath the ossuaries of Saint-
Eustache on the seventh day of the first decade of the second month of
Year Two of the Republic, One and Indivisible.

The Society, having been invited by the Section de la Réunion to
participate in the inauguration of the two martyrs of liberty, met at
eleven o'clock with their symbols—an *oeil de vigilance,* a flag, and four
pikes. While they were waiting for the members to arrive, a *citoyenne*
reported to those present in the room concerning the measures our
enemies were taking to starve patriots. She reported on what had just
been found in the sewers of Montmartre and the Temple—a large
quantity of bread. A *citoyenne* in the galleries cried out that she would
not believe it until she had seen it. Several people attested to the truth of
the statement. Others cried out, "Down with red bonnets! Down with
Jacobin women! Down with Jacobin women and the cockades! They are
all scoundrels who have brought misfortune upon France!" The disorder

increased. The vice-president who was chairing [the meeting] tried in
vain to bring people back to their senses using the arms of reason; she
used them in vain. The fiercest [women] among them were drunk. As
they were unable to restore order, armed troops were requisitioned to
restrain the galleries, which were about to swoop down upon the Society. Six citizens arrived, sabres unsheathed, along with the justice of the
peace, named Lindet, who entered the gallery. He asked for the floor;
the President gave her consent. He said, *"Citoyennes,* in the name of the
law, silence; in the name of the law I order you to stop talking." Then
he said, *"Citoyennes,* what's at issue is not the red bonnet; you will stop
wearing it, and you will be free to put whatever you wish on your
heads." He left, taking the armed troops with him, although the Society
asked for assistance three times. A minute later the justice of the peace
returned, alone, and, proceeding to the President's desk, asked her to
remove her bonnet, assuring her that in doing so she would restore
order. She obeyed. She took it and placed it on the head of the justice
of the peace. Then the people in the galleries applauded with the
greatest outburst of feeling. The justice of the peace, addressing himself
to the spectators, said to them: "The *citoyennes révolutionnaires* are not in
session; everyone can come in." At this point a crowd of countless
numbers of people came into the room and heaped the filthiest abuse
upon the members. They pounced upon the symbols: the *oeil vigilant,*
the flags, the pikes. They wanted to break everything to pieces. The
citoyennes, unfaltering in the midst of dangers, not wanting to abandon
their symbols, were struck and most shamefully attacked. Preferring to
become victims of a people led astray, thinking no longer about their
own persons but rather about imposing respect for the figure of Liberty
represented by the flag, one of them cried out, "Massacre us, if you like,
but at least respect the rallying point of Frenchmen." The *citoyenne* in
charge of the flag, mistreated to the point that she could resist no
longer, turned to the judge. She said, "I place it in your hand. You will
answer to me for it with your life."

Several cannoneers from the Section arrived and helped save it [the
flag] from the fury of those who were trying to tear it to pieces. At this
instant these wild women, unable to slake their rage, threw themselves
upon the members a second time, beat them, [and] dragged them. One
of them was carried away unconscious by a member of the Revolutionary
Committee of the Section. Several *citoyennes,* seeing themselves pursued,
took refuge there. The surgeons who arrived there treated a badly
wounded *citoyenne* and gave treatment to several who were unconscious.
One citizen, a member of the Committee, suffered a knife wound as he

tried to save a *citoyenne* who was being knocked senseless with blows from sabots; she still bears the marks.

This happened in the street. The *citoyenne* vice-president, in the name of the Society, asked the Committee to consent to draw up the *procès-verbal* of what had just taken place. The members of this Committee sidestepped the issue for a long while.

Three women were brought in—a mother and two daughters— accused of assault and battery. Citizen Gérault suggested that they be released. In vain the wounded *citoyennes* protested against this criminal indulgence. This same citizen kept on insisting, saying that at the present time it was necessary to take the soft approach. The women were released as well as two citizens who had been arrested. Just then, Citizen Gérault proposed that the *Citoyennes Révolutionnaires* be taken to a turret and that they be told that they were running great risks; that the people were calling for them, and were ready to force their way through to the Committee; that once they were hidden, the people would be brought in so they could be assured they were no longer there. The *citoyennes* never agreed to go into hiding although the proposition was repeated several times. The Society again asked for the *procès-verbal*. A citizen made it clear that it was necessary, for the honor of the Committee, in whose *arrondissement* the Society had been insulted, to proceed to [drawing up the *procès-verbal*] immediately so that the *citoyennes* who were present could all put their signatures to all the facts they knew something about.

It [the *procès-verbal*] was begun at last. Just then two men who had been speaking with Gérault in low voices came over; right after that, an officer from the armed troops came in. After conversing in low tones with Gérault, the latter spoke up, raising his voice: "What do you want? These *citoyennes* insist that the *procès-verbal* be drawn up." The officer, addressing the Society, said, *"Citoyennes,* I have just left my post to warn you of the risks you are running. People are all heated up; there is a huge crowd. Right now they are crying, *"Vive la République!* Down with the *révolutionnaires!"* They are about to break through the guard. The public safety, and that of the Section, requires that you withdraw immediately. We have provided a passage for you to leave without risk. Time is short. I ask you for a yes or a no." The *citoyennes,* out of consideration for the general welfare, agreed to leave. The officer left. Someone was sent to tell us that we could go out two by two, that there would be no danger. We were able to see that for ourselves. They had us go through the church, through the passage de Saint-Agnès. All seemed to us to be peaceful.

The members present signed, having attested to all the statements in the *procès-verbal:* Victoire Capitaine, Baraez, Pebli, Vildecoque, Femme Lemonnier, Levasoeupe, C. Pigont, Bigant, Claire, Bigant the elder, Marlet, Solandre, Martin, Femme Dubois, Dubrente, Femme Moreaux, Victoire. . . .

20. The National Convention Outlaws Clubs and
Popular Societies of Women

Source: *Réimpression de l'Ancien Moniteur,* vol. 18, pp. 298–300.

The events of 7 Brumaire were a prelude to the dissolution of
the Society of Revolutionary Republican Women. On the 8
Brumaire a delegation of market women filed their complaint
with the Convention. An investigation was ordered. The
following day, 9 Brumaire, André Amar reported to the
Convention on behalf of the Committee of General Security. He
categorically condemned women political activists and
recommended the suppression of their political organizations.
That same day the Convention voted a decree outlawing
"women's societies and popular clubs."

National Convention
Moise Bayle, Presiding
Session of 9 Brumaire

. . . *Amar, for the Committee of General Security:* Citizens, your Committee
has been working without respite on means of warding off the consequences of disorders which broke out the day before yesterday in Paris
at the Marché des Innocents, near Saint-Eustache. It [the Committee]
spent the night receiving deputations, listening to various reports which
were made to it, and taking measures to maintain public order. Several
women, calling themselves Jacobines, from an allegedly revolutionary
society, were going about in the morning, in the market and under the
ossuaries of les Innocents, in pantaloons and red bonnets. They intended
to force other *citoyennes* to wear the same costume; several [of the latter]
testified that they had been insulted by them. A mob of nearly six
thousand women gathered. All the women were in agreement that
violence and threats would not make them dress in a costume [which]
they respected but which they believed was intended for men; they

would obey laws passed by the legislators and acts of the people's magistrates, but they would not give in to the wishes and caprices of a hundred lazy and suspect women. They all cried out, *"Vive la République, une et indivisible!"*

Municipal officers and members of the Revolutionary Committee of the Section du Contrat Social quieted people down and dispersed the mobs. In the evening the same disturbance broke out with greater violence. A brawl started. Several self-proclaimed Revolutionary Women were roughed up. Some members of the crowd indulged themselves in acts of violence towards them which decency ought to have proscribed. Several remarks reported to your Committee show that this disturbance can be attributed only to a plot by enemies of the state. Several of these self-proclaimed Revolutionary Women may have been led astray by an excess of patriotism, but others, doubtless, were motivated only by malevolence.

Right now, when Brissot and his accomplices are being judged, they want to work up some disorders in Paris, as was the case whenever you [the Convention] were about to consider some important matter and when it was a question of taking measures useful for the Fatherland.

The Section des Marchés, informed of these events, drew up a resolution in which it informs your Committee that it believes several malevolent persons have put on the mask of an exaggerated patriotism to foment disturbances in the Section and a kind of counterrevolution in Paris. This Section requests that it be illegal to hinder anyone's freedom of dress and that popular societies of women be strictly prohibited, at least during the revolution.

The Committee thought it should carry its investigation further. It raised the following questions: (1) Is it permissible for citizens or for an individual society to force other citizens to do what the law does not prescribe? (2) Should meetings of women gathered together in popular societies in Paris be allowed? Don't the disorders already occasioned by these societies argue against tolerating their existence any longer?

Naturally, these questions are complicated, and their resolution must be preceded by two more general questions, which are: (1) Can women exercise political rights and take an active part in affairs of government? (2) Can they deliberate together in political associations or popular societies?

With respect to these two questions, the Committee decided in the negative. Time does not allow for the full development to which these major questions—and the first, above all—lend themselves. We are going to put forward a few ideas which may shed light on them [these questions]. In your wisdom you will know how to submit them to thorough examination.

1. Should women exercise political rights and meddle in affairs of government? To govern is to rule the commonwealth by laws, the preparation of which demands extensive knowledge, unlimited attention and devotion, a strict immovability, and self-abnegation; again, to govern is to direct and ceaselessly to correct the action of constituted authorities. Are women capable of these cares and of the qualities they call for? In general, we can answer, no. Very few examples would contradict this evaluation.

The citizen's political rights are to debate and to have resolutions drawn up, by means of comparative deliberations, that relate to the interest of the state, and to resist oppression. Do women have the moral and physical strength which the exercise of one and the other of these rights calls for? Universal opinion rejects this idea.

2. Should women meet in political associations? The goal of popular associations is this: to unveil the maneuvers of the enemies of the commonwealth; to exercise surveillance both over citizens as individuals and over public functionaries—even over the legislative body; to excite the zeal of one and the other by the example of republican virtues; to shed light by public and in-depth discussion concerning the lack or reform of political laws. Can women devote themselves to these useful and difficult functions? No, because they would be obliged to sacrifice the more important cares to which nature calls them. The private functions for which women are destined by their very nature are related to the general order of society; this social order results from the differences between man and woman. Each sex is called to the kind of occupation which is fitting for it; its action is circumscribed within this circle which it cannot break through, because nature, which has imposed these limits on man, commands imperiously and receives no law.

Man is strong, robust, born with great energy, audacity, and courage; he braves perils [and] the intemperance of seasons because of his constitution; he resists all the elements; he is fit for the arts, difficult labors; and as he is almost exclusively destined for agriculture, commerce, navigation, voyages, war—everything that calls for force, intelligence, capability, so in the same way, he alone seems to be equipped for profound and serious thinking which calls for great intellectual effort and long studies which it is not granted to women to pursue.

What character is suitable for woman? Morals and even nature have assigned her functions to her. To begin educating men, to prepare children's minds and hearts for public virtues, to direct them early in life towards the good, to elevate their souls, to educate them in the political cult of liberty: such are their functions, after household cares. Woman is naturally destined to make virtue loved. When they have fulfilled all these obligations, they will have deserved well of the Fatherland. Doubtless they must educate themselves in the principles of liberty in order to make their children cherish it; they can attend the deliberations of the Sections [and] discussions of the popular societies, but as they are made for softening the morals of man, should they take an active part in discussions the passion of which is incompatible with the softness and moderation which are the charm of their sex?

We must say that this question is related essentially to morals, and without morals, no republic. Does the honesty of woman allow her to display herself in public and to struggle against men? to argue in full view of a public about questions on which the salvation of the republic depends? In general, women are ill suited for elevated thoughts and serious meditations, and if, among ancient peoples, their natural timidity and modesty did not allow them to appear outside their families, then in the French Republic do you want them to be seen coming into the gallery to political assemblies as men do? abandoning both reserve—source of all the virtues of their sex—and the care of their family?

They have more than one alternative way of rendering service to the Fatherland; they can enlighten their husbands, communicating precious reflections, the fruit of the quiet of a sedentary life, [and] work to fortify their love of country by means of everything which intimate love gives them in the way of empire. And the man, enlightened by peaceful family discussions in the midst of his household, will bring back into society the useful ideas imparted to him by an honest woman.

We believe, therefore, that a woman should not leave her family to meddle in affairs of government.

There is another sense in which women's associations seem dangerous. If we consider that the political education of men is at its beginning, that all its principles are not developed, and that we are still stammering the word liberty, then how much more reasonable is it for women, whose moral education is almost nil, to be less enlightened concerning principles? Their presence in popular societies, therefore, would give an active role in government to people more exposed to error and seduction. Let us add that women are disposed by their organization to an over-excitation which would be deadly in public affairs and that interests of state would soon be sacrificed to everything which ardor in passions can generate in the way of error and disorder. Delivered over to the heat of public debate, they would teach their children not love of country but hatreds and suspicions.

We believe, therefore, and without any doubt you will think as we do, that it is not possible for women to exercise political rights. You will destroy these alleged popular societies of women which the aristocracy would want to set up to put them [women] at odds with men, to divide the latter by forcing them to take sides in these quarrels, and to stir up disorder.

Charlier. Notwithstanding the objections just cited, I do not know on what principle one could lean in taking away women's right to assemble peaceably. (Murmurs.) Unless you are going to question whether women are part of the human species, can you take away from them this right which is common to every thinking being? When a popular society is negligent with respect to general order, to laws, then the members, accused of the offense, or the entire association, if it has made itself guilty, will be pursued by the police. And you have examples of the dissolution of several societies which had been taken over by the aristocracy. But may fear of a few abuses to which an institution is susceptible not force you to destroy the institution itself? For what institution is exempt from inconveniences?

Bazire. There is not anyone who does not sense the danger of abandoning to the police the surveillance and the overseeing of the popular societies. Thus, this remedy, which is itself an abuse, should not be cited against the all too real drawbacks of women's societies. Here is how the suspension of these societies can be justified. You declared yourselves a revolutionary government; in this capacity you can take all measures dictated by the public safety. For a brief period you have thrown a veil over principles out of fear that they might be abused to lead us into counterrevolution. Therefore, it is only a question of knowing whether women's societies are dangerous. Experience has shown these past days how deadly they are to the public peace. That granted, let no one say anything more to me about principles. I ask that in a revolutionary spirit and by way of a measure of public security these associations be prohibited, at least during the revolution.

The decree proposed by Amar is adopted in these terms:

The National Convention, after having heard the report of its Committee of General Security, decrees:

Article 1: Clubs and popular societies of women, whatever name they are known under, are prohibited. [Article] 2: All sessions of popular societies must be public.

21. Women Protest the Suppression of the Society of Revolutionary Republican Women

Source: *Réimpression de l'Ancien Moniteur,* vol. 18, p. 350.

The following two documents illustrate women's protest against the closing of the Society of Revolutionary Republican Women and the radical establishment's successful campaign to silence that protest with arguments grounded in theories of feminine nature.

———————

National Convention
Continuation of Session of 15 Brumaire

A deputation of *citoyennes* is admitted before the bar, which announces itself as having a very important petition to present concerning an urgent matter.

One of them [a *citoyenne*]. The Society of Revolutionary Republican Women, this society, composed in large part of mothers of families, no longer exists. A law obtained on the basis of a false report prohibits us from meeting. . . .

Several voices. The business of the day.

The Convention moves on unanimously to the business of the day. The room resounds with applause.

The women petitioners leave the bar hurriedly.

22. Women's Deputations Barred from Sessions of the Paris Commune

Source: *Réimpression de l'Ancien Moniteur,* vol. 18, pp. 450, 451.

Commune of Paris. General Council. 27 Brumaire.

A deputation headed by women wearing red caps comes before the Council. There is furious hooting in the galleries, where they cry out: *Off with the women's red caps!* The noise increases; the president dons his hat and calls the galleries to order; calm is restored.

Chaumette: I demand a civic mention in the *procès-verbal* of the murmurs that have just broken out; this is an homage to morals. It is horrible, it is contrary to all the laws of nature for a woman to want to make herself a man. The Council must recall that some time ago these denatured women, these *viragos,* wandered through the markets with the red cap to sully that badge of liberty and wanted to force all women to take off the modest headdress that is appropriate for them. The place where the people's magistrates deliberate must be forbidden to every person who insults nature.

A member: No, the law allows them to enter; let the law be read. . . .

Chaumette: The law orders that morals be respected and that they be made to be respected. And here I see them despised. Well! Since when is it permitted to give up one's sex? Since when is it decent to see women abandoning the pious cares of their households, the cribs of their children, to come to public places, to harangues in the galleries, at the bar of the senate? Is it to men that nature confided domestic cares? Has she given us breasts to breast-feed our children? No, she has said to man: "Be a man: hunting, farming, political concerns, toils of every kind, that is your appanage." She has said to woman: "Be a woman. The tender cares owing to infancy, the details of the household, the sweet anxieties of maternity, these are your labors; but your attentive cares deserve a reward. Fine! You will have it, and you will be the divinity of the domestic sanctuary; you will reign over everything that surrounds you by the invincible charm of the graces and of virtue."

Impudent women who want to become men, aren't you well enough provided for? What else do you need? Your despotism is the only one our strength cannot conquer, because it is [the despotism] of love, and consequently the work of nature. In the name of this very nature, remain what you are, and far from envying us the perils of a stormy life, be content to make us forget them in the heart of our families, in resting our eyes on the enchanting spectacle of our children made happy by your cares. (The women wearing the red cap immediately replace this respectable badge by a headdress suitable to their sex.)

Ah! I see it, you do not want to imitate women who no longer blush; the sentiments that are the charms of society are not extinguished in you. I pay homage to your sensitivity, but I must make you see the full depth of the abyss where a moment's error was plunging you.

Remember this haughty wife of a stupid, perfidious husband, *la Roland,* who thought herself fit to govern the republic and who rushed to her downfall; remember the impudent Olympe de Gouges, who was the first to set up women's societies, who abandoned the cares of her household to get mixed up in the republic, and whose head fell beneath the avenging knife of the laws. Is it the place of women to propose motions? Is it the place of women to place themselves at the head of our armies? If there was a Joan of Arc, that is because there was a Charles VII; if the fate of France was once in the hands of a woman, that is because there was a king who did not have the head of a man and because his subjects were worth less than nothing.

Chaumette ended by demanding that the deputation of women not be heard, and that the Council not receive any more deputations of women except following a decree passed *ad hoc,* without this prejudicing the right of *citoyennes* to bring their requests and individual complaints before the magistrates.

Chaumette's speech is frequently interrupted by warm applause, and his indictment [*réquisitoire*] is adopted unanimously.

V

Citoyennes *in the Jacobin Republic:* September, 1793, through July, 1794

THE MONTAGNARDS led by Robespierre proclaimed the creation of Revolutionary Government on October 30, 1793, one day after the dissolution of the Society of Revolutionary Republican Women. The Montagnard minority dominated the National Convention and the Jacobin Society for the next ten months, suspending the June Constitution "until the peace" (it was never put into effect) and assuming dictatorial powers to defend the Republic against its internal and external enemies. It was no accident that the Jacobins suppressed the women's club before making such an alteration in government. They did not want organized women continually pressing for greater enforcement of their economic regulations, demanding greater autonomy in local government, and repeatedly criticizing what they called Montagnard cowardice and unwillingness to fulfill the promises of their June Constitution. For the Montagnards wished to set up a controlled state, a Republic of Virtue and a Reign of Terror. The documents in this section illustrate the reactions of the women to this government. They were sometimes supporters and sometimes citizens enjoying their time of glory, but they were also—especially towards the end of the Jacobin dominance—victims of the new morality and the Terror.

The executive power in Revolutionary Government was vested in a twelve-man Committee of Public Safety, whose acknowledged spokesman was Robespierre. The subordinate Committee of General Security served as the domestic police entrusted with the enforcement of political orthodoxy among all citizens. The Jacobin Society popularized the regime and prescribed the appropriate activities for the popular societies in Paris and its daughter societies in the thousands of communes throughout France.

The laws of the Jacobin government that affected women especially concerned economic policy, social customs, morals to establish the Republic of Virtue, and the instruments of the Reign of Terror. The most important economic law was the General Maximum, which set price ceilings on fifty basic necessities. Women maintained their constant vigilance to insure rigorous enforcement of this law.

The social legislation was intended to create a Republic of Virtue, in which laws would define the public interest and regenerate civic morality to promote the basic values of liberty, equality, and fraternity. Anything which detracted from an individual's participation in public affairs had to be eliminated, especially allegiances to the church or the privileged way of life. Prostitution and libertine manners were explicitly defined as expressions of aristocratic conduct. Other decrees stipulated the proper republican forms of speech (the use of the informal *tu* in direct address instead of the formal *vous*), dress, diet, and even marital relations expected of citizens. Christian time was replaced with the republican calendar. Months were renamed after seasonal characteristics and divided into three ten-day periods, with the tenth-day of each set aside for national festivals. The ultraradical Paris Commune surpassed the national Revolutionary Government in its assault on the church. Its campaign was designed to convert churches into national shrines, metal from church bells into weapons, and nuns' habits into bandages for wounded soldiers.

Terror was justified as vital in guarding the Republic against internal subversives and external enemies. Most comprehensive was the Law of Suspects, which listed all categories of enemies subject to investigation and imprisonment and authorized the forty-eight Sections in Paris and the communes in the Departments to elect Revolutionary Committees which would conduct interrogations, confiscations, arrests, and imprisonments of "suspects." The Committee of General Security supervised the Revolutionary Committees and received copies of all their proceedings.

Initially the women of Paris were enthusiastic about the Jacobin government, and they responded with many acts symbolizing their loyalty. For the first time, the women of the people were exalted as paragons who set the standards of morality in republican society. They felt a sense of involvement at the civic festivals. They cherished the moments when their children recited the Declaration of the Rights of Man and Citizen. The central economic planning and relatively steady supply of foodstuffs to Paris deepened the Parisian women's allegiance to the Revolutionary Government. As one woman in the spectator galleries of the Jacobin Society put it, "Damn it all, we're *républicaines,* nothing else. The aristocrats expect some uprising, but as long as the Seine flows and there is bread, we will be *républicaines.* . . . Long live the Republic!"[1]

Year II was also to go down in the collective female memory as a time when women exercised their political rights. In November, 1793, supporters of the disbanded Society of Revolutionary Republican Women went to the National Convention to obtain permission to reinstitute their Society, but the deputies refused even to hear their demand, and they had to withdraw hastily. Chaumette, the *procureur* of the Paris Commune, proposed a law, unanimously adopted on November 17, that prohibited deputations of women from coming to the Commune unless an *ad hoc* permission was granted. Despite these setbacks to the radicals, other women were active in the local clubs and Section assemblies, and they valued and used their right to present petitions there and at the National Convention. The documents in this chapter indicate that even the most inarticulate and illiterate women had learned to contact the appropriate authorities if they had personal grievances. Naturally, women's trust was increased by the economic policies that eased their dread of destitution.

However, the Republic of Virtue did not bring about a total transformation in the attitudes and behavior of *citoyennes.* Throughout Year II misunderstandings arose between the Jacobins and women regarding interpretations of revolutionary legislation and ideology. Attitudes about private morality are a case in point. The middle-class Jacobins preached the virtues of monogamous marriage and deplored libertine manners, drinking, gambling, and prostitution. By contrast, the *menu peuple* found enjoyment in the cheap wineshops, and gambling filled their leisure hours with a modicum of relief from their monotonous jobs and constant fears for subsistence. Montagnard puritanism was incompatible with the more tolerant moral outlook among the *sans-culottes* and non-elite women.

It was the Terror that finally undermined the unity between the Republic of Virtue and the women. The policies of the Jacobins created an atmosphere of fear and tension for poor as well as rich. Children were used to spy upon their teachers. Women found themselves arrested for a passing remark made in a bread line. They could not understand why the government enforced the Law of Suspects against humble people as harshly as it did against former nobles.

[1]Report of Bacon, February 22, 1794, in Pierre Caron, ed., *Paris pendant la Terreur: Rapports des agents secrets du ministre de l'Interieur* vol. IV, p. 307.

This distrust intensified in the spring of 1794 when male and female Hébertistes were arrested for protesting inadequate enforcement of the economic laws. In June, more than 40 percent of those convicted under the Law of Suspects came from the common people, an increase from only 15 percent in April.[2]

The documents in this chapter sample responses of Parisian women in Year II to various expressions of the Jacobin ideals. The first cluster elucidates the pride which women took in the first months of Revolutionary Government when they believed themselves to be model *citoyennes;* the second cluster concerns feminine reactions to the Law of Suspects; and the final cluster illustrates opinions among the minority of women who dared to speak out against the Jacobin machine and its terroristic legislation.

Montagnard centralization eroded women's autonomy in political institutions. Their participation in popular societies and clubs was welcomed, provided they stayed within government-supported limits. Violent incidents were infrequent because women were generally satisfied that the Jacobin government was guaranteeing their subsistence. But women also faced confusion, fear, and even death as government intervened in all dimensions of their lives.

[2]J. M. Thompson, *The French Revolution* (Oxford, 1964), p. 495.

1. CITOYENNE FEMME FAVRE TESTIFIES CONCERNING HER
REPUBLICAN PATRIOTISM AND JACOBIN ALLEGIANCES

Source: A.N., F⁷ 4704, dossier Femme Favre.

Femme Favre's testimony on the military situation in the spring
of 1793 reveals how women could be involved in the war.
Femme Favre was one of dozens of women who enrolled in the
Revolutionary armies. In the spring of 1793 the Convention
passed legislation which stipulated that they be eliminated.
Nonetheless, at least some of these women received high praise
from Revolutionary authorities for their services and were
rewarded with pensions.

   Note Femme Favre's awareness of complex, interrelated
military and political developments; her concern for the welfare
of patriotic soldiers; and her fear of *émigrés* and foreigners.

. . . The above-named *citoyenne* declares that having learned that her
husband, as well as other defenders of the frontiers, were totally without
underwear, clothing, and shoes, she made up her mind to make the
greatest sacrifices to assist her husband. Consequently, she sold most of
her possessions to go join him and left last February second, reaching
him at Liège on the eleventh.

   On the sixteenth her husband received orders to leave for the siege of
Maestricht, and she went with him. Firing began on the twenty-second
at 11 P.M. with the first shot, which her husband fired off, and it
stopped at 5 A.M. Because the shot and shells were not up to caliber,
they were reduced to shooting only twelve times a day. The munitions
were so poorly supplied that there were no cartridge boxes ready; there
was not a single twenty-four pounder mounted when the attack began,
and there were different-caliber shot mixed pell-mell, so it was necessary
to sort them out. When there were shot, there was no powder; and
when someone had powder, he lacked shot and there was no fire grate

ready for use. It was impossible to heat the shot until the night before the siege was lifted. There were several complaints made to General Miranda, but in vain. The moment the order for lifting the siege arrived, the whole army was lost in tears of despair. Rage provoked all the gunners to bite their ammunition. The advantage which the Army of the Republic had was not in doubt. If General Miranda had been sincere, and a loyal patriot, an easy victory would have resulted. No one could doubt that [the outcome] was the result of treason. Until Liège, the army had always behaved in an orderly fashion, but [at Liège], the troops, lacking any order whatever, disbanded and were pursued by a large enemy force which took advantage of the weakness of the orderly troops and forced them to retreat to Tirlemont. Then, having been taken as a prisoner of war dressed in the uniform of the National Guard which she [Femme Favre] had been wearing as a *capitaine en second* (the rank held by her husband) and which the Company of Gunners had conferred upon her out of esteem for him, a rank in which she was doing her military service, she could not say what took place after the first of March.

At first she was relieved of everything she owned, specifically a sum of 860 *livres* in assignats, 50 *livres* in hard coin, her watch, clothes, and in general everything she had, even her cravat, and she was then taken to the dungeons of Tirlemont, where she would have lost her life like the other prisoners, whom the enemy slaughtered by slicing them up with their swords to save on gunpowder.

She was awaiting this sad end when it was discovered by pulling off her vest that she was a woman. Then Captain Houlans, who commanded the enemy expedition, took her under his personal protection, and he had to arm himself with a pistol and his sword to prevent the others from killing her.

She was sent to the headquarters of the enemy army at Tongres, where she was imprisoned. All possible means were used to force her to divulge the *mot d'ordre* and other information about the Republican Army, but she answered all questions by saying that she knew nothing about all that. Believing that she could not understand German, they held many different conversations in her presence. The sense of what she remembered was that if National Guards were taken, there would be no mercy for them, while the prisoners from the troops of the line would be spared. The plan was to return to the city of Lille, to encircle it with the army, . . . and to be in Paris within two weeks.

While in prison she had seen many *émigrés* receive letters stamped from Paris and written by persons who kept up a safe correspondence with the enemies, informing them of everything that occurred and letting them know either the campaign plans or the proceedings of the National Convention and the ministry or, lastly, the state of our resources. She had also seen one of the letters addressed directly from Paris to Clairfait, which, unfortunately, she was unable to lay hold of, although she would have risked it even if it had cost her her life. What is all the more surprising is that the postal service does not work for the soldiers of our armies, since she had received none of the four letters sent her by Citizen Lindet, the justice of the peace of this Section [Contract Social]. It appears that some scheming is going on in the postal service. These *émigrés* occupy all the routes taken by the enemies and encourage them to massacre, burn, and commit every imaginable type of atrocity. . . . The gunners in her company are so poorly equipped right now that they do not have a single pistol, and the majority lack even sabres. A part of the army has no guns, and the rest have very poor ones which are either hammerless or without batteries. . . . Entire battalions are without *culottes,* dressed only in cloaks that are in such miserable condition that most of them are held together only by pins. Notably, the Seventh Battalion of Paris passed in review in this miserable condition of absolute destitution right before the eyes of Citizens Danton and La Croix, who could not refrain from remarking out loud, "O! for the final blow, those men over there are all without *culottes."* When the above-mentioned battalion requested arms from Dumouriez, he was content to answer in an impatient tone, "Good, good, we'll see to that." Lastly, most gunners have only their fists left to protect their guns. . . .

[She signed her declaration: "Elizabeth François Dubois: Femme de Pierre Louis Favre, *capitaine en second,* Gunners of the Seventh Battalion of Paris, Army of the North."]

2. CITOYENNE SCHOOLTEACHERS MOLD USEFUL CITOYENNES
   FOR THE REPUBLIC

Source: A.N., F⁷ 4635.

In Year II all male and female primary school teachers were
required to take an oath of loyalty to the nation; they then
received *certificats de civisme* from local authorities. Casin and
Laruly, *institutrices*, describing their efforts to establish a school
for needy young *citoyennes*, attempt to assure citizens in the
Section Gravilliers of their patriotic ardor in order to establish a
case for collecting unpaid salaries.

———————

Citizen and Citoyenne,
    I am going to recount, with my natural openness, how we went about
organizing the work in our classroom. We were resting peacefully in our
room when we learned that the children in Section Gravilliers, and in
other Sections, had been abandoned by their teachers. We gave up
our calm to rush to their aid and to prevent their going without an
education.
    We entered this establishment on April 7, 1790, and finding your
young students disposed against us, we worked to gain their confidence
with kindness and a few gifts. Having no money of our own, we cut up
our own clothing, and using it, we dressed twenty [students]. With this
tactic we succeeded in holding their attention. From then on our happiness consisted solely in providing for their well-being. Having realized
that because of their youth they could not concentrate exclusively on
studying, and that work yielding a profit that could be used for their
support could not help but excite competition among them, we took on
a seamstress, a lace mender, a wholesale linen maker, a stocking darner,
and a laundress who came during the summer from 8 A.M. until noon
and from 2 P.M. until 7 P.M. and during the winter from 9 A.M. until
noon and from 2 P.M. until 4 P.M., which, counting the evening,

allowed the children at least an hour of recreation. These six vocational instructors each had twenty students and received six *livres* a day, which we paid from our stipends. We considered ourselves fortunate to give our country this token of our love. This work was done in a large classroom where there was a mistress located in each corner. My companion, serving as the inspectress, was in a position from which she could see everyone at work, and she also showed students how to embroider.

Every morning the students were asked to boil a cauldron of bran water to wash their hands. A green cloth was placed on the worktable, and the sides of the cloth fell on the laps of the students, and some bibs were placed on them only while they were working to protect their completed pieces. At 9 A.M. I gave a lesson in writing. Then I made those at each worktable read, and they read a second time in the afternoon, for they read regularly twice a day.

We had the satisfaction of outfitting twelve of them in 1792 and fourteen in 1793, six with winter weight and eight in summer muslin, and of giving out four dozen bonnets and nice ribbons—not counting the parties we gave them twice weekly when we gave them all a little taste of their earnings—and the pleasure of seeing these young students leave us with the skill to earn their own living.

But we have not been paid for the past fourteen months; nor have we received the 400 *francs* I put up for this school. We have become heavily indebted. We are forced to restrict ourselves to a single linen maker, who, because she is a relative, is willing to wait. For ourselves there remains the satisfaction of having shaped impressionable hearts. Citizen and Citoyenne, we recommend to you these young students, who merit, by virtue of their gratitude, to be the children of the Republic and the hope of the Fatherland.

[signed] The teachers of the Section des Gravilliers,

Casin and Larouly, at the Presbytery.

Note. In the month of July, they [the students] presented their patriotic gift. The young person who gave the speech asked for support for [our] work. She was warmly applauded and greeted by the president, who assured her he would look into the matter. We were accorded the honors of the meeting, and Haudoin and several journalists mentioned this event. Haudoin added that they could be offered as a prize to the youth at the frontiers.

3. Citoyenne Jeanne Guillemette Galimard, Femme Poulet, Defends Herself Before the Jacobin Establishment Against the Charge of Guilt by Association

Source: A.N., F⁷ 4714, dossier 3.

The Law of Suspects (September 17, 1793) inaugurated the legal Terror. Revolutionary Committees in each Section were authorized to investigate and detain suspects; in such proceedings, rumored remarks and liaisons were often used as evidence of disloyalty to the Republic. Female domestics like Femme Poulet were particularly vulnerable, as many of them expressed sympathy for their former masters and mistresses. Unlike their employers, however, domestics rarely had an opportunity to escape or pay for privileged treatment in prisons. Femme Poulet's petition is indicative of the kind of effort a suspect might have to make to counter the circumstantial evidence that had led to her imprisonment.

———————

District Françiade, Department of Paris, Form to be filled out by the Committee of Surveillance of Auteuil, on its own responsibility, within eight days, counting the day it is received.

Name of detained; address before his detention; age; number of children; their age; where they are living; whether he [the detained] *is a widower, bachelor, married.*
Jeanne Guillemette Galimard, Femme Poulet, gardener at the Tuileries in the Commune of Auteuil; age thirty-four, married, with a son who is living in Auteuil with his father.

Place of detention; when and how long; by whose orders; why:
Detained since the twenty-sixth of the first month of Year II of the

Republic, first at Auteuil, and later moved to the prison of Section de l'Unité, and since 12 Brumaire at the prison of l'Abbaye, by order of the Committee of Surveillance of the Commune of Auteuil, following a number of denunciations for remarks unworthy of a citizen.

Profession before and since the Revolution:
A gardener for the house of La Tour du Pin, Governor, before and since the Revolution.

Revenue before and since the Revolution.
Living from her work before and since the Revolution.

Relations, liaisons.
None known except for those living in the house of La Tour du Pin, Governor.

Character and political opinions in the months of May, July, and October, 1789; 16 August; at the time of the flight and the death of the tyrant; 31 May, and during war crises; whether he signed any petitions or orders fatal to liberty [arrêtés liberticides].
Her character and opinions were unknown to us before today, when she was denounced, but it appears from denunciations that on August 10, far from being afflicted by the loss of patriots who perished during this *journée,* she had cried out that it had been advantageous, and that she much regretted the death of the tyrant.

Drawn up by us, members of the Committee of Surveillance of the Commune of Auteuil, meeting on 17 Floreal, Year II of the French Republic, One and Indivisible.

[signatures appended]

[In an undated petition to the citizen members of the *commission populaire,* femme Poulet related her efforts to prove her patriotism:]

Liberty, Equality, Fraternity, or Death
                    To the citizens composing the *commission populaire*
Citizens,
Having always comported myself in a manner beyond any possible reproach whatever, even during the Revolution—because I have done for it everything a *citoyenne* could do whose only wealth is the strength of her arms and who will not allow herself to be dragged into involvement in any political matter—that did not prevent my being arrested eight

months ago following a denunciation made out of vengeance and malice. As several certificates will show, I always comported myself as an honest woman should. A reclamation to the Comité de Sureté Général [is] signed by thirty-three persons known for their *civisme* and good republican principles.

I reclaim, Citizens, your complete justice, so that a luckless husband may have his cherished wife back, [and] a young child a mother who will take care that he become a good and honest republican.

Salut et fraternité,

[signed]
Jeanne Galimard,
Femme Poulet, gardener

4. PATRIOTISM MEASURED BY THE SHAPE OF DESSERTS
   SERVED AT A PARTY IN YEAR II

Source: A.N., F⁷ 4774, box 64, case of Citoyenne Marie-Anne
Scholastique Macé, Femme Paul, Américaine.

Everything had political connotations in the Year II. Local
authorities were suspicious of Citoyenne Macé, Femme Paul,
Américaine, in August, 1793, because she served "royalist"
heart-shaped desserts, allowed her children to sing "royalist"
songs at a party, and associated with foreigners and libertines.

———

. . . Then we called Citoyenne Marie-Anne Scholastique Macé, Femme
Paul, a native of Cap Français, living on rue de Bondy, no. 51, in Paris,
for the past three years, but on rue de Bondy for only two years, and
before that on rue St. Thomas de Louvre, near the church.

Q. Did she serve a meal for a *fête de marie,* prepared and served at her
   home?
A. Yes.
Q. How many guests were present?
A. About twenty-five, including her children.
Q. Did she know all those present?
A. She knew the musician who was her son's tutor and who also did the
   entertaining. This musician was named Guérin and was the oldest
   son; [he,] along with two of his brothers, was associated with some
   Italians. Also at the meal were Madame Béguin and her family as
   well as Citoyenne Béguin's brother; Citoyenne Gavaudin; an actress
   at the Opera . . . and several others, brought along by one or an-
   other [of the guests, and] whom she didn't know. . . .
Q. Was there something extraordinary served at the meal?
A. No.
Q. Among the desserts, wasn't there a dish everyone was talking about?
A. No.

Q. Wasn't there a white heart?

A. It was a *fromage à la crème,* shaped in the form of a heart.

Q. Didn't someone make some joke about the *fromage à la crème?*

A. No. And besides, if some jokes were made, they were made in such low voices that she hadn't heard.

Q. Was there singing at the meal?

A. Yes, but it was done by her children, who had composed a few short couplets for her party.

Q. Weren't there some other songs sung?

A. None had been sung.

Q. When patriotic songs were sung, weren't there some supplementary couplets sung, like *Va t'en voir s'ils viennent, Jean,* and wasn't the refrain very warmly applauded?

A. No. The singing of patriotic songs was not in question, nor the above-mentioned refrains. . . .

[She signed her statement.]

[Then Citoyenne Victoire Marie Heurtin, the cook and *femme de chambre* for Citoyenne Paul, appeared. Like many domestic servants during Year II, Citoyenne Heurtin supported her mistress:]

Q. Was she at the meal?

A. Yes, she was present.

Q. What was the dessert?

A. Biscuits, fruit, and *fromage à la crème.*

Q. What was the shape of the *fromage?*

A. Heart-shaped.

Q. What was said about the heart?

A. She knew nothing about this. And as she was doing the serving, and was coming and going, she couldn't know.

Q. Were there some songs sung?

A. There were some, but they were couplets sung by Citoyenne Paul's children.

[She signed her statement.]

[Citizen Douillet and his wife and Citizen Dombey, guests at the party, were also interrogated. The Douillet couple left the party early. Although neither gave much information, Citizen Dombey, their neighbor, overheard Citizen Douillet say:]

. . . at the meal there was a white heart concerning which a comparison was made. It was said that only Louis XVI's heart was as white. Aristocratic songs were sung which everyone applauded except him, Douillet. He crossed his arms and was very bored and grumbled at finding himself the only patriot. He also said, "As my wife was pregnant and feeling indisposed, we left before the end of the meal." In addition, the above-mentioned Douillet said, "In society the word 'citizen' must not be used," and [he said] that he believed that they were all aristocrats. . . .

[Citizen Douillet reappeared and added to his earlier testimony, acknowledging that he was told that there was a *crème en forme de coeur* for dessert; that while he was at the party, he had heard the words *roi* and *coeur blanc* spoken; and that during a conversation later on between him and Citizen Dombey, he had himself called attention to the connection between the two phrases *roi* and *coeur blanc*.]

5. Patriotism and Antipatriotism in the Classroom:
The Case of Citoyenne Raubour

Source: A.N., F⁷ 4774, dossier 87.

The question of female education was an important issue within
the Paris Sections. The crux of the problem was that there were
too few laywomen qualified to staff the public schools; frequently
former nuns in teaching orders were allowed to remain as
teachers in the newly created secular schools. Although former
nuns were required to swear an oath of loyalty to the Republic,
parents, children, and revolutionary authorities were quick to
question their patriotism. In the case of the *institutrice* Raubour,
a former nun with the teaching order of the Filles de Saint-Croix,
students testified to local authorities that Raubour was reluctant
to teach the Declaration of the Rights of Man and Citizen
properly; she administered whippings, and she gave preferential
treatment to paying students.

———————

[Citoyenne Catherine Potel, twelve and one-half years old, who lived
with her parents at rue de la Tisseranderie, no. 127, was called upon to
testify.]

Q. Whose writing was this [on the copy of an exercise that was sub-
   mitted to her for identification]?
A. It was hers.
Q. Who had given her this exercise?
A. Les Filles de la Croy.
Q. Who made her hand over her papers?
A. Her teachers.
Q. Was this sheet [the one in the *commissaires'* possession] the only one
   there was when it was turned over to the citizen *commissaire?*
A. There were three of them.

Q. Did she still have the two others?

A. No.

Q. Were the same words used on the other two sheets?

A. She does not remember.

Q. Who had obtained this exercise from her?

A. Her Aunt Charlotte.

Q. Where was this exercise?

A. Her Aunt Charlotte took it away.

Q. Why was this exercise still among her papers?

A. Because she always recopied the same thing.

Q. Did Citoyenne Raubour correct it when she wrote it out?

A. Yes, but she said only, "You do not write in a straight line, you must write more correctly."

Q. For how long had she been writing it [this exercise]?

A. For about four years.

Q. Why did she have only three sheets in the classroom?

A. Whenever she filled them, she picked up three more.

Q. Had she written the three sheets in the classroom?

A. Yes.

Q. At the time the *commissaires* made their inspection of the schools, were these the most recent exercises she had written?

A. Yes.

Q. Were all the sheets [?] dated?

A. She had dated them the way they were because she did not know the dates for the days. . . .

Q. Is the "Declaration of Man" [*sic*] on the exercises the children copy?

A. She saw it the other day.

Q. Did she hear that the children told the four *commissaires* that it was Aunt Raubour who opposed putting down "Rights of Man and Citizen" and who said to put only "Declaration of Man"?

A. Yes.

Q. Were there students in the class who were paying students?

A. Yes. Little Vincent had sixty *sous* or three *livres* in reserve to pay for a month of schooling, and Soeur Raubour made the nonpaying students sweep the classroom while not forcing the others [the paying students] to do so.

Q. Do the paying students leave at the same time as the others?

A. No, and she always stayed one-half hour or an hour at the disposition of Soeur Raubour.

Q. Did Soeur Raubour use the stock of a cat-o'-nine-tails?

A. Yes. She hit young Dumoy with it; his arms were black from it.

Q. Had Soeur Raubour been to her parents' home?
A. Yes. She had been there yesterday, in fact, to solicit them. . . .

[Catherine Potel's parents were questioned about Soeur Marie-Jeanne Raubour. Then the *commissaires* interrogated Citoyenne Raubour, former nun with Les Filles de la Croy, and presently a teacher in the schools in the Saint-Gervais Parish.]

Q. Why did she allow students to copy antirevolutionary exercises after she had sworn an oath to teach students confided to her care in accordance with revolutionary principles?
A. She had only the young Potel copy this exercise, and she was not aware that the style of this exercise was contrary to the principles of the Revolution.
Q. Since when had the Potel girl been copying this exercise, which she admitted was in the Potel child's hand?
A. Since she entered the class.
Q. Through whom had this exercise gotten there?
A. The Potel girl, in an interview with her, told her that she received it from Soeur Charlotte, sister in the above-named establishment. Last Tuesday, the thirteenth of this month, according to what the Potel girl told her, the *commissaires* determined that the aforementioned exercise was contrary to the principles of good citizenship. Citoyenne Raubour told her to tear it up, at which point the above-named Potel told her that she already had done so.

Observation on this matter: The above-named Raubour went to the home of Citizen Potel, a wine merchant, on Sunday, the twenty-first of this month, between 10 and 11 A.M. She begged his daughter, in particular, for assurance in her own words that the stated exercise no longer existed. To this the young Potel answered that she had torn it up, and Raubour, in addition, told the Potel girl to forget about it . . . and not to avow this exercise or read it herself or [allow it to be read] by any of her friends. . . .

Q. What did young Potel's mother tell her when she [Raubour] went to see her? What was the conversation about?
A. The conversation was about the accusation against her of alleged behavior unbecoming to a good citizen. And the above-named Raubour declared that she engaged and solicited the above-named

Citoyenne Femme Potel to appear yesterday before the General Assembly of this Section in order to discredit this opinion.

Q. Why, having come to the above-mentioned General Assembly, and having been given the floor so that she might justify herself, didn't she see fit to acknowledge this exercise?

A. She intended to, but because she was confused, she didn't think of it.

Q. What exercise replaced the one she had ordered torn up about the sixteenth of this month?

A. She gave them the "Rights of Man and Citizen" to copy.

Q. Why, when the *commissaires* visited the above-named school, did the children complain that the above-named Raubour was opposed to their putting "Rights of Man and Citizen" [at the beginning of the exercise], and why did she want them to write instead only "Declaration of Man"?

A. The allegation is false.

Q. Why did she have paying students in her school?

A. Because there wasn't any law against it; she had five who paid forty *sous* each and one who paid fifty *sous*.

Q. Why did she keep the children who paid at their lessons one hour later [than the children who were nonpaying]?

A. As she was obliged to supervise the children's reading and writing, she was unable to give to those who paid all the care which her conscience dictated, which obliged her to keep them later than she kept the others.

Q. Why did she discipline her pupils with the stock of her cat-o'-nine-tails?

A. She did not use the above-mentioned stock, but she did use the cat-o'-nine-tails.

Q. Did she have anything to add?

A. No.

After this testimony was read back to her, she declared that it contained the truth and persisted in this, and signed with us.

Citoyenne Raubour's colleague, Citoyenne Jeanne Esterre Dufour, Femme Bertran, was called and testified that she had found the antipatriotic exercise in young Potel's notebook. She also confirmed the testimony of others concerning Raubour's method of disciplining her pupils and her discrimination in favor of paying pupils. Other colleagues, Citoyennes Marie-Anne Dierri, Femme Souffletaux, and Citoyenne Louise Nicole Deschamps, also offered incriminating testimony. [At this point the *commissaires* decided to visit the school.]

. . . And then we, the *commissaires* of the integrated Sections des Droits de l'homme and de la Maison Commune, on July 23, at 9 A.M., went to the school of the children of this Section in a house situated on rue des Bard in the former Communauté des Filles de la Croy. We went up to the first floor. We entered a room looking out on two courtyards. We found twenty children there. Having called upon them to tell us the name of the teacher, they answered that it was Citoyenne Raubour. We called upon one of them, young Citoyenne Charlotte Victoire Poule. She appeared. We asked her to tell us what exercises she had been given to copy. She replied that she would show us her notebook. Having examined it and found nothing contrary to principles, we called upon her to tell us whether she knew whether there were still any paying children in the school.

A. She knew nothing about it.
Q. Did she recall whether she had the money in reserve to pay for the month on the day the *commissaires* made their visit?
A. She offered 50 *sols:* She added that she [Raubour] hit the children with the stock of the cat-o'-nine-tails and that she struck them in the face with books.
Q. Could she tell us which children wrote the exercise with *monarque des monarques* written in it?
A. Young Potel. It was taken from her, and she, Fille Raubour, tore up the [illegible] of a page she was still working on.

She told us she had nothing further to declare and signed. After [her testimony] was read back to her, she added nothing and did not want to retract anything and signed as follows: Charlotte Victoire Poule.

And as a natural consequence of our procedures, we called up Marie Geneviève Auvergne to declare and state before us whether she had cause to complain of bad treatment by the above-mentioned Raubour, either towards her herself or towards her classmates.

A. She had nothing to reproach her with since the *commissaires'* visit, except that she forgot or didn't want to put "Declaration of the Rights of Man" into her exercises; that she was satisfied with putting "Declaration of Man." She, the Auvergne girl, had pointed this out to her, and then the above-named Raubour had put it at the top [of the exercise]. She scolded them . . . when they deserved it, but no longer hit them with the stock of her cat-o'-nine-tails.

We then asked to see her bruise, which she showed us on the spot, and we observed the truth of her statements. We read it to her. She stated that it contained the truth and persisted in this and signed as follows: Marie Geneviève Auvergne.

Then we read out loud the above-mentioned two statements to all the assembled students, thirty in number, and they were asked to state whether what was contained there was true. They said yes and added that there were still preferred students. Those who paid did not have to sweep or clean the classroom, and they added that Citoyenne LeBlanc, who is sick and walks with a cane, was still being mistreated, notably yesterday, when she [Raubour] dragged her the length of the classroom and made her spend part of the time on her knees.

[pupils' signatures appended.]

[The *commissaires* visited a second classroom on the first floor.]
   . . . We asked the pupils present [which teacher] was usually at the school, and they answered that Citoyenne Deschamps was. We asked the students to tell us the truth, consulting their hearts and their consciences, and having, as in the other [classroom], made an inspection and search, we found nothing contrary to principles. They [the pupils] told us, after we asked them whether they had any complaints about Citoyenne Deschamps, that they had none. Asked if she hit them, they answered no. They were then asked whether they learned how to read well, and they answered, yes, and that they liked her a lot; and not one of them was able to sign [her name].

Then we went down to the ground floor to the classroom of Citoyennes Dufour and Souffletaux. Having completed an inspection and search, we found only the constitution along with the "Rights of Man" and other patriotic manuscripts. We asked the children present, more than forty little girls, to tell us whether they had any complaints to make concerning Citoyenne Dufour and Citoyenne Souffletaux and whether they were wicked and whether they liked them. They answered unanimously that they liked them a lot and that they were good and that they taught them how to read well. Moreover, we saw the "Rights of Man" framed in the said school, which proved the truth to us; and none of them was able to sign her name. . . .

[The *commissaires* visited Citoyenne Raubour's classroom and found no incriminating evidence. They made visits to the teachers' homes. At the homes of Citoyennes Souffletaux, Deschamps, and Dufour, they turned up no evidence of antipatriotism. They then decided to make a second visit to Citoyenne Raubour's home, which had been visited earlier in the day.]

We went there again at 6 P.M. to go through her papers and books once again. We did that. We found a brochure entitled: *Second Preface,* or *Conversation about Novels,* and inside was marked *La Nouvelle Héloïse.* We went through it, and having seen that it contained burlesque things, we had it numbered and sealed with wax by Citoyenne Raubour. And we confiscated it and deposited it with the Committee of Section de la Maison Commune, given that Citoyenne Raubour, being a teacher, should not be moved by any other passion than that of dedicating her every minute to moral education and [given] that this libidinous book might fall into the hands of her pupils.

Q. How did she get this book?
A. She bought it along with others.
Q. When did she become the owner of it?
A. She made no note of the date.

Notation made that this book was found in a room on the second floor which she was occupying and noted in addition that the last [page?] is inscribed as having belonged, it would appear, to Madame Bozaire de Groslai.

After having read her [statement] to her, and as we were on the verge of leaving, a neighbor came in who wanted to make the above-named Raubour listen to reason, but she refused to listen. And then, with this last statement, we called upon her to speak to us from her heart and her conscience and to tell us where the book was which we had seen in the morning. She replied that she had no others. Whereupon we, the *commissaires,* being in the aforementioned room and having entry to a little closet abutting the fireplace, found an obscene brochure there entitled *The Monk of St. Denis,* which we numbered and sealed with wax from the first to the last page. With it there was another brochure entitled *New Love Letters and Travels in the Isle of Love,* which we likewise numbered and sealed with it. Fourth, a motto from St. Theresa, which seemed to us to be suspicious. We numbered and sealed all of it. We made a bundle which we took to our brothers sitting on the Revolutionary Committee of [the Section] de la Maison Commune. We asked Citoyenne Raubour a second time if she was agreeable to having these aforementioned objects, listed in the present *procès-verbal,* numbered and sealed; she answered yes. And after her [statement] was read to her, having acknowledged that it contained the truth, she signed with us, M. J. Raubour . . . and we concluded the present *procès-verbal* at 9 P.M. on July 23, 1792, Year Two of the French Republic, One and Indivisible, leaving to the Sections, meeting in General Assembly, the right to legislate definitively on the result of this affair by drawing distinctions between vice and virtue.

6. The Jacobins Shore Up Republican Families

Source: A.N., F⁷ 4696, dossier 2.

The Jacobins subscribed to bourgeois values on the importance·of
the nuclear family, the virtues of domestic tranquility, and
maternity. The Revolutionary Committee of the Section des Amis
de la Patrie exemplified Jacobin views on model family life in its
reconciliation of the runaway Jeanne Angot with her mother.
Even though Jeanne was twenty years of age, the Committee
believed it important that she live with her mother until she
came under the protection of a husband. (Note that date,
addresses, and other information are missing from this
manuscript.)

———————————

We, the Commissaire of the Revolutionary Committee of Section des
Amis de la Patrie, asked Citizen Durandeau, mayor of La Catre, in the
Department of Indre, to be present in Paris along with the young
citoyenne in order to appear before our committee. We asked him the
name of the young person who was with him and who her family was.
He told us that she was one of his nieces and that she had a mother in
Paris, but that this girl was not pleased with where her mother had put
her; she had come to live with him. Next we interrogated the young
person, asking for her name and age. She stated that she was Jeanne
Angot, age twenty years and three months. We asked her whether she
would be content to return to the home of her father and mother, and
she answered, "Yes," but on the condition that her mother would be
willing to forget all the past with respect to her, and [as for herself,] she
will always try to earn her mother's love with good conduct.

Then Citoyenne Angot, now Femme Lembin, appeared and showed
her extreme joy at seeing her daughter. We asked her whether she
would be pleased to have her daughter with her. She answered that this
would be her crowning wish. After having seen the good disposition

they showed toward one another, we believed it was our duty to reunite them; to discharge the uncle, Citizen Durandeau, from his wardship over the young Citoyenne Angot; and to restore her to the hands of her mother. We asked them to sign the present conciliation with us.

[signature appended.]

Consequently, we have undertaken to write to the constituted authority in the place where Citoyenne Angot is living with her mother so as to inform ourselves concerning the comportment of mother and daughter respectively.

[signature appended.]

7. STATEMENTS OF SEAMSTRESSES ASKING RELEASE FROM PRISON

Source: A.N., F^7 4754, dossier 3.

On 23 Pluviose, Year II, the Revolutionary Tribunal freed three women who had been charged with making counterrevolutionary remarks tending to the reestablishment of royalty. The women were Victoire Gaudin, thirty-seven years old, a native of Provence; Rose Laborderie, twenty-one years old, a native of Champagne; and Françoise Deleus, thirty years old, a native of Abbeville. They were all *culottières,* all living at the same address, rue Ste. Antoine, no. 353. While technically freed by the judgment of the Tribunal, they were ordered to appear once every ten days before the Revolutionary Committee in their Section. One of them protested this arrangement in a petition to the Committee of General Security.

———————————◆———————————

To be sent to the Committee of General Security

Citizens:

Rose Laborderie, Victoire Gaudin, and Françoise Deleus, having been, during a five-month period, victims of a denunciation, although it was devoid of any evidence, were given their liberty by the Revolutionary Tribunal on 23 Pluviose, Year II of the Republic; [the tribunal] stated that there was no basis for the accusation against us and ordered our liberation on the condition that we appear once every ten days before the Revolutionary Committee of our Section, called La Maison Commune, and subsequently, de la Fidelité. And that is what we are still doing. Until now we have satisfied [the conditions of] this judgment.

But citizens, I leave it to you to judge whether it is cruel for citizens who always were [citizens], and who were placed under arrest only through the work of calumny, to have to moan in enslavement for a year now, notwithstanding our release from prison, or, to put it better, under a tyranny which is cruelest for pure hearts—under a suspicion

which, notwithstanding our innocence, exposes us to vexations by ignorant or intriguing persons. It can be seen from our verdicts that the
Revolutionary Tribunal recognized the jealousy which drove these
women to inculpate us.

Citizens, I write in the name of my companions. We ask you for our
full liberty. It is not necessary for us to reclaim your compassion for our
condition, which is becoming a continual subjection for us and which
often impedes us from carrying on our personal business. The purity of
our cause requires only that your justice be invoked; it must speak in our
favor.

It is our hope, citizens, that you might be willing to deliberate
speedily on this case.

Salut et fraternité
[signed] Rose Laborderie

8. A Woman of the People Asks the Revolutionary Establishment for Justice for Her Husband and Herself

Source: A.N., F⁷ 4775, dossier 1.

The legal terror confused and frightened many *femmes sans-culottes*. They approved laws which punished enemies of the people, but they could not understand why laws punished citizens like themselves. In letters on behalf of male relatives they asked for justice tempered by compassion and for speedy decisions—so that the family economy would not be shattered as male bread-winners awaited trial in jail. Femme Sauges, the wife of a *jacqueroutin*, depicted the plight of her family during her husband's long imprisonment. Although she did not understand fully the political quarrel between Jacobins and *jacqueroutins*, she did know that she and her children were doomed if her husband's case was not decided immediately.

———————————◆———————————

1 Nivoise, Year Two of The French Republic, One and Indivisible, 1793.

Citizen President:

It is to your committee that a poor *citoyenne* [appeals], a mother with a family who awaits only the time for giving birth to a republican, who is deprived of all means, who even finds herself in the greatest indigence since her husband's detention on the night of 6/7 Frimaire for a very minor cause, and that can only be that he held views [dictated by] his too-zealous patriotism [which] caused him to forget the respect he owed to the laws. Citizens, I request of you in your wisdom that he be interrogated in order to prove to you that he is a republican and that his only objective is to merit the esteem of his fellow citizens. Having only the resource of his strength for my subsistence and my children's, I appeal to your generous hearts; render me this important service which my distressing situation demands. With the most fervent gratitude,

[signed]

Femme Sauges

9. CITOYENNES CHALLENGE THE JACOBIN ESTABLISHMENT
   TO DEMONSTRATE THE JUSTICE OF SUMMARY ARRESTS

Source: A.N., F⁷ 4601, plaque 9, dossier Bizeau.

Female domestics received lower wages than their male
counterparts and were often employed by middle-class families of
moderate means who could not afford male servants. Such
women were frequently insulted in the marketplace during the
Year II for serving "unpatriotic" families. Several lost their
positions when their employers were imprisoned. The letter of
Citoyenne Carre, the domestic for a family arrested under the
Law of Suspects, suggests her confusion over the aims of
revolutionary justice since her family had, in her opinion, always
served the public interest and the Revolution.

———————————

Citizen President:
    . . . The *citoyenne* [Carre] with these titles [enumerated in the first
paragraph of her letter, omitted here] dares reclaim a family abducted
from its home on 3 Vendémiaire by a mere *mandat d'arrêt* issued by the
Committee of Surveillance in Section de l'Arsenal. This unfortunate
family, obedient, as it must be, to the law, does not make [any com-
plaint] and did not have any complaint made against the Committee. It
believes that severe measures which the Committee's vigilance dictates it
take are directed only toward serving the public interest. But, Citizen
President, this measure is perhaps too severe—carrying off an entire
family, composed of a grandfather, a father, a mother, and two children,
who breathe only to do good. All those in the Section in charge of
collecting for the expenses of the Vendée, or for the Section's poor, have
always found their purses open, as much as was possible [and] with the
pleasure which a good republican must feel when he is useful to his
Fatherland. [This family] never signed anything opposing the decrees of
the National Convention and took pleasure only in supporting the un-

fortunate. Citizen President, I am an example [of the good they have done]. I am without riches, and I have, for several years, owed my existence, I and others, to them. Their abduction deprives me of every- thing, but I do not complain for myself. The gratitude I owe to this unfortunate family dictates to me that I die to save them if there is no other way, but I speak to legislators who hold the balance of justice in their hands, and my despair is calmed.

This is a summary, Citizen President. The excess of our ills would be at its limit if all the unfortunate did not have a right to your justice and to your equity. Obedient to the laws, I ask to be heard. This is the cry of all good citizens and true *sans-culottes*.

10. CITOYENNE DUCROQUET SURVIVES UNDER THE JACOBIN
    REGIME

Source: "Lettre de la mère de Ducroquet à son fils," in Walter
Markov and Albert Soboul, eds., *Die Sans-culotten von Paris:
Dokumente zur Geschichte der Volksbewegung, 1793–1794,* pp.
340–42.

This letter from a mother to her son indicates that the Jacobin
economic legislation did not end the housewife's struggle to
provide daily necessities for her family. It also indicates the
underlying tensions these women lived with: confusion over the
requirements of documentary proof of hardship and fear of
sudden arrest. Note that Mme. Ducroquet's fear that her son
might have been arrested was in fact borne out. He was
guillotined on 4 Germinal.

———————

                         Damiens, this fourth of Ventose,
                         Year Two of the Republic
My son:
    I write you to let you know that tomorrow, or the day after tomor-
row, I will send off a small package of old things for your children. I
wanted to have something better; for the moment, I have nothing else.
The postage will be paid. As for me, I am not yet doing very well. Good
food is unavailable. There is nothing to be had. I was waiting patiently
for the first of Ventôse, hoping it would have brought back a little
plenty—but nothing. To get four eggs you have to get in a line with
six hundred people to wait your turn, and for everything, generally.
They say nothing about soap either, except that there will not be any
more. All that is taking a long time to come. You have to stay filthy for
lack of it.
    Our *prévôt* cousins send best regards. He asks you as soon as you have
received [it, a procuration mentioned below] at M. de Verdun's, to send

[it] to him. You shouldn't wait to receive [one] for Sagnier and Quiotte. They aren't in need. With them, the death of their mother separates them, but as for those who remain at home, very much in need, there are still three. As I told them, there is a delay concerning the arrest of Verdun. I told them we were in need, as they are; that as soon as you receive [it] at Citizen Verdun's, you would sent it to us.

She brought me a little cake. I send you a piece. It will be a bit hard, but you can heat it up. About a certificate, August answered. He told me he knew all about it, but that these favors are only for those who can prove they have nothing and that their children provide for their subsistence. Nonetheless, he said that if they were willing to give us one, he would send it to us; but your father says he will not show his face in town because he will be disgraced.

You will find several books that I am sending back to you. In one you will find a ten-*livre* bill. Three *livres* of this comes from Sophia [for] your pomade and the money for your bottle. The rest is for your children. This book will be tied up with string. Look out for it. Let me know, I beg you, when you have received it at Citoyenne Roucoult's address, and don't delay, because I'll be uneasy.

I saw in the paper that someone named Ducroquet was arrested. I'll admit to you that that obsesses me, although I know full well, and I am quite sure, that you are a good patriot. This name, Ducroquet, caught my eye, but I was told that it was a deputy in the assembly. Let me have some news from you. That would give me pleasure, as I think you know. I send you my love, and I am,

Your mother, Harlay Ducroquet

Undoubtedly you received the letter and the procuration from Sagnier. Today, Monday, I will put the package in the carriage. It is possible that it will leave tomorrow.

11. THE TRIAL OF A FEMINIST REVOLUTIONARY, OLYMPE DE GOUGES

Source: *Bulletin du Tribunal criminel révolutionnaire* (Paris, n.d.
[1793]), nos. 66, 67, pp. 264–68, in Bibliothèque historique
de la Ville de Paris, 104,843, vol. 2.

One of the famous victims of the Terror was Olympe de
Gouges, author of the Declaration of the Rights of Woman
(chapter two, above, document 10). De Gouges claimed she was
happy about the Republic once she convinced herself that the
King was a traitor. But in 1793 she circulated tracts critical of
the Terror. In July she was arrested and imprisoned in the
Abbaye for having published a document suggesting a popular
referendum on the form of government France should have.
After an interrogation before the Revolutionary Tribunal on 11
Brumaire (November 1, 1793), de Gouges was condemned to
death. She stated that she was pregnant. That appeal, had it
been accepted, would have delayed her sentence until the birth
of the child. The court ordered a medical examination, and her
appeal was denied. She was guillotined on 13 Brumaire.

Audience of . . . 12 Brumaire, Year II of the Republic.
Case of Olympe de Gouges.
Questioned concerning her name, surname, age, occupation, place of
birth, and residence. Replied that her name was Marie Olympe de
Gouges, age thirty-eight, *femme de lettres,* a native of Montauban, living
in Paris, rue du Harlay, Section Pont-Neuf.
The clerk read the act of accusation, the tenor of which follows.

Antoine-Quentin Fouquier-Tinville, public prosecutor before the
Revolutionary Tribunal, etc.
States that, by an order of the administrators of police, dated last July

25, signed Louvet and Baudrais, it was ordered that Marie Olympe de Gouges, widow of Aubry, charged with having composed a work contrary to the expressed desire of the entire nation, and directed against whoever might propose a form of government other than that of a republic, one and indivisible, be brought to the prison called l'Abbaye, and that the documents be sent to the public prosecutor of the Revolutionary Tribunal. Consequently, the accused was brought to the designated prison and the documents delivered to the public prosecutor on July 26. The following August 6, one of the judges of the Revolutionary Tribunal proceeded with the interrogation of the above-mentioned de Gouges woman.

From the examination of the documents deposited, together with the interrogation of the accused, it follows that against the desire manifested by the majority of Frenchmen for republican government, and in contempt of laws directed against whoever might propose another form of government, Olympe de Gouges composed and had printed works which can only be considered as an attack on the sovereignty of the people because they tend to call into question that concerning which it [the people] formally expressed its desire; that in her writing, entitled *Les Trois urnes, ou le Salut de la patrie,* there can be found the project of the liberty-killing faction which wanted to place before the people the approbation of the judgment of the tyrant condemned by the people itself; that the author of this work openly provoked civil war and sought to arm citizens against one another by proposing the meeting of primary assemblies to deliberate and express their desire concerning either monarchical government, which the national sovereignty had abolished and proscribed; concerning the one and indivisible republican [form], which it had chosen and established by the organ of its representatives; or, finally, concerning the federative [form], which would be the source of incalculable evils and which would destroy liberty infallibly.

. . . The public prosecutor stated next that it is with the most violent indignation that one hears the de Gouges woman say to men who for the past four years have not stopped making the greatest sacrifices for liberty; who on August 10, 1792, overturned both the throne and the tyrant; who knew how to bravely face the arms and frustrate the plots of the despot, his slaves, and the traitors who had abused the public confidence — to men who have submitted tyranny to the avenging blade of the law — that Louis Capet still reigns among them.

There can be no mistaking the perfidious intentions of this criminal woman, and her hidden motives, when one observes her in all the works to which, at the very least, she lends her name, calumniating and spewing out bile in large doses against the warmest friends of the people, their most intrepid defender.

In a manuscript seized in her home, on which she placed a patriotic title only in order to get her poisons circulated more freely, she places in the mouth of the monster who surpasses the Messalinas and the Medicis these impious expressions—"the placard-makers, these paper scribblings, are not worth a Marat, a Robespierre; in the specious language of patriotism, they overturn everything in the name of the people; they appear to be serving propaganda and never have heads of factions better served the cause of kings; at one and the same time they serve two parties moving at a rapid pace towards the same goal. I love these enterprising men; they have a thorough knowledge of the difficult art of imposing on human weaknesses; they have sensed from the beginning that in order to serve me it was necessary to blaze a trail in the opposite direction; applaud yourself, Calonne, this is your work."

Lastly, in the work in question one sees only provocation to the reestablishment of royalty on the part of a woman who, in one of her writings, admits that monarchy seems to her to be the government most suited to the French spirit; who in [the writing] in question points out that the desire for the republic was not freely pronounced; who, lastly, in another [writing] is not afraid to parody the traitor Isnard and to apply to all of France what the former restricted to the city of Paris alone, so calumniated by the partisans of royalty and by those of federalism.

On the basis of the foregoing exposé the public prosecutor drew up this accusation against Marie Olympe de Gouges, widow Aubry, for having maliciously and purposefully composed writings attacking the sovereignty of the people (whose desire, when these were written, had been pronounced for republican government, one and indivisible) and tending towards the reestablishment of the monarchical government (which it [the people] had formally proscribed) as well as the federative [form] (against which it [the people] had forcefully protested); for having had printed up and distributed several copies of one of the cited works tending towards these ends, entitled, *Les Trois urnes, ou le Salut de la patrie;* for having been stopped in her distribution of a greater number of copies as well as in her posting of the cited work only by the refusal of the bill-poster and by her prompt arrest; for having sent this work to her son, employed in the army of the Vendée as *officier de l'état major;* for having, in other manuscripts and printed works—notably, in the manuscript entitled *La France sauvée, ou le Tyran détrôné* as well as in the poster entitled *Olympe de Gouges au Tribunal Révolutionnaire*—sought to degrade the constituted authorities, calumniate the friends and defenders of the people and of liberty, and spread defiance among the representatives and the represented, which is contrary to the laws, and notably to that of last December 4.

Consequently, the public prosecutor asks that he be given official notice by the assembled Tribunal of this indictment, etc., etc.

In this case only three witnesses were heard, one of whom was the citizen bill-poster, who stated that, having been asked to post a certain number of copies of printed material with the title *Les Trois urnes,* he refused when he found out about the principles contained in this writing.

When the accused was questioned sharply about when she composed this writing, she replied that it was some time last May, adding that what motivated her was that seeing the storms arising in a large number of *départements,* and notably in Bordeaux, Lyons, Marseilles, etc., she had the idea of bringing all parties together by leaving them all free in the choice of the kind of government which would be most suitable for them; that furthermore, her intentions had proven that she had in view only the happiness of her country.

Questioned about how it was that she, the accused, who believed herself to be such a good patriot, had been able to develop, in the month of June, means which she called conciliatory concerning a fact which could no longer be in question because the people, at that period, had formally pronounced for republican government, one and indivisible, she replied that this was also the [form of government] she had voted for as the preferable one; that for a long while she had professed only republican sentiments, as the jurors would be able to convince themselves from her work entitled *De l'esclavage des noirs.*

A reading was provided by Naulin, the public prosecutor's substitute, of a letter written by the accused to Herault-Séchelles in which principles of federalism are found.

The accused replied to this fact that her intention had been, as she had said already, pure and that she wanted to be able to show her heart to the citizen jurors so that they might judge her love of liberty and her hatred of every kind of tyranny.

Asked to declare whether she acknowledged authorship of a manuscript work found among her papers entitled *La France sauvée ou le Tyran détrôné,* she replied yes.

Asked why she had placed injurious and perfidious declamations against the most ardent defenders of the rights of the people in the mouth of the person who in this work was supposed to represent the

Capet woman, she replied that she had the Capet woman speaking the language appropriate for her; that besides, the handbill for which she was brought before the Tribunal had never been posted; that to avoid compromising herself she had decided to send twenty-four copies to the Committee of Public Safety, which, two days later, had her arrested.

The public prosecutor pointed out to the accused, concerning this matter, that if her placard entitled *Les Trois urnes* had not been made public, this was because the bill-poster had not been willing to take it upon himself. The accused was in agreement with this fact.

Questioned about whether, since her detention, she had not sent a copy to her son along with a letter, she said that the fact was exact and that her intention concerning this matter had been to apprise him of the cause of her arrest; that besides, she did not know whether her son had received it, not having heard from him in a long while and not knowing at all what could have become of him.

Asked to speak concerning various phrases in the placard entitled *Olympe de Gouges, défenseur de Louis Capet,* a work written by her at the time of the former's trial, and concerning the placard entitled *Olympe de Gouges au Tribunal Révolutionnaire* as well, she responded only with oratorical phrases and persisted in saying that she was and always had been a good *citoyenne,* that she had never intrigued.

Asked to express herself and to reply precisely concerning her sentiments with respect to the faithful representatives of the people whom she had insulted and calumniated in her writings, the accused replied that she had not changed, that she still held to her same opinion concerning them, and that she had looked upon them as ambitious persons.

In her defense the accused said that she had ruined herself in order to propagate the principles of the Revolution and that she was the founder of popular societies of her sex, etc.

During the résumé of the charge brought by the public prosecutor, the accused, with respect to the facts she was hearing articulated against her, never stopped her smirking. Sometimes she shrugged her shoulders; then she clasped her hands and raised her eyes towards the ceiling of the room; then, suddenly, she moved on to an expressive gesture, showing astonishment; then gazing next at the court, she smiled at the spectators, etc.

Here is the judgment rendered against her.

The Tribunal, based on the unanimous declaration of the jury, stating that (1) it is a fact that there exist in the case writings tending towards the reestablishment of a power attacking the sovereignty of the people [and] (2) that Marie Olympe de Gouges, calling herself widow Aubry, is proven guilty of being the author of these writings, and admitting the conclusions of the public prosecutor, condemns the aforementioned Marie Olympe de Gouges, widow Aubry, to the punishment of death in conformity with Article One of the law of last March 29, which was read, which is conceived as follows: "Whoever is convicted of having composed or printed works or writings which provoke the dissolution of the national representation, the reestablishment of royalty, or of any other power attacking the sovereignty of the people, will be brought before the Revolutionary Tribunal and punished by death," and declares the goods of the aforementioned Marie Olympe de Gouges acquired for the republic. . . .

Orders that by the diligence of the public prosecutor this judgment will be executed on the place de la Révolution of this city [and] printed, published, and posted throughout the realm; and given the public declaration made by the aforementioned Marie Olympe de Gouges that she was pregnant, the Tribunal, following the indictment of the public prosecutor, orders that the aforementioned Marie Olympe de Gouges will be seen and visited by the sworn surgeons and doctors and matrons of the Tribunal in order to determine the sincerity of her declaration so that on the basis of their sworn and filed report the Tribunal can pronounce according to the law.

Before pronouncing his judgment, the prosecutor summoned the accused to declare whether she had some observations to make concerning the application of the law, and she replied: "My enemies will not have the glory of seeing my blood flow. I am pregnant and will bear a citizen or *citoyenne* for the Republic."

The same day [12 Brumaire], the health officer, having visited the condemned, recognized that her declaration was false.

. . . The execution took place the same day [13 Brumaire] towards 4 P.M.; while mounting the scaffold, the condemned, looking at the people, cried out: "Children of the Fatherland, you will avenge my death." Universal cries of "Vive la République" were heard among the spectators waving hats in the air.

12. Disillusionment of Femmes Sans-Culottes with the Jacobin Regime

Source: A.N., F⁷ 4748, reproduced under "Affaire Sibilot, Millard, Perrenay, Ducastellier, et autres. Interrogatoire de la Citoyenne Benoit Trivel, Femme Jannisson: Procès-verbal de la Citoyenne Jannisson," in Walter Markov and Albert Soboul, eds., *Die Sans-culotten von Paris: Dokumente zur Geschichte der Volksbewegung, 1793–1794*, pp. 398–404. Another copy in A.N., W 385, plaque 895.

In Ventôse of the Year II, Hébert (Père Duchesne) launched an abortive coup to oust the Jacobins from the National Convention and install more militant *sans-culottes* like himself. Hébert appealed for female support by conjuring up fears of a famine and a new aristocratic plot. The Jacobins retaliated, and Hébert and his associates were sent to the guillotine. Disturbances in the national workshops for women and in the marketplace were labeled "hébertiste," and several *femmes hébertistes* were imprisoned for unpatriotic behavior.

The next two documents help explain why many common women lost their zeal for the Jacobin Republic in the spring of Year II. In this interrogation of women in a Paris workshop, frightened women testified against their coworker, Femme Jannisson, who was alleged to have enlisted the support of Hébert for a petition demanding better wages and working conditions. Jannisson's case came before the Revolutionary Tribunal; a jury found her not guilty. She was freed on 25 Prairial, Year II.

Procès-verbal of Citoyenne Jannisson.

Q. . . . Asked name, age, profession, residence.

A. Benoit Trivel, Femme Jannisson, working at the spinning mill for three and one-half years, at the place of the former Jacobins, rue

Jacques; residing at rue Perdue, no. 2, place Maubert, Section du Panthéon français; age, fifty-six.

Q. Had she not submitted complaints about different people employed by the administration in the workshops at the former Jacobins, rue Jacques?

A. No, she had submitted no complaint except against Citizen Coquet and Citoyenne Cachois. . . . At 9 A.M., on 3 Floreal, Citizen Coquet, accompanied by Citoyenne Cauchois, came to find her, the *citoyenne* declarant, at her place [in the workshop], and after having ascertained that she was really Citoyenne Jannisson, he told her, the declarant, that subchief Citoyenne Cauchois was complaining that she, the declarant, was forcing her [Cauchois] to pay her more for her spinning than it was worth. Whereupon the declarant, addressing herself to Citoyenne Cauchois, said: "Quiet! I already forced you, and grabbed you by the neck for paying me more for my work than it was worth." Whereupon, Citizen Coquet, the director, said that in the future he would pay no more than six *livres* for a tow and that if the thread was not good he would pay only four. Right there, Citizen Coquet pulled out a package of thread, saying it was the declarant's. He threw it into the middle of the workshop and summoned all the workers so they could see whether the thread was worth the price paid for it, saying to her, the declarant, that there were two or three of them who were counterrevolutionary women in the workshop.

Q. Some days before the arrest of Hébert, nicknamed Père Duchêne, hadn't she said that she didn't give a damn, that her affairs were going well, that Hébert was at the head of it?

A. No, but on [16 Ventôse], having met up with Hébert, nicknamed Père Duchêne, on the Boulevard du Temple, she spoke with him about affairs having to do with spinning workers at the Jacobins. He instructed her to prepare a petition [and] to present it to the Commune, and he [Hébert] would compel them, if he could [to consider their demands]. A few days later, when Citoyenne Catherine Larmet had come over to her and asked her how things were going, she, the declarant, answered, "Our affairs are going well. I met Père Duchêne on the Boulevard du Temple. I spoke with him about it [these affairs], and he told me that he will help us."

Q. On the day Hébert, nicknamed Père Duchêne, was executed, or the next day, had she not said that he was a good patriot, a good Jacobin, who had done a great deal for the Republic and that for thanks he was sent to the guillotine?

A. She did not say that, and she had no knowledge of these allegations.

Q. Had she been with other *citoyennes* from the workshop in the Section de Marat? Why was she there?

A. She went there one time with a *citoyenne* from the cotton workshop, and that was in order to present a petition, the contents of which she did not know, as she had neither read nor signed it. However, she had heard that it was for the purpose of reclaiming the two pounds of bread they were being denied.

Q. Why did they go to Section de Marat rather than to Section de Châlier, where the workshops in the Jacobins are located?

A. The *citoyenne* cotton workers whom she, the declarant, accompanied told her that they also presented [a petition] in the Section de Châlier.

It is pointed out to her that she is not telling the truth, because she had signed the petition for the Section de Marat.

A. If she signed, she has no recollection of it, but she does not believe she signed it, and if she saw it, she would recognize her signature well enough.

Q. Wasn't she the individual who went to the home of the *commissaires* in the Section de Marat to ask them to come to the workshops at the Jacobins?

A. Three of them asked their [the *commissaires'*] opinion about the workshops in the Jacobins. The *citoyenne* declarant added that Citoyenne Foucheret told her that the doorkeeper told her that five carriages had left the place of the former Jacobins loaded down with furniture and effects which were said to have belonged to Citoyenne Marianne Fouchot and that two or three days before, she, the declarant, had seen two packages taken out which were said to be the belongings of the above-named Marianne Fouchot, who was moving. She added, further, that at the beginning, when *citoyennes* wore cockades, the above-named Marianne Fouchot went over to Citoyenne Catherine Larmet and said to her, "So, you are wearing a cockade." When [Citoyenne Larmet] answered, "Yes, and why aren't you wearing one?" the above-named Fouchot replied, "As for me, I don't want to wear one." Whereupon, she [Larmet] told her [Fouchot], "You're leaving yourself open to being arrested." Citoyenne Fouchot answered, "I'll slit open the stomach of the first one to arrest me, with my knife."

The declarant [Citoyenne Jannisson] also added that in 1791 the above-named Fouchot came to the workshop where the declarant works and asked to buy some silver. Not having found any to buy that time, she came back a second time to ask whether someone would be willing to sell her some silver. She, the declarant, answered that spinners did not earn enough to sell silver. Whereupon Citoyenne Fouchot said she wanted only pieces worth twelve or twenty-four *sols*. Then she, the declarant, Citoyenne Jannisson, asked her want she wanted to do with this silver and whether she intended to send it to the *émigrés*. Whereupon the above-named Fouchot answered, laughing, "Yes," and right there she purchased forty-eight *livres* in silver from two *citoyenne* workers who had earned this during harvest season, and she gave each of them a fifty-*sol* profit. She made the same purchase from another *citoyenne*, but she did not know what the profit was which [Fouchot] gave her.

She also declared that on the day a barrel of powder blew off the door of the guardpost situated on rue de la Lingerie, the above-named Fouchot came to the workshop and announced that cannon volleys were being fired onto the patriots, exclaiming, "See what your nation does for you; as for me, as long as it does me no more good than it's been doing me now, I'm not going to concern myself with it at all. I've stuffed it up my ass, and I'm shitting on it."

She [Citoyenne Jannisson] added that Citoyenne Bougrot told her, the declarant, that the above-named Fouchot told her that if she had a million, she would offer it to save the King's life and that on the day of the former King's death she came to the workshop all in tears. The declarant added that with respect to Catherine Larmet, last December 9 she told her that Marianne Fouchot's brother, on the day of La Coutelet's execution, took from his sister a fifty-*alder* piece of linen and twelve pieces of cloth and a sack filled with six *franc ecus*. Since that day she herself had not heard anything more said about it. Several days later the above-named Larmet told this to her out loud in the workshop. This same day, the above-named Larmet told her, the declarant, that she was in a position to prove that Citoyenne Fouchot was Madame d'Argent, since she herself told her so on two occasions.

With respect to Citoyenne Valentine, she states that the day la Neuve Eglise was executed, she came to the workshop all in tears. She fell ill and was sent to l'Hôtel Dieu; she was released only three or four days ago, and that is all the declarant said she knew. . . .

On 15 Prairial, Year Two of the French Republic, One and Indivisible, at 10:30 A.M., we had Citoyenne Jannisson brought in. She asked to be heard. She stated that about three months ago she and two other *citoyenne* cotton workers had presented a petition to the Popular Society of the Section de Marat. She also stated that about two months ago she

and three other *citoyennes* from the workshop at the Jacobins also presented a petition to the Committee of Public Safety of the National
Convention for the purpose of reclaiming two supplementary pounds of
bread which they were receiving every week and which had been taken
away from them at the same time that a fixed rate was being set for their
work. The aforementioned petition was sent to the Comité des Marchés.
She added that on 29 Floreal they met two members of the Committee
of Public Safety, one of whom was Citizen Collot d'Herbois, and told
them that the pay for their work had been lowered. They asked the two
citizen representatives of the people to consider the reclamations contained in their petitions. They answered, telling the declarant and her
companions that to refresh their memories concerning the memoir they
need only give them a memo. They did that. That is all she said she had
to declare. . . .

[signed] Jannisson

Year Two of the French Republic,
One and Indivisible, 14 Prairial, 11 A.M.

[Testimony was taken from Citoyenne Jean Cecile Galet, unmarried,
and living in the Section du Panthéon-français, rue Traversine, no. 6,
formerly a worker in the workshop at the Jacobins:]

Q. Hadn't she heard it said by workers in the workshop of the Jacobins
   and especially by Citoyenne Jannisson that their affairs were going
   well and that they didn't give a damn, that they had Père Duchêne
   at their head?
A. No.
Q. Hadn't she heard Citoyenne Jannisson say that Hébert was a good
   patriot and a good citizen and that he had been executed for good
   services he had rendered to the Republic?
A. Two days after Hébert's execution, Citoyenne Jannisson said that he
   had always done good work for the Republic, and in return, he had
   been executed. . . . [Citoyenne Galet was unable to sign the transcript of her testimony.]

[Next appeared Citoyenne Rousseau, twenty-seven years old, residing
in the Section de la Cité, rue Cristophe, no. 3, and working in the
workshop at the Jacobins:]

Q. Hadn't she heard it said by various workers in the workshop at the
   Jacobins, and notably by Citoyennes Jannisson and Troussard, that
   Hébert, called Père Duchêne, had been executed as repayment for
   good services rendered to the Republic?

A. Yes.

Q. Had she heard Citoyennes Jannisson and Troussard say that their affairs were going well, that they didn't give a damn, that they had Père Duchêne at their head?

A. Yes. . . .

[She was unable to sign the transcript of her testimony.]

[Next appeared Citoyenne Marie-Elizabeth Fleurantine, twenty-two years old, residing in the Faubourg St. Jacques and working in the workshop at the Jacobins:]

Q. Had she heard it said to various workers in the workshops at the Jacobins, and notably by Citoyennes Jannisson and Troussard, that Hébert, called Père Duchêne, had been executed in repayment for good services rendered to the Republic?

A. Yes, she had heard this said to Citoyenne Jannisson.

[She was unable to sign her transcript.]

[Other *citoyennes* appeared, including Veuve Galet and Veuve Mignan, and their testimony corroborated testimony already offered. Then appeared Citoyenne Elizabeth Charpentier, twenty-eight years old and a worker in the workshop at the Jacobins, residing in the Section de l'Arsenal, rue des Prêtres St. Paul, no. 8:]

Q. On the day of the execution of Hébert, called Père Duchêne, was she aware that anyone said that he was a good patriot who had given a great deal of service and that for recompense he had been executed?

A. She had not heard these words spoken, but Citoyenne Galet, *fille*, told her she had heard these remarks made by Citoyenne Jannisson. The *citoyenne* added that Citoyenne Larmet told her that having asked Citoyenne Jannisson how her affairs were going, she answered, "They are going well, because we have Père Duchêne at our head," and these remarks were made a few days before the arrest of Hébert, called Père Duchêne.

[She was unable to sign for herself.]

[Next, Françoise Charpentier, thirty-two years old, a worker in the workshop at the Jacobins, living in Section de l'Arsenal, rue des Prêtres St. Paul, no. 8, appeared. After her appeared Citoyenne Catherine Larmet, femme Bernard (wife of a) *gendarme*. She was twenty-eight years old, a worker in the workshop of the former Jacobins, living on rue d'Aras, no. 3, Section du Panthéon français:]

Q. Was she aware that several days before the arrest of Hébert, nicknamed Père Duchêne, Citoyenne Jannisson said that their affairs were going well because they had Père Duchêne at their head?

A. Yes, in fact she had asked Citoyenne Jannisson whether her affairs were going well, and Citoyenne Jannisson answered that they were going well because Père Duchêne, who was a good *sans-culotte* and a Jacobin, was at their head, and one or two weeks afterwards, when the declarant learned that Père Duchêne had been arrested, she said to Citoyenne Jannisson, "You told me Père Duchêne was a good *sans-culotte* and that he was at the head of your affairs, but nonetheless here he is under arrest." Citoyenne Jannisson replied that he wasn't dead yet.

Q. What affairs of Citoyenne Jannisson was she talking about?

A. She didn't know what the affairs of Citoyenne Jannisson were, but only that Citoyenne Jannisson told her, the declarant, that she wanted to reclaim the two pounds of bread a week that had been taken away from them as well as the spools of thread and yarn that hadn't been paid for at the price they were worth.

Q. Did she know that the day of the execution of Hébert, nicknamed Père Duchêne, Citoyenne Jannisson said he was a good patriot who gave much service to the Republic and that as his reward he was sent to the guillotine?

A. It was not to her, the declarant, that Citoyenne Jannisson made these remarks, but to Citoyennes Galet, mother and daughter, to Citoyenne Rousseau, and to Citoyenne Fleurantine, who repeated them to her the next day. . . .

[She signed.]

[Testimony was taken from four more people.]

13. THE WOMEN OF THE PEOPLE REVOLT AGAINST THE
JACOBIN REGIME

Source: A.N., F^7 4707, dossier 2.

This document depicts a woman's reaction to the repressive
atmosphere in the Jacobin Republic following Hébert's coup.
Wearied by long waits on food lines, Femme Guinée, wife of an
unemployed wig maker, repaid the insult of a Jacobin official.
Her retort cost her several months in prison. In her letter,
written shortly after the fall of the Jacobins, Femme Guinée
describes conditions in female prisons and treatment of poorer
female suspects.

———————

Liberté, égalité
                    This 25 Fructidor, Second Year of the French Republic,
                                                One and Indivisible,
Citizens,
     Citoyenne Anne Félicité Guinée, twenty-four years old, married to
Citizen Fillastre, a wig maker on rue des Vieilles Auduette, no. 3,
Section de l'Homme Armé, informs you that she was arrested on [22
Germinal] at the Place des Droits de l'Homme, where I [sic] had gone to
get butter. I point out to you that for a long time I have had to feed the
members in my household on bread and cheese and that, tired of complaints from my husband and my boys, I was compelled to go wait in
line to get something to eat. For three days I had been going to the same
market without being able to get anything, despite the fact that I had
waited from 7 or 8 A.M. until 5 or 6 P.M. After the distribution of butter
on the twenty-second, some citizens said to me, "Are you still here?" I
replied, "For three days I have been coming without getting the least
thing." A citizen came over to me and said that I was in very delicate
condition. To that I answered, "You can't be delicate and be on your
legs for so long. I wouldn't have come if there were any other food." He

replied that I needed to drink milk. I answered that I had men in my house who worked and that I couldn't nourish them with milk, that I was convinced that if he, the speaker, was sensitive to the difficulty of obtaining food, he would not vex me so, and that he was an imbecile and wanted to play despot, and no one had that right. Here, on the spot, I was arrested and brought to the guard house. I wanted to explain myself. I was silenced and was dragged off to prison, where I was left for six hours without anyone's asking whether I needed anything. About 7 P.M. I was led to the Revolutionary Committee of Section des Droits de l'Homme, where I was called a counterrevolutionary and was told I was asking for the guillotine because I told them I preferred death to being treated ignominiously the way he was treating me. I asked to write to my husband. I was refused. I saw a citizen wig maker whom I begged, in low tones, to go alert my husband.

When my husband arrived, he was told that he was not needed. He went to Section de l'Homme Armé. Two *commissaires,* the *commissaires de police et d'accapparement,* reclaimed me. It [the Revolutionary Committee of Section des Droits de l'Homme] informed the *commissaires* that a counterrevolutionary could not be returned, and the *commissaires* answered that they had never known me to be such. About midnight my *procès-verbal* was read to me. I was asked if I knew whom I had called a despot. I answered, "I didn't know him," and I was told that he was the commander of the post. I said that he was more [a commander] beneath his own roof than anyone, given that he was there to maintain order and not to provoke bad feelings. During this [time] one of the members called me a counterrevolutionary and an aristocrat. I answered that I was surprised that he insulted me that way and that even though I was a prisoner, they had to respect me.

From the answers in my *procès-verbal* I was told that I had done three times more than was needed to get the guillotine and that I would be explaining myself before the Revolutionary Tribunal. The next day, I was taken to the Revolutionary Committee of my Section, which, without waiting to hear me, had me taken to the Mairie, where I stayed for nine days without a bed or a chair with vermin and with women addicted to all sorts of crimes who wanted everything from me. And when I complained, they put a knife to my throat. One day a bakeress who was under arrest for having given out bread without a [ration] card said, in tears, that she would have done better to throw her bread away than to give it away without a card. Despair prompted her to speak so. Three prisoners called me and asked me whether I wanted my liberty. My first impulse was to say yes. They told me, "You have heard what the bakeress just said. We will denounce her before the Revolutionary Tribunal, and we will have our liberty. I said that I would have my liberty because justice owed it to me, but that I would prefer death to having [liberty] at the expense of the liberty or the life of anyone else. I warned the bakeress to be more circumspect, and from that moment I became their sworn enemy. There was no longer any rest for me, and they invented all kinds of things to inflict pain on me, and I was told my head would roll, by decree.

One evening, eight or nine days after my arrest, I wrote a letter to my husband to ask him for linen and for money. In the morning I gave it to a female *commissaire*. I told her, "Have it read by the administrators." And I gave her some money for taking it to its address. Neither my husband nor myself ever heard anything more about this letter, and we do not know what became of it.

On the ninth day I was transferred to the prison of La Force, and I had to sleep on straw, as I had no money, and I was asked for fifteen *sous* on the first night. I said that whenever I received the money, I would give it to them. I wrote to inform [people] where I had been transferred. My letters were intercepted. In the evening I was getting ready to sleep in the same room I had slept in the previous evening. With the lowest of inhumanity, they came to take me away. It was useless for me to beg, shed tears, and say that I would not be without money for long. It was all useless, and I was placed in a room for troublemakers [? in French *chambre des galleusse*]. The next day, when the *commissaire* brought my food from the house, I wanted to give [them] a letter. One of the turnkeys pushed me back with such brutality that I was unable to hand over my letter. In the end, . . . my husband received only two of them. I received some money. I had to give it to the authorities for the room with straw where I had slept. I was already being threatened, and I would have been attacked had I not given over everything that was being asked. I went into my cell, and in spite of the fact that I had paid for my bed, I still had to hand over money to this same woman who had me put into the room for troublemakers.

In the end I can give you only the very slightest idea of all the horrors that are committed in these terrible prisons. The details would take too long. I was thrown together not with women but with monsters who gloried in all their crimes and who gave themselves over to all the most horrible and infamous excesses. One day, two of them fought each other with knives. Day and night I lived in mortal fear. The food that was sent in to me was grabbed away immediately. That was my cruel situation for seventeen days. My whole body was swollen from chagrin and from the poor treatment I had endured; finally, on the seventeenth day I was called to appear before the municipal police. How taken aback I was when I heard the national guardsman say that I was charged with having made remarks that were unbecoming to a citizen [and] tended to stir people up in the Place des Droits de l'Homme. I was stricken to the point that it was impossible for me to speak a word, and I lost the use of my senses. My case had been placed before the correctional police while I was under arrest. The General Assembly of my Section named *commissaires* to work for my liberation. The condition I was in gave my husband and my relatives reason to believe I was pregnant. A brief was presented, and this was mentioned, and that was the reason I obtained my provisional discharge on double bail.

From this period on I have been ill continually. I had bile in my blood, and I have had a great deal of difficulty restoring my health. I am informing you that I am the mother of a family and that I have not stopped being persecuted by fate, considering that my husband lost his position and the little he had saved from his work. This most recent trial has just crowned our misfortune because of the expenses my detention gave rise to and [because of] my illness, and I find myself overwhelmed on all sides. For a long time now I have been looking for a position, in view of the fact that my husband's situation has deteriorated. I cannot find anything. My conduct is free of all reproach. I have always comported myself following republican principles, and I have always sought to merit the esteem [due] a good citizen.

I count on your justice to get a definitive judgment handed down as speedily as possible for my tranquility and for that of the two citizens who are posting bail for me, and I dare flatter myself that your humanity will not view with indifference the fate which overwhelms me and that it [humanity] will do everything possible to obtain a position for me—or whatever employment seems suitable to you. That would give me and my family the means to subsist. I am counting on your justice and your humanity.

> Salut et fraternité
> written by me,
> [signed] femme Filhastre [*sic*]

VI

Women's Final Political Efforts:
July, 1794, through May, 1795

REVOLUTIONARY GOVERNMENT came to an abrupt end in July, 1794. The incoming Thermidorians disbanded or transformed the institutional bases of women's political power and limited their influence as citizens. The popular classes of Paris had reason to regret the defeat of the Jacobins despite their disillusionment during the trial of Hébertists and the acceleration of the Terror against members of their own group, for the Thermidorian government eroded both their political power and the economic legislation that protected their livelihood.

The drive for reform of the legal and social condition of women had ended. There were no further petitions and speeches asking for educational innovations, divorce, or civil equality. Women's leaders from earlier periods were in eclipse. Olympe de Gouges had been guillotined. Théroigne de Méricourt had been flogged in March, 1793, by women who supported the Montagnards and resented her championing of the Girondins. She went mad and died in the Salpêtrière in 1817. Etta Palm d'Aelders returned to Holland. Claire Lacombe was arrested April 2, 1794, and imprisoned until August 20, 1795. Upon her release she became the proprietress of a tobacco shop and later returned to acting in Nantes. Pauline Léon and her husband, Théophile Leclerc, were also arrested in April, 1794, and served terms until August 19, 1794. No new heroines arose to speak out for women's issues.

The Thermidorians broke up the institutions that had given the common people of Paris their political influence in Year II. The public galleries in clubs and Section assemblies where women had been so prominent began to exclude common women, and the Section committees, once filled with *sans-culottes,* became an arena for "respectable" citizens. In October, 1794, clubs lost the right to affiliate, correspond, and petition. In May, 1795, the Convention decreed that women were to be kept out of the galleries.

Socially, the Thermidorians replaced the austerity of Jacobin virtue with salon life, gambling, and similar pleasures. Thérèse Cabarrus, mistress and later wife of the leading Thermidorian, Tallien, became the model woman, setting fashions and hair styles. She and her social set, the Merveilleuses, and their male escorts, the Muscadins, held extravagant balls to commemorate the victims of Year II, restricting invitations to those whose relatives had died under the guillotine.

Once again women suffered hunger and want. Laissez-faire economic policies were restored by the Thermidorian government. The Law of the Maximum on prices was cut back in October, 1794, and finally eliminated in December. Free trade brought back hoarding and speculation and especially massive inflation. Municipal regulation of provisioning was continued, but it was unworkable because authorities stopped forcing reluctant peasants to accept the rapidly depreciating *assignats* as payment for their products. In the winter and spring of 1795, women faced shortages of basic commodities, long bread lines, and the accompanying insults of magistrates and bakers. To make things worse, workshops were closed down in February.

The popular insurrections which exploded in the spring of Year III, the Germinal Days and the Prairial Days, were the people's reaction to Thermidor. The economic hardships of that spring prompted women to take the initiative in the insurrections as they had in the October Days, the Sugar Riots, and the February Days.

The documents in this chapter illustrate the women's reactions to the bourgeois régime in Year III. Contemporaries noted the prominence of women in the crowds and their virulent manner in demonstrations at the Section assemblies and the National Convention. The women of Year III employed all the tactics they had developed since the beginning of the Revolution: they initiated processions to the local and national authorities to demand bread and the rights of the people; they created disturbances in bread lines and began operations of *taxation populaire;* they collaborated in conspiracies; and they poured invectives on the Thermidorian police, magistrates, and National Guards.

During the Prairial Days the women called for bread and the Constitution of 1793. These symbols show that their revolutionary experience had confirmed their traditional roles as protestors when their subsistence was threatened. But they had now joined to their economic concerns a new consciousness of the revolutionary doctrines of rights and equality.

Thermidorian society was outraged by the "furies" and "shrews" in the spring insurrections. The government took harsh measures to repress a recurrence of such popular uprisings and made special efforts to humiliate the women involved. The repression was thorough and successful. There were no insurrections comparable to the Prairial Days until 1848. A generation of revolutionaries was silenced, including those who had spoken so loudly and so strongly on behalf of women.

1. Citoyenne Arnoux Challenges the Thermidorians in Nivôse, Year III

The acute subsistence crisis during the winter of Year III led to continual disturbances in the marketplaces, and *sans-culotte* women were overheard complaining about shortages and inflated prices. Citoyenne Arnoux was a particular threat to Thermidorian officials because she did not fear making her criticism public. Note the Thermidorian commissioners' conspicuous emphasis upon her remarks about women's power to make or break revolutions.

———————◆———————

1*a*. Source: Copy of a report by police inspectors Ollivier and Baron concerning Citoyenne Arnoux, dated 26 Nivôse, Year III, in A.N., F⁷ 4581, plaque 4, dossier Arnoux.

Liberté   Egalité
Paris, this 26 Nivôse of the Third Year of the French Republic, One and Indivisible.
Administrative Commission of the Paris Police.

We found ourselves around 3 P.M. on the rue de la Tabletterie, at the place of Citizen Dufour, a baker, as the final distribution of bread was being made. Many people were in the shop, among others Citoyenne Arnoux, living at Bâtiment Neuf, Stᵉ Opportune, who was making a lot of noise. . . . [in text] We tried to bring her to order. She showered us with insults, telling us that "things would not be going on like that for long," that "they would get us sacked first," that "the women were going to rise up," that "all we had to do was to turn in our report," and that she "didn't give a damn." She's a woman who's been involved in several legal proceedings. . . . [in text]

We proceeded next to the house of Citoyenne Robinot, on the rue de la Tabletterie. She [Ollivier and Baron are apparently referring here to Arnoux] said that "the counterrevolution was going to take place before the end of the month," that "it would be very necessary that things change," that "there were several of them in the *quartier* whom it would be necessary to get sacked," and that "she would have them sacked."

Signed: Ollivier
Baron

———————

1*b*. Source: Copy of interrogations before the Revolutionary Committee of the Quatrième Arrondissement, 29 Nivôse, Year III, in the case of Femme Arnoux, in A.N., F⁷ 4581, plaque 4, dossier Arnoux.

. . . On said day [29 Nivôse, Year III], we heard Marie Angélique Porcher, Femme Arnoux, residing at Bâtiment Neuf, [Ste.] Opportune, a button-mold seller.

Q. Where did she go to get her bread on 26 Nivôse?
A. To rue de la Tabletterie.
Q. Were there a lot of people there?
A. At least thirty women were there.
Q. Did she have any difficulty getting bread?
A. Yes, and she waited her turn, but she complained about being forced to line up, saying that if all the women were like her, there would be no more lines, because she could get along very well for a day without bread. Then Citizen Ollivier, whom she knew to be a *commissaire* on the bridges, told her to keep quiet. She told him that that was none of his business; that she recognized as *commissaire* only Citizen Boulanger, co-member of the Comité de Bienfaisance, who handed out her [bread] cards to her, and that he [Ollivier] would do better to mend his britches than to meddle in this.
Q. Hadn't she said that she would get Ollivier sacked first and that there would be an end to that?
A. She had not made these remarks.
Q. Hadn't she said that the women were going to rise up?
A. No. All she said was that by setting up lines, they were looking to stir up the people, and that there was ill will there, on one side and the other, because there was no shortage of bread.
Q. Hadn't she already had some legal case?

A. In truth she had been involved in a case where there was a question of four hundred *livres* in counterfeit *assignats,* but her innocence was recognized, as she had been acquitted by order of the directors of the jury for the Département de Paris, dated August 22, 1793, old style, which she showed us and which was returned to her.

Q. Had she been to see Citoyenne Robinot, the laundress, that same day, and what was she doing there?

A. She went there to get her workers' shifts, which she brought to her for bleaching.

Q. Hadn't she made some remarks while she was there?

A. She said that she had come from standing in line at the baker's, that she had seen her [Robinot's] crony while she was there, and that she had had a run-in with him there. She [Arnoux] noted that the crony was the aforementioned Citizen Ollivier. Citoyenne Robinot told her he was a police spy. She [Arnoux] told her [Robinot] that he could be the devil if that was what he wanted; she wasn't afraid of him.

It was pointed out to her that at the aforementioned Robinot's place she said that the counterrevolution would take place before the end of the month, that it would be very necessary that things change, that there were several people in the *quartier* who would have to be sacked, and that she would get them sacked.

A. All these allegations are false, and she never got herself mixed up in political matters; she doesn't have the powers of a diviner to be able to foretell all that and to say it.

Q. Where was her husband?

A. He was in Malancourt in the Département de la Meuse on family and business matters.

The present interrogation was read back to her. She said it contained the truth and added that if remarks were reported at Citoyenne Robinot's, it is only she [Robinot] who could have made them up, because the two of them had had a few run-ins when she was living in the same house [as Robinot], notably when she, the deponent, did not want to get involved in a fight that took place at the aforementioned Robinot's between her and one of her workers by coming to her [Robinot's] aid, and because she did not want to be the one to separate the two of them. On this day she [Robinot] came up to her [Arnoux's] room to insult her, reproaching her with wanting to let her be murdered. The remarks held against her are so obviously hers [Robinot's] that she [Arnoux] warned her not to sleep at her own place because she would be arrested.

She was given a new reading [of her deposition] and she held to it and signed:

Signed: Femme Arnous [*sic*]

On said day appeared Marie-Louise Orey, wife of Joseph Robinot, a laundress on rue de la Tabletterie, no. 103, who stated that on 26 Nivôse of this month Citoyenne Arnoux came to her place specifically to tell her about the fight she had had with Citizen Ollivier at the baker's. At that time she told her that "civil war could break out before the end of the month," that "it was the women who had started the Revolution," that "it was up to them to bring it to an end," that "they would go and seek out the women in their rooms," and that "those who weren't willing to march would be chopped up, so much the worse for those with children, because they wouldn't be given any special treatment." Those she had it in for would be the first ones she'd get to, especially Ollivier, her [Robinot's] crony, and his [Ollivier's] wife. When she, the deponent, pointed out to her that she herself would be exposed, she answered, "That will be okay with me; I'd bet a thousand-*livre* bill on that happening." The deponent pointed out to her, in addition, that if something like the tenth of August took place, her husband would be found out. She answered, "He is out in the country now, and if he showed up, she would be sure to make him get out right away." All these remarks were made in the presence of her daughter, age thirteen, and her worker, named Angélique, who doesn't stay at her place but at Vieille rue du Temple, at a hatter's, opposite the rue de Bercy.

We asked her whether she didn't harbor some resentment against the aforementioned Femme Arnoux and whether she hadn't had some fights with her, above all about her [Arnoux's] not coming to her aid the day she had a fight with one of her workers. She answered that this allegation was false, that she never had fights with her workers, and that, in addition, Citizen Fouyol Michel also heard this woman's remarks concerning which he can make a statement. He lives on the first floor of her house.

She said this was all she knew. Her present declaration was read back to her. She said it contained the truth and signed.

Signed: F. Robinot

On said day Citizen Michel Fouyol, called Michel, appeared. He works for the furriers, resides at rue de la Tabletterie, no. 103, Section des Marchés. He stated that he had not personally heard Citoyenne Arnoux making any remarks on these particular days; that he only knows second-hand that on several occasions she said that she "was shitting on the Nation," and [made] other remarks as unworthy of a good citizen as they were crude. He said that was all he knew, and signed.

Signed: Fouyol

On said day, Marie Françoise Millot appeared, a worker in dressmaking, living on Vieille rue du Temple, house no. 108, occupied by Citizen Bourgoin, who declared that she knew Citoyenne Arnoux and that she was at Citoyenne Robinot's on 26 Nivôse when the aforementioned Citoyenne Arnoux came up there specifically to tell her about the fight she had at the baker's with Citizen Ollivier. This woman told her that "civil war would break out," that "she knew when it would begin and where they would go," and that "they would be pillaging at the homes of rich people and those she had it in for [and] where she knew there was something [to take]." "Femme Ollivier and her husband would be chopped up"; "it was the women who had started the Revolution"; "it was up to them to bring it to an end." They would be going to seek the women out in their houses, and if they didn't want to "march, she would have them chopped up." "She would stake a thousand-*livre* note on that happening, sooner rather than later"; "it would take place at the end of the present month or in the course of next month." She knew full well how it would start. She told Citoyenne Robinot that when this *événement* took place, if her husband returned from the country she would make him get out immediately so that he wasn't part of it, and [she made] other remarks of this kind which she doesn't recall.

She said that was all she knew. Her declaration was read back to her. She said it contained the truth and signed.

Signed: Millot

2. CITOYENNE CLAUDEL, ACCUSED OF CONSPIRACY, DEFENDS HER PATRIOTIC PRINCIPLES

In the spring of Year III, women were in the avant-garde of protest as subsistence problems became acute once again. They helped organize the abortive popular insurrection in Germinal, · Year III, and took major roles in the Lagrelet conspiracy in the last days of Germinal, possibly to organize a general insurrection. Femme Claudel, the wife of a former member of the Revolutionary Committee for the Section Pont Neuf, was singled out by a renegade member of the conspiracy as the most bloodthirsty of the group. In her letter reclaiming her release from prison she clearly sets forth her principles as a devoted wife, mother, and *citoyenne.*

———————

2*a*. Source: Special session of the Comité civil of the Section de l'Indivisibilité during which evidence in the case of Femme Claudel was recorded, 7 Thermidor, Year III, in A.N., F[7] 4649, dossier Claudel.

The Comité civil, assembled in conformity with the order of the Committee of General Security dated 30 Prairial in order to provide it with knowledge about various denunciations as well as with information concerning the morality of citizens disarmed or incarcerated—all either by order of the Committee of General Security or by order of the General Assembly of the aforementioned Section—after having examined the registers both of the Comité civil and of the Committee of Surveillance of the Eighth Arrondissement, with which it acts in concert, and the *procès-verbaux* of the General Assembly for 5, 6, 7, 8, 9, 10, and 11 Prairial, as well as the documents deposited with the commission set up to receive denunciations, gathered the following denunciations:

Femme Claudel, arrested by order of the General Assembly of 5 Prairial.

Meeting of 5 Prairial. A literal extract from the report of the Commission of Six.

It follows from the declaration of André Pavon that it is a certain thing that ever since a wavering terrorism has been trembling before the justice which has been pursuing it and which has just brought it down, the blood-drinkers have been holding secret meetings. It is certain, according to this declaration, that their assemblies were of the disgusting nature of those of man-eaters and all the more criminal because there were agitation and orders for liberating prisoners during the night of 29 Germinal and for dividing the conspirators into several detachments in order to direct them to various prisons. . . . [in text]

These assemblies were being held for about the last four months, from six or seven o'clock until ten o'clock in the evening, regularly every three or four days, most often at the house of François, a wine merchant, rue du Parc; at the house of Lagrelet, a dealer in stoves, rue de Bretagne; three or four times at the house of a wine merchant at the corner of rue des Amandiers and rue de Popincourt, Faubourg Antoine; two times at the house of a wine merchant near the middle of rue de Bercy; and several times at the Auberge de l'Aventure, place de Grève.

Of all the people at whose homes the conspirators were meeting, only Lagrelet, according to André's deposition, knew the reasons for the gatherings. The others, who are wine merchants, were unaware of the purpose.

The people who were ordinarily there numbered altogether between sixty and eighty, and those from the Section, whom he named, are: [A list of the outstanding conspirators follows. Number six on the list was Femme Claudel.] Sixth: The wife of Claudel, a former member of the Comité révolutionnaire (was never absent, and André denounces her as the most sanguinary). . . .

André declared that he didn't know how to sign his name.

It is with much satisfaction (the *rapporteur* continues) that the commission has noted that the result of the work with which it has been preoccupied, and to which it has assigned the importance it merits, is that only those persons are called to your attention concerning whom your opinion has been pronounced.

Following deliberation, it has been decided unanimously to propose to you the arrest and immediate arraignment before the Committee of General Security of the aforementioned Janson, Vernourye, Blondeau, Canot, and Femme Claudel.

The assembly's pronouncement was in conformity with the recommendation of the commission.

There exists at the Comité de Surveillance of the Eighth Arrondissement a denunciation dated 10 Germinal against Femme Claudel for being part of a gathering which took place at the home of François, a wine merchant, rue du Parc. . . .

2*b*. Source: Undated memoir by Citoyenne Claudel to the citizen
        members composing the Committee of General Security, in
        A.N., F⁷ 4649, dossier Claudel.

Memoir of Citoyenne Claudel,
Section de l'Indivisibilité,
Prison de la Pelagie.

To the Citizen members composing the Committee of General Security,
Section de police.

Citoyenne Claudel, residing in Paris on rue Payenne, Section de Indivisibilité, informs you that as per the extract from the report of the Commission of the aforementioned Section, she sees herself denounced for having been in the clubs which had been meeting for the past four months every three or four days, most frequently at the house of François, a wine merchant, living on rue du Parc; three or four times at the house of a wine merchant at the corner of rue des Amandiers and rue Popincourt, Faubourg Antoine; two times at the home of a wine merchant near the middle of rue de Bercy, and several times at the Auberge de l'Aventure, place de Grève. It was stated that she was never missing and was the most bloodthirsty.

Reply.

Citoyenne Claudel declares that on the basis of the complaints made by her to the Committee of General Security concerning false inculpations made against her by some individual in the Section, she was expecting the justice she had a right to expect. And so as not to leave any doubt concerning the purity of her intentions and the proofs of her innocence, she has no fear about allowing her conduct to be known. At first she was very astonished by the accusation brought against her relative to the secret meeting held at the home of Citizen François. Citoyenne Claudel is sincere enough to acknowledge that she has been in that house nearly thirty times. And although she was seen, her attention was never directed to the persons who might have been gathered there, but rather to the interests of this wretched family, where the unfortunate mother could hardly provide her children with bread. This touching scene would have melted a heart of iron. She states this reluctantly because she does not like to put a value on the good she does, but the circumstances compel her to say that this afflicted mother had her [Claudel] come to her home in order that she might receive some consolation. Citoyenne Claudel can add to her innocence still more by giving information about a document on file with the Civil Committee of the Section and [which] is most appropriate for her justification. This is what it states, in substance: Citizen François, wine merchant, also denounced by some individual from the Section for holding secret meetings at his house, addressed a memoir on this subject to the aforementioned Committee in which he justified himself fully, and on the basis of which the Civil Committee has declared that he had no knowledge of this.

And as for the other allegations, she swears on everything she holds most sacred that they are false and absurd and that she never knew the other wine merchants named in the statement of reasons for her arrest. And to provide the greatest certainty of this, she asks to appear before those who denounce her.

Citizen Representatives, deign to look at these miserable denunciations: you will see that they can only have been dictated by a thirst for vengeance, in that they are altogether lacking in proof. And you cannot give credence to denunciations from which the names of those who authored them are withheld.

She depends entirely on your justice to return to her the liberty which was ravished so unjustly—a mother of three young children, pregnant, deprived for the past eight months of her unfortunate husband, and exposed to the persecution of her enemies only in order to punish her for her civic-mindedness, her obedience to the laws, her love for the Republic, and for the national representation which she has sworn to uphold until her last breath.

Salut et fraternité. . . .

3. MEN AND WOMEN AT THE PONT NEUF REGRET THE
   DISAPPEARANCE OF THE POPULAR SOCIETIES IN YEAR III

Source: Archives de la Préfecture de Police, Paris, AA 216,
Section Pont Neuf, 29 Germinal, Year III.

The Thermidorians managed to apprehend the chiefs of the
Lagrelet conspiracy on the night of 29 Germinal, but they
found it more and more difficult to control popular protest in
the streets. This account, occurring on the night that the
Lagrelet conspiracy was uncovered, shows that rebellious spirit
was spreading. Popular orators like Soret found little trouble in
attracting female crowds to applaud his criticisms of the
undemocratic features of Thermidor.

———————◆———————

. . . Then Citizen François Le Febvre, an artist living in Paris at no.
1620, rue Guénégaud, Section de l'Unité, appeared and testified that
having left the Théâtre de la Cité opposite the Palais and while walking,
between 9 and 9:30 P.M., through the entry court that leads from the
cour Chapelle to the rue de la Calandre, he heard a citizen who was in
the middle of a discussion with several *citoyennes* and who said, among
other things, "I am delighted to meet someone who thinks my way.
Eight months ago we had bread, and today we don't have any more. We
are living under slavery." One of the *citoyennes* added these remarks:
"Yes, I see women who, when they receive a quarter-pound loaf, not
having gotten any the night before, are really satisfied and very happy. If
you go to present a petition about it to the National Convention, you
are arrested. The popular societies have been closed. That was in order
to plunge us back into slavery. We are all suckers." And following these
remarks, the above-mentioned individual started applauding and repeated the same word, *suckers,* and with that they took leave of one
another, saying, "good night," and "until tomorrow."

The declarant, sensing in these remarks something suspicious and tending to Maratism and provocation, thought he ought to follow the above-mentioned individual. Seeing that there were several citizens gathered around him [Soret], he, the declarant, gave them his opinion concerning the above-mentioned individual, and they, the citizens, said immediately that it was an urgent matter that such an individual be arrested and escorted to the *commissaire de police*. Moreover, the declarant noted in addition that while the above-named individual was speaking with the *citoyennes* referred to above, he formally declared before the above-mentioned *citoyennes,* "Right now, no one can speak up any more. . . ."

The next person to appear was Citizen Louis Duhaupas, a goldsmith living in Paris in the cour Chapelle, no. 7, in this Section. He declared that, returning home around 9:30 P.M., via the entry to the Palais, opposite the rue de la Calandre, he saw an individual who was with three women and who said, "We are all suckers." This individual was observed by several people who were present and who regarded him as suspect and arrested him immediately. The above-mentioned individual, seeing himself apprehended by the above-mentioned citizens, began screaming, "Murder," and refused to go along, notwithstanding the request made to him by the above-mentioned citizens to come along peacefully. No violence was done to him. Notwithstanding the tremendous resistance he put up, the above-mentioned citizens brought him to us, and the declarant believed he should come and make the present declaration. . . .

[Similar eyewitness accounts were offered by Pierre Antoine Filliet (?), police officer; Pierre Thomas Nicolas Champion, an employee in the Bureau for the Liquidation of Émigrés; André Charles Chabroud, in charge of public instruction for the Department of Paris; and Louis Ribancourt the younger, a gunner for the reserve guard of the Section. The next interrogation was that of the suspect, Jacques-Philippe Soret, a domestic working for Citizen Grenier, an employee at the Commission des relations extérieurs. Soret was forty years old, a native of St. Clair, and presently living in Paris on the rue de Luxembourg, no. 180, Section des Piques.]

Q. Where was he coming from when he was arrested?
A. From supper.
Q. Where and with whom did he have supper?
A. He had drunk a pint of wine at the corner of the rue du Bout du Monde with Citoyenne Fanchette Duchesne.

Q. Who was this Citoyenne Duchesne?

A. She lives with her mother on the rue Neuve St. Eustache at the home of a linen maker, on the fifth floor.

Q. Wasn't it with the said Citoyenne Duchesne that he was having a conversation at the entry to the Palais opposite the rue de la Calandre?

A. He chatted with no one at this entry. When he arrived, he entered through the big iron gate of the Palais and passed under the arcade which leads from the Grand Cour into the second *cour,* [cour] de la Comptabilité, where he is on guard duty.

Q. While in this cour de la Comptabilité, had he not seen some women?

A. No.

Q. Did he not see people making their escape, crying, "Murder"?

A. No. But while in the center of the above-mentioned *cour,* several citizens approached him and put their hands around his neck. He was asked by one of them if it wasn't he who had just made some remarks. He answered that he had made no remarks and that he did not know what they were talking about.

Q. Upon returning to the *cour* he is referring to, did he not say to some women that he was delighted to meet someone who thought the way he did?

A. He spoke to no one.

Q. Did he not say, "Eight months ago we had bread, and today we don't have any"?

A. He spoke to no one, nor did he hear this said to anyone there.

Q. At what time did he leave the guard post that afternoon?

A. At 7:15 P.M.

Q. At what time was he arrested?

A. 9:15 P.M.

Q. Why had he cried, "Murder," when he was arrested by some citizens?

A. He cried, "Murder," because when he was surrounded by several citizens, and realizing that they were pushing him from behind and that he was disarmed, he began to scream, "Murder," not knowing why he was arrested.

It was pointed out to him that if he were not guilty, he shouldn't have been afraid, and that consequently the resistance he put up could only be viewed as suspicious in view of the fact that the people who had arrested him had neither the dress nor the appearance of thieves.

A. He was not at all afraid, but being defenseless, he wanted to be brought to the guard house where his post was, where he could be identified.

Q. Did he recognize as his the sabre we showed him which was brought to the bureau by one of the guards?

A. Yes, he recognized it. This sabre belonged to a friend who had lent it to him that morning for doing his guard duty.

Q. How long had he lived in Paris?

A. About fourteen years.

Q. Had he served any other masters during this period besides the one he was with presently?

A. He had served Abbé Matté for about seven years, and after that, he entered the service of the master he is now working for.

Q. Had he not been a carrier of fire and powder arms, in short, both defensive and offensive weapons?

A. No.

He was then asked to empty his pockets, and he complied. Nothing suspicious was found on him, and he was asked immediately to deposit the belt and sheath of the sabre in question. He agreed. He was asked whether he had any statements to make to us. He said he had nothing to tell us. . . .

Based on the testimonies that have been made to us . . . Jacques-Philippe Soret made remarks to several women in a group which made it seem plausible that the reign of blood and horror of Robespierre and Company was something to be wished back. It would appear from the same declaration of witnesses that the above-mentioned Soret had enthusiastically applauded the slanderous and atrocious remarks made by one of the women with whom he was speaking. Finally, the above-named Soret and the women who were speaking with him appeared to be wishing the popular societies back and planned a rendezvous for a later date.

On the stated day, the first of Floreal, at 2 A.M., we, the undersigned *commissaires de police,* having gone to the Revolutionary Committee mentioned above in order to deposit the above-named Soret there, and having found no one there, decided on the spot that the said Jacques-Philippe Soret would be taken to the Committee of General Security of the National Convention so that the Committee could take the most appropriate action concerning the above-named Soret.

4. Report by Beurlier and Duret, Employees of the Commission de Police Administrative in Paris, on Events of 6 Floréal, Year III

Source: Report filed on 7 Floréal in F.-A. Aulard, ed., *Paris pendant la réaction thermidorienne et sous le Directoire: Recueil des documents pour l'histoire de l'esprit public à Paris,* vol. I, pp. 683–85.

In Floréal, women were still able to challenge Section authorities by using violence to protest flour shortages. In this report police investigators state that women are the most serious threat to public order, and the investigators consider them the enemies of official bodies at all levels of government.

———————————————

The mood of the public. Groups.

It has been established from various reports relative to yesterday that groups in the squares, in the streets, and in public places, as well as gatherings at bakers' doors, were as numerous as they were tumultuous and extremely agitated. The women, above all, seemed to be playing the principal role there; they were taunting the men, treating them as cowards, and seemed unwilling to be satisfied with the portion that was offered to them. A large number of them wanted to rush into insurrection; even the majority appeared to be determined to attack the constituted authorities, and notably the government Comités, which would have happened were it not for the prudence and firmness of the armed troops. One can easily convince oneself of what has just been reported by glancing attentively and impartially at several reports which bear witness {to this understanding of the situation}.

1. In {the report} signed Marceau, who reports having heard it said, "That will make for civil war; that's all we're asking for; is it also possible to live with two ounces of bread? Aren't they doing this on purpose?" he adds that in other gatherings they all said, "The Conven-

tion had better put some order into all that; it's about time." He sums up by saying that heads are dangerously inflamed.

2. In [the report] signed Bouillon, here are the phrases, verbatim: "Yesterday a multitude of women from the Section des Piques, after having refused the portion of bread being offered to them, went to the Committee of the Section and from there to the Convention. They stopped all the women they met on their way and forced them to join up with them."

3. Citizen Compère, in his report, confirms the above assertion and adds more alarming occurrences. . . . Surveillance. . . . [*sic*] Bellier reports that at the horse market last night some women were saying that they must go *en masse* to the Convention to demand a king in order to have bread; the same report states that at 9 P.M., near the Pont Notre-Dame, there was a group of two hundred people who were speaking the same language. This inspector was called before the Convention to be reprimanded for his apathy or his carelessness in not having followed the individuals who were making these remarks. A special WATCH HAS BEEN SET UP FOR THIS PURPOSE; . . . . [*sic*].

[signed] Beurlier, Duret

5. Violence and Taxation Populaire in Floréal, Year III

Source: "Extrait du Registre des délibérations du Comité civil de la Section du Bonnet de la Liberté, Séance du 11 Floréal, an 3eme de la République Française une et indivisible," printed in B.N., Lb⁴⁰ 1747, and reprinted in Walter Markov and Albert Soboul, eds., *Die Sansculotten von Paris: Dokumente zur Geschichte der Volksbewegung, 1793–1794*, pp. 466–80.

Women led a market disturbance, described in this document, that was extensive enough to necessitate the armed force of several Sections to restore order. The women got results. They inspected the meeting place of the Comité civil for hidden bread ovens, and they got flour distributed only to those bakers they approved.

———————————

. . . The first load of flour left at 6 A.M. with allotments for nine bakers and was stopped by some wild women at the door of Citizen Beuchot, a baker. Only two bakers had received their allotments.

The women, whose numbers were growing visibly and among whom there were many outsiders, having stopped this flour wagon, took the liberty of walking around in the streets. In vain, the Commissaire de police and peaceful *citoyennes* tried to see that the laws were enforced and respected.

As more armed troops were required to restore peace at the market, the *révoltées,* supported by the refusal of the armed troops to march to keep order, became all the more violent. A troop of these frenzied women came before the Comité civil, saying that they would not allow this flour to be distributed to the bakers. They plunged their hands into the sacks, took the flour, and grumbled a lot about the quality, saying that this subsistence was not fit to be put into a human body.

These women, besieging the hall where the members of the Civil and Relief Committees were meeting, gave vent to the most atrocious insults. The neighborhood echoed with their horrible yells and with the most irritating and coarse slanders.

One of them, out of criminally exasperating motives, had carried audacity and bad faith to the point of picking up, from the corner of the committee room, some sweepings among which there were a few grains of rice. [She] passed off this refuse to her companions as the flour that the Committee was distributing to the bakers. Unfortunately this woman could not be identified. . . .

Citizen Parot, a warrant officer, informed the Committee that the National Convention, indignant over this insurrection, was determined to bring in armed force to restore order. He added that he thought it was appropriate to inform the women who were holding up the wagon of his intention so as to avoid the consequences of this harsh measure.

Therefore, some *commissaires* again went to the place where the wagon was being held up and in vain tried the most persuasive tactics. Wasted efforts. As their only reply to the words of peace they were lavishing, they received the most positive refusals and atrocious insults. Several voices were even heard saying, "That is going to have to go on for three more days, and then it will blow up."

Among those who were speaking this way was a man whom it was not possible to identify. This is the moment to note that several men, among whom there were several who are foreign to this Section, slipped in among the women.

From the midst of this group of rebels some women separated to go to the agency, where they were told that a sack of flour weighing 217 *livres* had been sent to the Committee to be given to nursing mothers. On the basis of this declaration they returned to the Committee like furies, saying that the *commissaires* had stolen a sack of flour. That might have taken place about 10 A.M.

[The women refused to listen to the Committee's explanation that the delay in shipping the flour for nursing mothers was due to administrative problems.]

. . . At this time, one Anfrey, a fireman, living at rue de Sevree, no. 1328, was heard calling out to Citizen Desplace, Section Drummer, "Go get your drum so the general alarm can be sounded and the Section declared in insurrection."

The women who stopped the flour wagon finally made up their minds to take it to the agency, where the sacks were weighed in the presence of Citizen Petit, the *commissaire*, who was very taken aback by this operation. After that, the women returned like furies, announcing to the Committee, "You have stolen two thousand and as many hundred *livres* of flour from us, and the agent is coming." Over against this slander the members put the calculation of flour received and distributed to several bakers; they defied them to find a single ounce missing, and then the Committee remarked that it was surprising that they were concerned about the flour that was on the wagon, as a second load remained at the Section.

. . . About 5 P.M., these women and some men took the liberty of placing the members of the Committee under arrest in the name of the sovereign people and the law. They [the women] went *en masse* into the [Committee] room, giving vent to the greatest vexations against the *commissaires,* threatening them like thieves, saying that they ate white bread while the people ate black bread. These women accused the Committee of having an oven and kneading trough and insisted that they be given the keys to inspect the house.

The Committee, forced to comply with their illegal demand, asked the office boy to let them see, twice over, all the apartments which belong to the Committee. The outcome of this minute inspection was that they found neither the oven nor the kneading trough nor dough, which they had been assured [they would find] by some women who claimed to have handled the dough and seen the said oven and the kneading trough.

An individual whom, unfortunately, the Committee was unable to identify said, "When the people is in insurrection, if it turns out that it has faithless mandatories, they must be accused and judged and punished on the spot. . . ."

The result of this *journée*, the first signs of which were evident the night before at the General Assembly, was that in the entire Section bread was distributed only by Citizens Défossé and Berger, as the women were opposed to its being distributed at the other bakers', having threatened to drag through the gutter those [men] or [women] who showed up to get their bread. Likewise, they had the butchers' stalls shut down, saying that when there was not any bread, there should not be any meat either. And they hindered commerce, forcing all the merchants to close up shop because of the trouble they instigated. . . .

[An armed force from the Section, accompanied by reinforcements from other Sections, finally restored order, and after assuring the women a supplement of flour, the commander of the armed troops reprimanded the women for their reprehensible behavior.]

Source: A.N., F⁷ 4548, plaque 5, p. 73, dossier Barbau (p. 11),
as reproduced in Walter Markov and Albert Soboul, eds., *Die
Sansculotten von Paris: Dokumente zur Geschichte der Volksbewegung,
1793–1794*, pp. 490–92.

The Prairial Days were better organized than those of Germinal;
the insurgents had military plans for taking over the National
Convention and a tentative plan for a popular government. The
rallying cry was Bread and the Constitution of '93.
Contemporaries have left vivid accounts of the initiative and
tenacity displayed by the women of the people. When the
insurrection was suppressed, the government established a special
military tribunal, and local authorities received hundreds of
denunciations of insurgent men and women. The following five
documents sample Thermidorian views of female rioters.

Section de l'Indivisibilité
Denunciation against Widow Barbau, 10 Prairial, Year III.
Because any citizen who is a friend of order and justice and humanity
must state what he saw and heard from the monsters composing the
infernal sect of Jacobin terrorists, blood-drinkers, etc. . . . I declare
that the Barbau woman from the Marché Saint-Jean, in the right-hand
corner, is one of these furies to be guillotined, vomited up from Hell to
destroy the French human race. The role she played during the reign of
the Robespierrists will bring her into the public eye. She was the secret
agent and confederate of Laine, Commissaire of the former Revolutionary Committee of this Section. Moreover, she was a sister *tricoteuse* in
the spectator galleries of the Jacobins, known from [these affiliations] to
the Revolutionary Tribunal. She said to whoever was willing to listen to
her, "I have had thirty-five of them guillotined by a simple declaration,

and this will not be the sum total. It wouldn't matter if someone were my best friend, I would have him guillotined if he did not think like a true Jacobin. . . ." About five or six weeks ago, at the door of Citizen Patriarche, a baker on the rue de Culture-[Ste.] Catherine, I saw and heard her making the most revolting, seditious, and bloody remarks you could imagine. She incited citizens and *citoyennes* to revolt, to throw their bread in the face of the Commissaires, and from there to go and fall upon the people in power. According to her account, it was they who were responsible for people's dying of hunger as much as the egotistical merchants, the former aristocrats, the rich. All who were and still are priests will not be guillotined or finished off *en masse;* everything will not be okay, etc. . . . She said, "They really had it in for our poor Robespierre, but in his reign, at least, one ate. For humane reasons executions took place promptly, but these people, they make us die languishing because if that kind of thing goes on we will die mad; but good patriots will get the upper hand, and if they do not, the Republic is lost." On the days which preceded 1 Prairial, I noted in her appearance and on her sinister face an extraordinary contentment. She was seen appearing late in the morning and returning very late and very excited because she believed her triumph assured. She already pointed out those whom she would have guillotined. She was often at the door of the Convent Filles-Bleues and for secret business at the door of the former Hôtel Carnavalet. . . . Whenever a so-called *muscadin* or other well-dressed persons passed before her, she cried out pretty loudly, "There goes yet another damned one for the guillotine." There is every reason to believe that she was paid off, since no one has seen her work. She contributed no small amount to bringing on the disastrous *journées* of 1, 2, and 3 Prairial. On the fifth, seeing that the battle was lost, she said good-bye and moved out that same day.

On my life, I will support everything stated above.

[signed]

Fontaine

rue de Culture Ste. Catherine, no. 529

Note. On Saturday, the fourth of the month, she danced *en ronde* at the door of the convent. She held up a red handkerchief as a rallying sign, and she called it her favorite handkerchief, or her handkerchief of blood.

Source: A.N., W. 546, dossier 29.

———————— ◆ ————————

Copy of a letter read to the General Assembly of the Section du
Muséum, 10 Prairial, Year III. Addressed to the President of this
Section.

Paris, 7 Prairial, 1795, Year 3 of
the French Republic

Citizen:

Believing neither that the respect due our sex is an authorization to
commit evil, directly or indirectly, nor that there can be exceptions to
the law made for women without some principles being violated, it is
time that these "furies" who for too long have dishonored a portion of
their sex with immoral and criminal conduct should come under the
arm of the law and that those who remain loyal to their duty should
stop being forced to be witnesses of their crimes or victims of their
oppression.

I sense the full importance of a denunciation stripped of all feelings of
hate, vengeance, and even of spite. The voice of duty imperiously orders
all ordinary individuals, above all in the crises we are in, to denounce
enemies of the public interest, to make them known, and to establish a
line of demarcation between them and respectable people.

Consequently, I declare that I saw the above-named Femme Periot, a
merchant at one of the gates of the Louvre, residing on rue des Lavan-
dières, at the hatter's house next to the baker's—I declare, I say, that I
saw the above-named, long before the Prairial Days, constantly showing
loyalty to the Jacobin system, preaching Marat's maxims to various
groups, and repeatedly demanding that heads roll. I saw her at the trial
of Carrier conspiring on behalf of the Jacobins at the Revolutionary
Tribunal. She was always threatening the convention with an imminent
dissolution and merchants with certain pillage. Revolted by the conduct

of this shrew, I have denounced her to the Committee of Police of the convention.

At the time of the Triumvirate, this woman never stopped haranguing everyone with a human face. A person had to be marked with the stamp of an assassin or be tainted with blood to dare pass before her stall without being insulted. For without knowing you or speaking to you, she insulted you concerning your face and appearance. She always had the same refrain, "Patience, the brigands will not always have the upper hand. The Mountain will return. The time is not far off."

During the recent *événements* [Prairial], I saw the above-named with all the scoundrels, exhorting them with all the gestures of a madwoman not to give in until the Constitution of 1793 was agreed to on the spot. They should ask for Billaud, Collet, and Barère and hold the convention under seige until they [the three men] were delivered back to Paris. She screamed, "Yes, we must eliminate these marsh-toads. We have on our side the troops, the good gendarmes, and the faubourgs. The *muscadin* guillotine will be called out. We must have the traitors' blood." And I point out that I heard her several times over. I have followed her constantly in the vicinity of the Tuileries and the convention. I have even seen her provoke men and defy them, and try to stir up a brawl.

For these reasons I have come to denounce her so that the constituted authorities will keep watch on such a shrew and put her out of the way of harming society.

Since it is correct that the constituted authorities check up on the morality of informants, I am ready to give full information on my conduct during the twelve years I have lived in Paris and to prove that since 1789–90 I have struggled continuously against the Jacobins and have become their victim several times.

But I affirm that no personal hate or vengeance has prompted my pen or my heart.

In this spirit I am, with fraternity, your fellow *citoyenne,*

> Anne Marguerite Andelle, Widow Ruvet,
> rue des Fossés [Ste.] Germain [des près], no. 13,
> home of Citizen Allard.

8. The Military Establishment in Year III Offers Its Perspective on the Prairial Days

Source: [General Kilmaine,] *Détails circonstanciés de ce qui s'est passé le 4 Prairial au Faubourg St. Antoine par le Général Kilmaine, Général de Division commandant la Colonne de droit* (n.p., n.d.), in B.N., Lb⁴¹ 1826.

———————————

. . . We started marching, and I appeared at the first barricade, accompanied by the Commissaires of Section Quinze-Vingts. We were received with howling and the most atrocious insults by a great many armed men and a greater number of women, or rather, furies, who wanted to butcher us alive, or so they assured us. I let these howls quiet down, and I summoned them in the name of law and the national representation to deliver up the assassin [a man suspected of murdering National Representative Ferand on 1 Prairial] along with those who saved him from execution and to open the barricade at once. I threatened, in case of refusal, to use cannon to blow it up, throwing back onto the rebels the full horror of the consequences of their stubbornness.

I will point out here that at that moment it would have been very easy for me to turn back and leave through the barrière du Trône without the slightest risk, but beside the fact that it is in my character to doggedly pursue an action I believe good, such a withdrawal, which would have looked like a retreat dictated by fear, would have increased the audacity of the rebels a hundredfold and would have notably discouraged the good citizens of Paris. I firmly resolved to force these same men who wanted to encircle us to tear down their barricades themselves, but this required a great deal of prudence and much tenacity. Considering that I had only twelve hundred men (whose courage and devotion, to tell the truth, could be relied upon absolutely), and [considering] that we were surrounded by twenty thousand armed men and forty thousand furies—for they cannot be referred to as women—this action will be judged as appropriate.

Finally, having used first threats, then reason, we succeeded in opening up a passage. We started marching and arrived at the second barricade, where we were received with the same howls. At my end I used the same methods I had {used} the first time, and strongly supported all the while by the two Commissaires from Section Quinze-Vingts, whose zeal and devotion cannot be praised sufficiently, we succeeded, at the end of a quarter of an hour, in breaking through, but when we began marching, rumor spread that the rear guard had gotten hold of a cannon in Section Montreuil. Immediately the rebels took it upon themselves to rebuild the barricade. The cries and howls started up again. Several climbed up to the windows to assail us from there with gunfire, which made the position of the cavalry, above all, very alarming, as it could not defend itself in barricaded streets against men who were firing on them from the first floor. On the spot, I sent out General Brune, whose firmness I had tested. I asked him to go to the back of the column and order that no cannon be taken. . . .

[General Kilmaine relates his consternation at not receiving reinforcements that had been promised him in the morning. He continues:]

Two of the people's representatives, Vernier and Courtois . . . , joined the ranks of the *avant-garde* of the battalion. I feared that the rebels would recognize them and that the assassins would concentrate all their efforts on them. We were firmly resolved to defend them or get ourselves killed, but there were only twelve hundred of us, and we were surrounded by a countless multitude of armed men and a horde of *mégères* a thousand times more atrocious than the men. Besides, we could compromise the success of the great expedition [planned for the evening] by precipitating hostilities with such inferior forces. The rear guard abandoned the plan to carry the cannon off, but it was done with good grace and not in the least forced by the rebels. Then the second barricade was reopened, and we again started marching through. Having arrived at the last barricade, we found a more stubborn resistance than at the first two, increased by a great number of citizens who had strayed from Section Indivisibilité and from the Grand Rue Saint-Antoine. The same cries, the same threats from the rebels' side. The same firmness, even *sang-froid*, on our side. At last, wearied by our minimal success in using reason, I ordered the cannon pointed against the barricade, quite resolved to fire in three minutes' time if our demand was not heeded. I was very calm about our success, because we had only one more barricade to open up and we had the boulevard after that to deploy, and with courageous and devoted men accompanying me, I did not fear fifty thousand brigands with only the audacity of crime, assassination, and pillage for objectives, and who easily lose courage when they have to risk their lives to achieve [these objectives]. Then, seeing the gunners ready to fire, and several citizens won over besides by the reasoning of the Commissaires from Section Quinze-Vingts, and backed by the arguments of several good citizens who had mingled with the crowd and who, finally, had taken a stance, they made up their minds to open the last barricade. We again resumed our march for the fourth time, and we reached the boulevard, where we would get ready for battle. . . .

While we were resting, some groups of women among those known as "furies of the guillotine," bribed to preach anarchy and pillage, surrounded us from all sides. They surrounded mainly the dragoons of the Third Regiment. Several persons expressed their anxiety to me about these groups. I confess that I had none. I knew this regiment, having fought with it in what was formally Champagne. I knew its republican feeling and hatred of brigandage and anarchy. . . .

[During the evening attack on the Faubourg, Kilmaine's column guarded the entrance to the Faubourg. Kilmaine read the proclamation warning the rebels to capitulate or face the consequences of an armed assault.]

During this time a prodigious number of women and armed men converged on us via the rue Saint-Antoine. I stopped them with one hundred dragoons, who operated in such a way as to leave no hope to partisans of revolt. Detachments from each column entered the Faubourg to cries of "Long live the Convention," "Long live Liberty," "Long live the Republic," "Down with the Jacobins," "Down with the Brigands."

9. Interrogation of a Suspected Instigator of Female Insurrectionary Activities During the Prairial Days

Source: A.N., W 547, dossier 46.

On 27 Prairial, Year III, a young girl, Catherine Louise Vignot, disguised as a man, was brought to the Commissaire de police in Section Montreuil by a volunteer guard at the Vincennes *barrière*. She was five-feet two-inches tall, with dark hair and eyebrows, grey eyes, and an ordinary face; she lived on the Grande Rue du Faubourg and worked as a charcoal-carrier.

———————

Q. Why isn't she wearing the clothes appropriate for her sex?
A. The trade she is in does not allow it, as women's clothes would constrain her in working.
Q. On 1 Prairial, wasn't she leading some women, and didn't she have an open sabre in her hand?
A. No.
Q. On 2 Prairial, wasn't she also leading some women who went to the Convention?
A. As she was going to work around 6 A.M. the day in question, she was taken there by force by some women from Faubourg Marceau. She was obliged to march with them, and she left them near the Champs-Elysées.
Q. Hadn't she gone with the women to the doors of the Convention?
A. No.
Q. When she left the Faubourg with these women, didn't she have an unsheathed sabre in her hand?
A. She had a sabre in her hand, but it was in its scabbard.
Q. On the way, had she not drawn the sabre from its scabbard?
A. No.
Q. At what time did she leave the women?

A. She left them around 1 P.M.

Q. Where did she go after she left them?

A. She went to drink a pint of wine in the cabaret at the waterfront, near Pont-Marie. She was with a young woman and a single girl.

Q. Does she know the names of the two women?

A. She doesn't.

Q. Does she know where they live?

A. One of them lives near the Vincennes gate—she does not know the number of the house or the Section—and the other told her, while they were drinking, that she lived near the Porte-Antoine, but she doesn't know anything else about it.

Q. At what time did she return to the Faubourg?

A. She returned there around 5 P.M.

Q. Did the women come back with her to the Faubourg?

A. The married woman accompanied her to the rue de Reuilly, and it was there that she left her; the other went off after they left the cabaret, and then she, the declarant, returned to her place, where she remained until the next morning.

Q. Where was she on 4 Prairial?

A. She left her place at 5 A.M. to go to work above the rue Montmartre, where she unloaded a wagonload of charcoal at a restaurant owner's place.

Q. At what time did she return to the Faubourg?

A. At 10 A.M.

Q. Had she not been among the women who wanted to stir up citizens to keep the troops in the Faubourg from leaving?

A. She was on the boulevard then, and she met the troops at the Porte-Denis.

Q. Was she in the Faubourg at the time of the proclamation of the Convention ordering the return of the cannon, and did she not stir people up in an attempt to prevent them from being returned?

A. She was walking on the Grande Rue du Faubourg, but she said nothing.

Her interrogation was read back to her. She said her answers were truthful. When she was asked to sign, in accordance with the law, she stated that she didn't know how.

Then we, the above-named Commissaire [Louis Gille], suspecting that the above-named Vigniot was not telling us the truth, asked Citizen Garnier, *chef de brigade,* residing at Grande Rue, no. 109, to come to our office so we could find out from him whether he had some information to give us concerning the above-named Vigniot. Citizen Garnier, having arrived, stated that on 1 Prairial, a *citoyenne* dressed as a man and whom he recognized as the one who was now in our office was at the head of the first mob of women, at least four hundred in number, which set out for the Convention. The above-named woman, dressed as a man, marched at the front of the above-mentioned women with an open sabre in her hand and was leading them. She was also wearing a three-cornered hat with a red and blue plume, and she was next to the drummer, who was beating double-time. He, the declarant, went to the head of this crowd and asked this woman dressed as a man on whose order she was marching to drumbeat. Then she, as well as the other women, shouted to him to let them pass. He does not know how she comported herself at the Convention, but he, the declarant, having been degraded by the furies that morning and dragged along, nonetheless was at the guard post at the gate of La Place d'Armes at the stated time of 7 P.M. Seeing the above-named disguised woman coming back, he ordered her arrested and brought to the guard post. He upbraided her in the sharpest tones concerning her comportment and principally about how, through her instigation, she had exposed many mothers with families and had imperiled them. After that, he, the declarant, dismissed her. . . .

[Extract from the minutes of the meeting of the General Assembly of Section Montreuil on 5 Prairial:]

Several members denounced a woman usually dressed as a man who worked as a charcoal carrier for being one of these [women] who incited rebellion by going into houses and, through sheer force, dragging away respectable *citoyennes* content to stay in their households and mistreating those who refused to march against the National Convention. The assembly decreed that the Committee of General Security be notified, and in the event that the charcoal carrier has any arms, they will be taken from her. . . .

10. The Case of Femme Mandrillon, Referred by Section Tuileries to the Military Tribunal for Violent Behavior During the Prairial Days

---

10*a*. Source: Copy of the report of Citizen Hosteau concerning Femme Mandrillon, Paris, 8 Prairial, Year III, in A.N., W. 546, dossier 23.

Commission administrative de la Police de Paris.
Report of Citizen Hosteau concerning Femme Mandrillon

Liberty   Equality

Paris, 8 Prairial, Year III of the
French Republic, One and Indivisible

I made a report on the fourth of this month concerning a woman who outraged all good citizens by giving vent to force and to terrible acts of violence. On the first of this month this woman ran to all the doors of the various bakers in the Section preaching revolt, preventing peaceful women from getting bread, and saying, "It's today that all those rascals there will fart," and she threw stones into the shop of Citizen Woitai, a shoemaker. And the last brick nearly killed a citizen who was there. She also forced all the women she found to start marching. This wretched woman was seen with a white-handled knife in her hand, saying, "I'm really going to get inside their hearts and spill their blood, even wash my hands in it," and she incited all the women to murder a representative's wife, nineteen to twenty years of age, who was passing by on the rue de Chartres, by saying, "There's a deputy's wife; she'll have to be killed."

This woman was accompanied by Femme Touraugot, by Femme Flament, by someone from off the streets called Manette, by someone named "Mon Rose," and by several other prostitutes like herself. The chief is named Adelaide, a former prostitute and subsequently claiming marriage to a gendarme named Mandrillon. And as witness to these facts, we have: Citizen Harbonnier, the former *commissaire de police;*

Challier, a merchant—soft-drink peddler on the rue de Chartres; Citizen Bougarel, a merchant-grocer on the rue de Chartres, and his wife and his daughter; Citizen Beaugrand, rue Honoré, no. 144; Citizen Le Bon, *fils,* a wig maker on place de la Réunion, no. 1; as well as several others, who will be indicated for you either by witnesses or by several women who were compelled to march with her by force.

Some time ago I arrested this woman, and she was judged by the correctional police for having hit and roughed up Citizen Widow Gentie, a merchant-butcher on rue de Rouen, and the daughters of Citizen Gagniot, a merchant—soft-drink peddler on rue de Rouen. This woman is very dangerous.

Submitted as a report. Signed: Hosteau. . . .

———————

10*b*. Source: *Procès-verbal* of interrogation of Femme Mandrillon before the Commission de Police administrative de Paris, 9 Prairial, Year III, in A.N., W. 546, dossier 23.

Commission de Police administrative de Paris

Liberté   Egalité

Paris, 9 Prairial, Third Year of the
French Republic, One and Indivisible

Before us, the members of the commission, by virtue of a mandate which we issued yesterday on the basis of reports made to us, an individual appeared whom we proceeded to interrogate as follows:

Q. Last name, first name, age, place of birth, profession, and residence.
A. Marie-Jeanne Adelaide LeGrand, wife of Claude-Michel Mandrillon, a lieutenant in the Thirty-First Division of the Gendarmerie nationale, Army of l'Indre et Meuse; age, thirty-two years; native of Passy-les-Paris; a laundry worker; living on rue de Chartres Honoré, no. 384, for the past six years. She showed us her marriage certificate dated the nineteenth of the second month of Year Two.
Q. On the first of the month, hadn't she run to all the doors of the various bakers in the Section, preaching revolt and preventing peaceful women from getting their bread?

A. No, she never threatened anyone, and she herself was threatened with a whipping if she got her bread.

Q. Hadn't she said, speaking about the deputies, "It's today that all those rascals must fart"?

A. No.

Q. Hadn't she thrown stones into the shop of Citizen Voitier [*sic*], a shoemaker, and hadn't a brick thrown by her nearly killed a citizen who was there?

A. No.

Q. Hadn't she forced all the women she found to march?

A. No.

Q. Hadn't she had a white-handled knife in her hand as she said, "I'm really going to plunge it into their heart, spill their blood, and wash my hands in it"?

A. No.

Q. Hadn't she incited all the women to murder a representative's wife, aged nineteen to twenty years, who was walking by on rue de Chartres by saying, "There's yet another one; she's the wife of a deputy; she must be killed"?

A. She can't answer this accusation, and it's the epitome of villainy.

Q. Did she know Femme Flament? Someone from off the streets, called Manette?

A. And this person from off the streets declared that she didn't know who they were.

It was pointed out to her that she was not impressing us with her negative answers, and that there were citizens and *citoyennes* who could attest to the facts which she was denying.

A. She fears nothing, and she is innocent.

Q. Hadn't she been arrested and arraigned before the correctional police?

A. She had been arrested for having roughed up citizen widow Gentie, a butcher on rue de Rouen, but she was acquitted.

It was pointed out to her that in the Section des Tuileries she had a reputation for being a wicked woman, and that at all times she gave herself up to violent excesses towards peaceful citizens.

A. She never did any harm to anyone, and these rumors are ill-founded.
                    Signed: LeGrand, Femme Mandrillon, and LeRoy

Given what is stated above, we declared that Citizens Charbonnier, Bougarelle, Beaugrand, and Beaufils, witnesses of the excesses in which Femme Mandrillon indulged, will be called upon to make their declarations concerning the deeds imputed to her, and that provisionally, the aforementioned Femme Mandrillon will be placed in the prison so that, following the declarations, measures judged necessary can be taken with respect to her.

> At Paris, this 9 Prairial, Year III.
> Signed: Le Roy. . . .

10c. Source: Interrogation of Femme Morey before the Commission de Police administrative de Paris, 9 Prairial, Year III, in A.N., W. 546, dossier 23.

Commission de Police Administrative de Paris
Liberté   Egalité
Paris, 9 Prairial, Year III of the
French Republic, One and Indivisible

Before us, members of the Commission of Police, appeared Citoyenne Françoise Morey, shop girl for Citizen Bougarelle, merchant-grocer, residing at rue de Chartres, no. 473. She told us that on 1 Prairial, at 9 A.M., she arrived at the door of the baker's to get the quantity of bread due her, as noted on her card. Citoyenne Mandrillon appeared during this time. She lived, as far as the deponent knew, on rue de Chartres. She told the deponent and those who were there that if anyone received bread he would be whipped and roughed up by her and her supporters—which prevented the distribution of bread and forced the deponent to return home without bread.

In the afternoon, while the deponent was outside her shop, about 2 P.M., the aforementioned Mandrillon passed by armed with a knife, saying she would plunge her knife into the stomach of the first person to come near her.

Her declaration was read back to her, and she attested to its being sincere and truthful, adhered to it, and signed with us: Françoise Morey. . . .

Following the declaration contained elsewhere, Citoyenne Françoise Morey adds that on 28 Floreal, at the home of Citoyenne Nems, living on rue des Boucheries Honoré on the second floor, she met the aforementioned Flamant, who lives on rue de Chartres [Marguerite d'Arras, wife of Michel Cormans, and called Flamant—another woman implicated in the alleged conspiracy to incite rebellion]. She asked her whether her bourgeois had any pease flour, to which the deponent replied, "Yes," and that her bourgeois was selling it for twelve *francs* a *livre*. To this reply the aforementioned woman burst out with [her] remarks, saying that her bourgeois, the deponent's, was a hoarder; that she had supported him, but that very soon looting would break out; that he would be looted, as the others; and that she would be at the head when they came to the shop of the deponent's bourgeois.

On 1 Prairial, at 3 P.M., the deponent was busy shutting up her shop, and a minute after the aforementioned shop was shut down, Citoyenne Flamant passed by, or came by by design, [and] through a grill made insulting remarks to the deponent, saying that "she and her bourgeois were going to be strung up that very day."

Just after these infamous remarks [were made], the deponent went up to the fifth floor in her house, and having arrived there, she looked out the window and saw the body of the representative who was being dragged through the streets, and at the same time she noticed Femme Flamant opposite, on the fifth floor, looking out through the casement window, saying, "Bravo! bravo! Soon it will be the merchant's turn, and they will get the same, that has to happen."

Her declaration (what was added) was read back to her, and she attested to its being sincere and truthful, and adhered to it, and signed: Françoise Morey. . . .

11. The Dissolution of the National Workshops for Women

Source: Report in Messidor, Year III, by the Commission d'agriculture et des arts to the National Convention, in A.N., F¹⁵ 3594–95, published in Alexandre Tuetey, *L'Assistance Publique à Paris pendant la Révolution française,* vol. IV, entry no. 505, pp. 734–38.

Thermidorian fears of women congregated in large groups led to the dismantling of the national workshops for women shortly after the Prairial Days. From then on, women were encouraged to work at home, and the government touted the patriarchal line: domestic work for women will allow them to be better wives and mothers as well as more productive workers.

———

The spinning workshops of Paris were set up in the month of May, 1790, in order to provide work for women and children who had no other means of existence and who, without this resource, would have been reduced to begging. The Commission d'agriculture et des arts, which has been in charge of administering them [the workshops] for several months now, has been treating them more as manufactories than as relief agencies, and from this point of view it [the Commission] has sought to make them serve commerce and the progress of trades.

In executing this project it [the Commission] has conceived the idea of transforming the workshops into training schools in order to turn out working women able to do work in manufactures and, with this objective, compel spinners [who are] already trained to work at home. With this in mind it [the Commission] drew up a draft of a decree and a very detailed list of rules that it submitted to the Comité d'agriculture last Frimaire, on the twelfth.

The ideas of the Commission d'agriculture have been partially realized, for already the women workers in the Atelier du Midi have moved out, and on the responsibility of the owners or principal tenants, materials, spinning wheels, and necessary tools have been entrusted to them to allow them to spin at home. The women workers of the Atelier du Nord have not been as docile; they continue working in the workshop.

Among the means employed by the Commission d'agriculture for the new organization of the ateliers, that of having work done at home by the spinners and of admitting inside the workshop only apprentices seems necessary to adopt, as it combines several advantages.

First, it provides more efficaciously for the amelioration of the working and unfortunate class while avoiding long and miserable journeys for the workers, which saves precious time they could use for their work or in the care of their households.

Second, it yields the greatest quantity and a better quality of spinning. Indeed, for five years during which the workshops have existed, there have always been some outside workers, and it has often been observed that they produce more beautiful thread than workers in the shops.

Third, it prevents inconveniences that might result—for morals or for public tranquility—from numerous gatherings of simple people who are credulous and easily led astray by perfidious suggestions of malevolence and seduction.

Fourth, it simplifies and facilitates the administration of the workshops, lessens expenses considerably, and applies all possible economy and precision to their maintenance.

Conclusion

———————

FOR THE MODERN FEMINIST this collection of documents may appear disturbing. After June, 1795, it seemed that the women of Paris were a failure as a political force. First of all, they had lost their supporting institutions. Their clubs were closed, they were shut out of the galleries of the Convention, popular societies were disbanded, and workshops were closed. After that there was no longer any way to coordinate the political efforts of women of all social ranks. Furthermore, once the Jacobins had co-opted populist principles and programs, the radical left disintegrated. Finally, the repressive tactics of the Thermidorians were effective. In the aftermath of the Prairial Days a special Military Tribunal and Section committees ordered the arrest and imprisonment of the most articulate and dedicated male and female leaders among the common people. Police had become adept at unearthing clandestine organizations, spying, infiltrating bread lines and marketplaces. While such tactics also dissolved the political power of the male *sans-culottes* and prevented the mutual support between men and women that had been effective in the Year II, one could also assert that the male revolutionary leadership deliberately reduced women to a narrow but exalted role— that of bearing, nurturing, and educating future citizens.

Successive governments under the Directory and Napoleon made deliberate efforts to prevent crowds from congregating and women from having any impact on public affairs. Even the legal and civic gains women had made in the first six years of the Revolution were eroded after 1795. During the Directory, laws pertaining to the establishment of primary schools for girls were poorly enforced, and *citoyenne* became an exclusive title for respectable ladies and female friends of the national representatives. The Napoleonic Code did not perpetuate most of the revolutionary advances in women's legal equality, such as in property administration and child custody. The Code did keep equal inheritance and did permit divorce, until the Restoration. In general, married women were considered legal minors and were denied ownership of property. Moreover, married women were forbidden to make contracts without their father's or husband's consent, and the double standard of morality was incorporated in private law dealing with divorce, child custody, and alimony. The Napoleonic Code rendered the position of French women less advantageous than it had been in the Old Regime. Before the Revolution, women of the religious and lay aristocracy had been able to handle property and legal matters which pertained to their estates and families; the Napoleonic Code treated *all* women equally and prevented those of high social status from exerting any power in public and familial matters.

But the involvement of the women of Paris in the Revolution did have a lasting impact on French politics and society in spite of the numerous setbacks to women in the aftermath of Year II. Furthermore, women of the middle and lower classes acquired new outlooks about themselves and their role in society which could not be erased by patriarchal attitudes and laws.

First, women in the Revolution accentuated their impact on government officials in times of crisis. In fact, the involvement of large numbers of women in protest was taken by both national and local authorities as a signal of the seriousness of the breakdown of control. When scarcity and prices made women desperate, there was no way to control the streets. Furthermore, after the Revolution any war policy had to accommodate the particular needs of women: pensions for widows or wives of disabled soldiers, adequate uniforms and provisions for husbands and sons in the army, workshops for women, and so on. If such demands were neglected, women would be sure to come threatening and shouting into the galleries of national legislatures and local assemblies. Thus, the Revolution carried forward and intensified the roles of women as barometers of political crises and as potent threats of a breakdown in control of the city. The Revolution did not create these roles for women, but it magnified the national political repercussions of their protest.

A second legacy of revolutionary women is their contribution to political education. Women had become conscious of their roles as makers of patriots and had come to put a high value on education in general and education for politics in particular. Women who were political oddities, like Olympe de Gouges or Etta Palm d'Aelders, may not have originated a feminist movement, but they did help to legitimate the idea that women had something to say about politics that could not be discounted or laughed off by those in power. Women were influential as the main transmitters of political values to their children, especially attitudes toward authority and toward political participation.

The content of French political vocabulary and myth was permanently transformed by women in revolutionary Paris. Political style is an important element of any political culture because it determines the ways in which the content of politics will be felt, transmitted, and understood. French political style is both highly verbal and highly visual. Modern French political analysts have often commented on the persistence of revolutionary rhetoric in the twentieth century. Much of this symbolism is associated with women: their knitting needles, their wooden shoes stamping approval or outrage in the galleries of the National Convention or the Jacobin Society, the tricolored ribbons in their bonnets, the pikes in their hands. As we have seen in the documents, these symbols were meaningful within the context of revolutionary politics and remain in the political culture as evocative symbols of approval, disapproval, or disgust.

To the 1848 generation of Parisian revolutionary women, the women of the eighteenth-century Revolution were important for more than their symbolic inspiration. The Society of Revolutionary Republican Women became the prototype of political clubs for women that flourished in 1848. The two presidents, Lacombe and Léon, were extolled for their attacks on the bourgeoisie and their championship of the interests of working women.

In this anthology we have argued that prerevolutionary political nationalization was carried forward by the revolutionary leadership and most fully by the Jacobins, with a significant innovation in the form of institutions for mass political participation. The national legislatures, the Commune, the National Guard, the Section assemblies, the societies, the clubs, and so on, brought people together to act on their needs and demands. Some of the women of Paris demanded and acted upon their rights to full political participation in these institutions. Women were not mere tools of male agitators and radical journalists, as so many conservative historians and writers have argued. It is clear in the documents that men and women had differing perceptions and expectations of women in the new society. Male revolutionaries had granted women the honorary title of *citoyennes* without expecting that women would want to try to exercise full rights of political autonomy. But the women took their title seriously.

Sometimes the women demanded literal equality in modern political power: the right to bear arms, the vote, a national assembly of women.

They were most effective, however, when they made their traditional demands for subsistence and economic security. On these issues they were able to forge an alliance with the radical left in Parisian politics, culminating in their closeness to the Enragés in 1793. These issues were their traditional economic grievances, but it is our contention that these issues became a bridge to modern political activities. In the early months of the Revolution, demands for bread and subsistence were presented through symbolic acting out, as if the women were in rehearsal trying out new roles. In their marches early in the fall of 1789, and when they played legislators for a day at Versailles in October, they were emerging as autonomous political actors.

As the Revolution unfolded, such behavior became institutionalized in galleries, clubs, and popular societies. Once the Revolutionary Government had consolidated power, it did not or could not share authority with the new structures of political democracy while fighting a simultaneous international and civil war and combatting subversion. Ultimately, of course, the people were empowered only as plebiscitory supporters of a dictator. Thus, fully egalitarian democracy was ephemeral in French politics for the women as well as the men. But it set a precedent. The lessons in civic behavior and exposure to public affairs were not forgotten. In the events of 1848 and 1871 women revived the spirit of the Parisian women of 1789 and 1793, although they learned to correct mistakes made by their predecessors in tactics, organization, and relations with male revolutionaries. They remembered that their eighteenth-century revolutionary forebears were becoming citizens with an articulate voice in their neighborhoods, their city, and their nation. The women of revolutionary Paris take their places in history as integral parts of the revolutionary legacy to the future; their influence was not to last, but it was not to be forgotten.

Selected Bibliography

Abensour, Léon. *La Femme et le féminisme avant la Révolution française*. Paris, 1923.

Abray, Jane. "Feminism in the French Revolution," *American Historical Review* 80 (February, 1975):43–62.

Alexandre, Charles A. "Fragments des Mémoires de . . . ," ed. Jacques Godechot, *Annales historiques de la Révolution française* 24 (1952):146–86.

Aulard, F.-A. *Le Culte de la raison et de l'Etre suprême, 1793–1794: Essai historique*. Paris, 1892.

———. *Paris pendant la réaction thermidorienne et sous le Directoire*. 5 vols. Paris, 1898–1902.

———. *Recueil des Actes du Comité de Salut Public avec la correspondance officielle des représentants en mission et le régistre du Conseil exécutif provisoire*. 28 vols. Paris, 1881–1951.

———. *La Société des Jacobins: Recueil de documents pour l'histoire du Club des Jacobins de Paris*. 6 vols. Paris, 1889–97.

———, ed. *Papiers de Fournier l'Américain*. Paris, 1898.

Bourdin, Isabel. *Les sociétés populaires à Paris pendant la Révolution de 1789 jusqu'à la chute de la royauté*. Paris, 1937.

Bouvier, Jeanne. *Les Femmes pendant la Révolution*. Paris, 1931.

Buchez, P. B., and B. C. Roux, eds. *Histoire parlementaire de la Révolution française, ou Journal des Assemblées nationales depuis 1789 jusqu'au 1815*. Paris, 1834.

Caron, Pierre. *Paris pendant la Terreur: Rapports des agents secrets du Ministre de l'Intérieur*. 4 vols. Paris, 1910–49.

Cerati, Marie. *Le Club des citoyennes républicaines révolutionnaires*. Paris, 1966.

Chassin, Charles-Louis. *Les Elections et les cahiers de Paris en 1789*, 4 vols. Paris, 1888–89.

Dawson, Philip, ed. *The French Revolution*. Englewood Cliffs, N.J., 1967.

Duhet, Paule-Marie. *Les Femmes et la Révolution, 1789–1794*. Paris, 1971.

Fleury, Michel, and Pierre Valmary. "Les Progrès de l'instruction élémentaire de Louis XIV à Napoléon III d'après l'enquête de Louis Maggiolo (1877–1879)," *Population* 12 (1957):71–92.

George, Margaret. "The 'World Historical Defeat' of the Républicaines-Révolutionnaires." *Science and Society* 40, no. 4 (Winter, 1976–77):410–37.

Gerbaux, F. "Les Femmes soldats pendant la Révolution," *La Révolution française* 47 (1904):47–61.

Godechot, Jacques. *La Prise de la Bastille*. Paris, 1965.

Goncourt, Edmond de, and Jules de Goncourt. *La Femme au dix-huitième siècle*. 2 vols. Paris, 1882.

Guillaume, J. *Procès-verbaux du Comité d'Instruction publique de la Convention nationale*. 6 vols. Paris, 1898–1907.

Hufton, Olwen H. *The Poor of Eighteenth-Century France, 1750–1789*. Oxford, 1975.

———. "Women and the Family Economy in Eighteenth-Century France," *French Historical Studies*, Spring, 1975, pp. 1–22.

———. "Women in the French Revolution," *Past and Present* 53 (November, 1971):90–108.

Kaplan, Steven L. *Bread, Politics, and Political Economy in the Reign of Louis XV*. 2 vols. The Hague, 1976.

Lacour, Léopold. *Les origines du féminisme contemporain. Trois Femmes de la Révolution: Olympe de Gouges, Théroigne de Méricourt, Rose Lacombe*. Paris, 1900.

Lefebvre, Georges. *The Coming of the French Revolution*. Trans. R. R. Palmer. New York, 1947.

Lytle, Scott. "The Second Sex (September, 1793)," *Journal of Modern History* 26 (1955):14–26.

Markov, Walter, and Albert Soboul, eds. *Die Sansculotten von Paris: Dokumente zur Geschichte der Volksbewegung, 1793–1794*. Berlin and Paris, 1957.

Mathiez, Albert. *Le Club des Cordeliers pendant la crise de Varennes et le massacre du Champ de Mars*. Paris, 1910 (reprint Geneva, 1975).

———. "Étude critique sur les journées 5/6 octobre," *Revue historique* 67 (1898):241–81.

Michelet, Jules. *Les Femmes de la Revolution*. Paris, 1854.

Monin, H. *L'Etat de Paris en 1789*. Paris, 1889.

Patrick, Alison. *The Men of the First French Republic*. Baltimore and London, 1972.

Portemer, Jean. "Le Statut de la femme en France depuis la Réformation des coutumes jusqu'à la rédaction du Code Civil," in *Recueils de la Société Jean Bodin pour l'histoire comparative des institutions*, vol. 12, pp. 447–97.

Reinhard, Marcel. *La Chute de la Royauté*. Paris, 1969.

Rose, R. B. *The Enragés: Socialists of the French Revolution*. Melbourne, 1965.

Rudé, George. *The Crowd in the French Revolution*. London, 1959.

———. *Paris and London in the Eighteenth Century: Studies in Popular Protest*. New York, 1971.

Soboul, Albert. *La Civilisation et la Révolution française*, vol. 1, *La Crise de l'Ancien régime*. Paris, 1970.

————. *Les Sans-culottes parisiens en l'an II. Mouvement populaire et gouvernement révolutionnaire (2 juin 1793–9 Thermidor an II).* Paris, 1959 (Trans. and abr. G. Lewis, *The Parisian Sans-Culottes and the French Revolution.* Oxford, 1964).

————. "Sentiments réligieux et cultes populaires sous la Révolution: Saintes, patriotes et martyrs de la liberté," *Annales historiques de la Révolution française* 29 (1957):193–212.

Stoddard, Julia C. "The Causes of the Insurrection of the 5th and 6th of October," *University of Nebraska Studies* 4, no. 4 (October, 1904):267–327.

Sullerot, Evelyne. *La Presse féminine.* Paris, 1963.

Tilly, Charles, Louise Tilly, and Richard Tilly. *The Rebellious Century, 1830–1930.* Cambridge, Mass., 1975.

Tønnesson, Kare. *La Défaite des Sans-Culottes: Mouvement populaire et réaction bourgeoise en l'an III.* Oslo and Paris, 1959.

Tuetey, Alexandre. *L'Assistance publique à Paris pendant la Révolution.* 4 vols. Paris, 1895–97.

————. *Répertoire général des sources manuscrites de l'Histoire de Paris pendant la Révolution française.* 11 vols. Paris, 1890–1914.

Villiers, Baron Marc de. *Histoire des Clubs de Femmes et des Légions d'Amazones, 1793–1848–1871.* Paris, 1910.

Williams, David. "The Politics of Feminism in the French Enlightenment," in *The Varied Pattern: Studies in the Eighteenth Century,* ed. P. Hughes and D. Williams. Toronto, 1971.

Woloch, Isser. *Jacobin Legacy: The Democratic Movement under the Directory.* Princeton, 1970.

Name Index

Subject Index

Active citizens (suffrage qualifications), 61
Amis de la loi, 63
Amis de la vérité, 68
Army, 104, 105, 147, 151, 172, 175, 225–27, 310
assignats, 188, 272
ateliers. See workshops
August 10, 1792 (attack on Tuileries), 104, 159, 255

Bastille (conquest of), 29, 30, 66, 97, 158, 168

cahiers (revolutionary grievance lists), 7, 22–26
Cercle social, 62, 71
Champ de Mars Massacre, 5n, 64, 80–85, 97, 106, 113, 159
Club monarchique, 63
cockade, national (revolutionary headgear), 39, 40, 49, 52, 146–48, 169, 197, 198–202, 205–12, 262
Committee of General Security, 160, 179, 180, 182–84, 187, 190, 194, 213, 214, 217, 221, 222, 246, 279, 281, 286, 301
Committee of Public Safety, 180, 221, 258, 264
communauté (for women), 22–26
Constituent Assembly. *See* National Assembly
Constitution of 1791, 61, 64, 65, 72, 85, 86, 109
Constitution of 1793, 145–47, 160, 172, 173, 221, 272, 292, 295

constitutional monarchy, 63, 64
Cordeliers Society, 61, 63, 64, 66, 67, 72, 81, 143, 145, 148, 150, 159

Declaration of the Rights of Man and Citizen, 4, 13, 56, 57, 64, 73, 87, 176, 222, 236, 237, 239–41
Declaration of the Rights of Woman, 4, 64, 65, 87–96, 254
De l'esclavage des noirs, 257
Directory, 309
divorce laws, 4, 61, 103, 310

education for women, 7, 19–21, 69, 70, 77, 123, 228, 229, 236–43
Enlightenment, 6, 7
Enragés, 105, 143, 145–47, 175, 182, 312
Estates General, 9, 13, 22–26

February Days (1793), 106, 107, 132–41, 272
Fédérés, 103, 168
Feminism, 309–12
femmes sans-culottes, 63, 65
Feuillants, 183, 187
fishwives. *See* poissardes
Floréal (1795), 287–91
fraternal societies, 106

Germinal Days (1795), 272, 279–86, 292
Girondin faction, 103–5, 108, 112, 143–46, 150, 154, 155, 161, 172, 177, 271

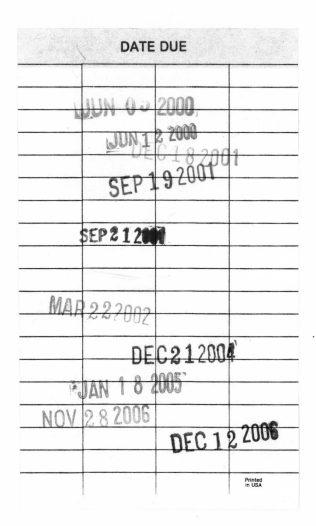